INVESTMENT AND FACTOR DEMAND

CONTRIBUTIONS
TO
ECONOMIC ANALYSIS

193

Honorary Editor:
J. TINBERGEN

Editors:
D. W. JORGENSON
J. WAELBROECK

NORTH-HOLLAND
AMSTERDAM • NEW YORK • OXFORD • TOKYO

INVESTMENT AND FACTOR DEMAND

Patrick ARTUS
Caisse des Dépôts et Consignations (CDC)
and Ecole Polytechnique, Paris

Pierre-Alain MUET
Observatoire Français des Conjonctures Economiques (OFCE)
and Ecole Polytechnique, Paris

1990

NORTH-HOLLAND
AMSTERDAM • NEW YORK • OXFORD • TOKYO

ELSEVIER SCIENCE PUBLISHERS B.V.
Sara Burgerhartstraat 25
P.O. Box 211, 1000 AE Amsterdam, The Netherlands

Distributors for the United States and Canada:

ELSEVIER SCIENCE PUBLISHING COMPANY INC.
655 Avenue of the Americas
New York, N.Y. 10010, U.S.A.

The present volume is a revised, expanded and updated translation of
'Investissement et Emploi', Paris, Economica, 1986
Translated by Jonathan Mandelbaum

ISBN: 0 444 88105 0

PRINTED IN THE NETHERLANDS

INTRODUCTION TO THE SERIES

This series consists of a number of hitherto unpublished studies, which are introduced by the editors in the belief that they represent fresh contributions to economic science.

The term "economic analysis" as used in the title of the series has been adopted because it covers both the activities of the theoretical economist and the research worker.

Although the analytical methods used by the various contributors are not the same, they are nevertheless conditioned by the common origin of their studies, namely theoretical problems encountered in practical research. Since for this reason, business cycle research and national accounting, research work on behalf of economic policy, and problems of planning are the main sources of the subjects dealt with, they necessarily determine the manner of approach adopted by the authors. Their methods tend to be "practical" in the sense of not being too far remote from application to actual economic conditions. In additon they are quantitative.

It is the hope of the editors that the publication of these studies will help to stimulate the exchange of scientific information and to reinforce international cooperation in the field of economics.

The Editors

Foreword

Economists differ as to the relative importance of the factors that determine business investment. Some analysts assign a key role to market prospects, others to realized profits, debt constraints and interest-rate levels. Until recently, econometric studies of investment pitted these different approaches against one another without ever successfully reconciling them in a coherent theoretical framework. One of the prime contributions of the disequilibrium theory to the econometrics of investment has been to furnish a clear and comprehensive behavioral interpretation for the main models used in empirical studies. By taking account of the constraints under which firms operate, we can describe the coexistence of several potential determinants of investment. The relative importance of these varies in response to the economic cycle.

More recently, refinements in econometric techniques have made it possible to produce numerical estimates of multi-regime models. This has enhanced economic analysis by enabling periods to be distinguished according to their prevailing types of behavior. In addition, the present authors have gradually incorporated into their studies on French data the advances of economic theory in such areas as decisions under uncertainty, behavior interdependence and adjustment dynamics.

The first part of the book presents an estimate of the conventional investment models, their interpretation in terms of disequilibrium, and their application to an assessment of economic policy during the 1970s. Chapter 2 opens with an investment-model typology based on the inclusion of constraints expected or perceived by firms, and on the extent of capital-labor substitution.

The chapter goes on to set out an estimate of the various models using annual time series. Chapter 3 elaborates on the hypotheses about production-technique choices and capital malleability by taking a new comparative look at the "putty-putty" and "putty-clay" models. Chapter 4 studies the fiscal, taxation and monetary policies that have affected investment since the first oil crisis, and assesses their macroeconomic impact with the aid of the METRIC model.

The second part illustrates the interdependence of decisions concerning investment, labor, and consumption of raw materials and energy. For this purpose, we use a joint estimate of factor demands. Chapters 5 and 6 study the joint determination of investment and labor in two alternative hypotheses : absence of constraints (notional demand) or, on the contrary, demand constraint (effective demand). Chapter 5 is confined to the technological dependence between labor demand and capital demand. We show that factor costs have a much more limited influence than demand, and that labor reacts more promptly than investment to the various explanatory factors. Chapter 6 explicitly introduces adjustment costs into the calculation of factor demand. It also incorporates an error-correction process into the formation of demand expectations. The conclusions of this chapter corroborate those of the preceding one: capital-adjustment costs are higher than labor-adjustment costs, and the model with no demand constraint does not yield credible results. Chapter 7 extends the analysis of substitution effects to include intermediate energy consumption. This factor is complex, for the influence of energy cost on capital accumulation depends not only on the substitution between the "capital + energy" bundle but also on the direct substitution between capital and energy. The influence can therefore be positive or negative. Chapter 7 presents an estimate of three-factor demand functions for the main OECD countries that enables us to interpret the contradictory results previously obtained through cost functions.

The final chapters implement the latest econometric theories and methods. These are first applied to the estimate of a multi-regime investment model incorporating output, labor, and financial constraints (Chapter 8), then to the joint determination of investment and labor in a context of demand uncertainty (Chapter 9).

Acknowledgements

This volume is a collection of theoretical and applied studies on the econometrics of investment and employment in France published by the authors over the past decade.

Most of these articles initially appeared in French journals : *Revue Economique* (Chapter 1), *Observations et Diagnostics Economiques* (Chapter 4) and, for the most part, *Annales de l'INSEE* (since 1985, *Annales d'Economie et de Statistique*) (Chapters 2, 3, 5, 6, 7 and 9). We are grateful to the editorial boards of these periodicals for permission to reprint our contributions.

We also wish to thank the co-authors of certain of these studies : Michel Boutillier and Pierre Villa (Chapter 5), Bernard Migus (Chapter 6) and Claude Peyroux (Chapter 7). Last but not least, we express our gratitude to Marie-Christine Hurault and Christine Carl for their efficient assistance during the production of this book.

Contents

CHAPTER 1
Theoretical foundations and main models*
by
Patrick Artus and Pierre-Alain Muet

Introduction

For the past two decades, the econometrics of investment has seen the development of two distinct approaches, which we shall respectively define as "explicit" and "implicit." Both derive the investment function from a behavior that consists of an intertemporal maximization of the firm's profit. The "explicit" approach pioneered by Jorgenson [1963] links investment to variables that determine its profitability — in particular by incorporating production-function parameters. By contrast, the "implicit" approach introduced by Tobin [1969] seeks to measure that profitability directly on the basis of the stock-market value of assets. While the second approach has recently given rise to new theoretical developments, its econometric relevance cannot be compared to that of the first approach, which has more successfully integrated earlier models such as the flexible accelerator, first empirically (Jorgenson [1963]; Eisner and Nadiri [1968]; Bischoff [1971]; etc.), then theoretically (Grossman [1972]).

The first section of Chapter 1 presents the theoretical foundations of the models. The second section compares the main econometric estimates by analyzing the impact of growth, factor costs and financial conditions on investment.

1. THEORETICAL FOUNDATIONS

We shall begin with a highly simplified presentation of the main investment models, using a model in which labor is instantaneously adjusted whereas the change in capital requires a one-period lag. Thus investment demand in period (t) results from the capital desired by firms for the period (t+1). Choosing as decision criterion the maximization of discounted profit, we

---

* Originally published as "Un panorama des developpements recents de l'econometrie de l'investissement," *Revue Economique* 35(5):791-830, Sept. 1984.

shall in turn describe the main investment models in terms of the constraints perceived or expected by firms in the markets concerned by the investment decision. This leads us to distinguish between *notional demand*, which depends solely on factor costs, and *effective demands*, which depend on expected constraints on the various markets. Lastly, by introducing uncertainty or adjustment costs, we can validate the main results obtained through the implicit approach (Tobin's q).

1.1. Conceptual framework

Q_t, L_t, K_t and p_t, w_t, q_t respectively designate the volumes and prices of output, labor and capital at the date t (stocks defined at the start of the period). I_t stands for investment volume. We assume that prices and costs (p_t, w_t, q_t) are given for the firm. The same obviously applies to the capital stock available at the start of the period (K_t). *The decisions of firms therefore concern the quantity of output* (Q_t), labor (L_t) and investment (I_t) for the period. I_t is linked to the capital stock desired for the period (t +1) by the standard equation:

$$(1) \qquad K_{t+1} = \frac{K_t + I_t}{(1 + \delta)},$$

which assumes an exponential depreciation at the rate δ .

Technical constraints are represented by the production function with substitutable factors:

$$(2') \qquad Q_t \leq f(K_t, L_t) ;$$

$$(2'') \qquad Q_{t+1} \leq f(K_{t+1}, L_{t+1})$$

In keeping with the conventional analysis, we assume that firms base their production, employment and investment decisions on the maximization of discounted profit. In the simplified framework used here, where capital is treated as perfectly homogeneous and malleable, this maximization is restricted to the current period and the period after it. Discounted profit over the two periods (in other words, the increase in the firm's value over the two periods) is equal to:

(3)
$$\Delta V = (p_t\, Q_t - w_t\, L_t) + [q_t\, K_t - q_{t-1}\, (1 + r_{t-1})\, K_{t-1}] - q_t\, I_t$$

| Profit in period t | Discounted capital gain in period t | Investment expenditure |

$$+ \frac{1}{1+r_t}\ (p^*_{t+1} - w^*_{t+1}\, L_{t+1}) \quad + \frac{q^*_{t+1}\, K_{t+1}}{1 + r_t} \quad - q_t\, K_t$$

| Expected profit | Expected discounted capital gain for (t + 1) |

with r_t the discounting rate (or nominal interest rate from period t to period t+1).

Maximizing (3) under constraints (1) and (2) therefore gives the supply of goods and the demand for labor and investment for period (t), as well as the supply of goods and the demand for labor and capital expected for period (t + 1). In this model, investment is the only variable linking the two periods together. It will be noted that the problem of determining the supply of goods and demand for labor in period (t) can be separated from the problem of calculating the quantities in t+1 (and — as a result — determining investment demand) by rewriting (3) as follows (the constant term d stands for the capital gain in period t, which is exogenous):

(3 a)
$$\Delta V = (p_t\, Q_t - w_t\, L_t) +$$

　　　Profit in period t

$$\frac{1}{(1 + r_t)}\ [p^*_{t+1}\, Q_{t+1} - w^*_{t+1}\, L_{t+1} - q_t\, (r_t + \delta - \dot{q}^*)\, K_{t+1}] + d$$

　　　Profit net of the cost of capital in period (t + 1)

This notation displays the user cost of capital:[1]

(4)
$$c^*_{t+1} = q_t\, (r + \delta - \dot{q}^*), \quad \text{with} \quad \dot{q}^* = \frac{q^*_{t+1} - q_t}{q_t}$$

---

1. This definition of user cost is indeed the one obtained by applying Euler's relation to the standard intertemporal maximization : $\int e^{-rt}\, (\,pQ - wN - qI\,)\, dt$. The concept of user cost precisely enables the dynamic intertemporal optimization to be reduced to the customary "static" optimization (in the absence of adjustment costs). See Jorgenson [1963].

and shows that the maximization of (3a) is decomposable.The maximization of period t profit determines output and labor in t on the basis of prices and any quantitative constraints observed in the two markets:

$$\text{Max } (p_t\, Q_t - w_t\, L_t)$$

$$Q_t \leq F\,(K_t\,,\, L_t)$$

$\left.\vphantom{\begin{array}{c}a\\a\end{array}}\right\}$ determines $Q_t\,,\, L_t$

The maximization of expected profit net of the cost of capital determines output, labor and expected capital for period t +1 on the basis of expected prices and any expected constraints:

$$\text{Max } (p^*_{t+1}\, Q_{t+1} - w^*_{t+1}\, L_{t+1} - c^*_{t+1}\, K_{t+1})$$

$$Q_{t+1} \leq F(K_{t+1}\,,\, L_{t+1})$$

$\left.\vphantom{\begin{array}{c}a\\a\end{array}}\right\}$ determines $Q_{t+1}\,,\, L_{t+1}$, K_{t+1} and I_t

In this last case, we are interested only in demand for capital K_{t+1}, which sets the demand for investment decided on in period (t):

$$(1a) \qquad I_t = K_{t+1}\,(1+\delta) - K_t$$

This simplification corresponds to the definition customarily used both in macroeconomic theory and in macroeconomic models. Subsequently, and in keeping with standard practice, we shall refer to K_{t+1} as desired capital.

Investment demand represents: (a) a demand for a "capital" good in the goods market; (b) a demand for loan funds in the financial market, equal to the net change in indebtedness. Ignoring share issues, we obtain the accounting equation:

$$(5) \qquad q_t\, I_t \;=\; A_t \;+\; B_{t+1} - B_t$$

	Gross	*Gross*	*Net*
	investment	*cash flow*	*indebtedness*

The complete model thus defined enables us to describe different situations, depending on the constraints perceived and anticipated in the various markets concerned by the investment expenditure:

- competitive markets (Walrasian equilibrium);

- expected constraint on demand (Keynesian situation);
- expected constraint on unemployment;
- financial constraint.

In the first situation, investment demand depends only on prices and determines the notional supply of goods for period (t+1) and desired indebtedness according to the following flowchart:

Expected prices for (t+1) $\rightarrow$ Notional investment demand $\rightarrow$ Desired output for (t+1)

$\downarrow$

Indebtedness

In the second and third situations, prices and the expected constraint for period (t+1) determine investment (and indebtedness):

Expected costs for (t+1) $\rightarrow$ Effective investment demand $\leftarrow$ Expected constraint for (t+1)

$\downarrow$

Indebtedness

In the final situation, financial constraints unilaterally determine investment:

Indebtedness $\rightarrow$ Investment

1.2. Notional and effective demands in the absence of financial constraints

Since we are interested only in investment here, we shall restrict ourselves to calculating optimal capital at the date (t + 1), omitting the index (t + 1) to simplify notations, since all quantities refer to this period. The program is written:

(6) $\quad$ Max $\{ \Pi(Q,L) - c^* K \}$
$\quad$ $Q \leq f(K,L)$
$\quad$ $Q \leq Q^*$ $\quad$ $L \leq L^*$

Using the production function, we can always express profit in terms of expected prices, capital and one of the two variables "labor" or "output":

$\Pi_1(K,L) = p^* f(K,L) - w^* L$
$\Pi_2(K,Q) = p^* Q - w^* L(Q,K)$

When financial constraints are absent, the maximization (6) will always cause the marginal profitability of capital to equal the user cost of capital:

(7) $\Pi'_K = c*$

but this marginal profitability will be expressed differently depending on the nature of expected constraints.

a. Notional demand or true neoclassical model

This model corresponds to the conventional hypotheses of the neoclassical general equilibrium: competitive markets and absence of demand constraints. Capital demand, which depends only on expected labor and capital costs, is obtained by resolving the first-order conditions:

$$\left.\begin{array}{l} \Pi'_{1K} = p* \, f'_K \ = \ c* \\ \Pi'_{1L} = p* \, f'_L \ - \ w* = 0 \\ Q \ = f(K,L) \end{array}\right\} \quad \Rightarrow \quad K = K(c*/p*, \, w*/p*)$$

The second-order condition requires non-increasing returns to scale[2]. Using marginal conditions and Euler's law, we can write a general expression of notional demand for capital in differentiated form (see Appendix 2 to Chapter 8 for the demonstration of differentiated equations 9, 10 and 11):

$$(9) \qquad \frac{dK}{K} = -\left(\beta\,\sigma + \frac{1-\beta}{1-v}\right)\frac{d\left(\frac{c}{p}\right)}{\frac{c}{p}} - \beta\left(\frac{1}{1-v} - \sigma\right)\frac{d\left(\frac{w}{p}\right)}{\frac{w}{p}}$$

β is the share of wage costs in total cost $[wN/(wN+cK)]$. This coefficient is equal to the coefficient $\beta/(\alpha+\beta)$ of the Cobb-Douglas function. v represents returns to scale of the production function (homogeneous and of degree v), σ elasticity of substitution. Equation (9) shows that notional demand is an always-decreasing function of capital cost and a usually-decreasing function of labor cost $(\sigma(1+v)<1)$. Coefficient β depends, in general, on the relative

---

2. This condition is obviously very restrictive. It can, however, be eased when the uncertainty on prices or adjustment costs is incorporated.

capital-labor cost (except in the case of a Cobb-Douglas function, where it is strictly constant). We can nevertheless verify that the variations of this coefficient are negligible compared to factor-cost changes (see Chapter 5). As a result, differentiated equations such as (9) can be used in practice for an econometric estimate of the models.

b. Effective demand for investment: exogenous expected demand

If demand is assumed to be constrained, the marginal profitability of capital equals the product of the wage rate by the marginal substitution rate. Optimal capital is obtained by resolving:

(7b) $\Pi'_{2K} = - w^* L'_K = c^*$

$\Rightarrow K = K(Q, c^*/w^*)$

(2) $Q = f(K,L)$

This last condition is quite simply the identity between the relative capital-labor cost and the marginal substitution rate. The second-order conditions merely imply that the isoquants are upwardly concave. They impose no restrictions on returns to scale. Writing returns to scale v , substitution elasticity σ , the share of wage cost in total cost β , and the rates of Harrod and Solow technical progress γ_n and γ_k , we get a general, differentiated expression of effective demand:

$$\frac{dK}{K} = \frac{1}{v} \frac{dQ^*}{Q^*} - \beta \sigma \frac{d\left(\frac{c^*}{w^*}\right)}{\left(\frac{c^*}{w^*}\right)} - [\beta \sigma \gamma_n + (1 - \beta \sigma) \gamma_K] \, dt$$

c. Expected constraint on labor

This situation appears when the labor demand corresponding to the investment demands studied above exceeds the expected supply of labor. This constraint leads to a demand for capital conditioned by the labor supply and the cost of capital:

(7c) $\Pi'_{1K} = p^* f'_K = c^*$

$\Rightarrow K = K(L^*, c^*/p^*)$

(2) $Q = f(K,L)$

As earlier, the response of investment to the interest rate depends mainly on the elasticity of substitution between capital and labor. The response equals zero if the function has complementary factors, and it increases in absolute value with the elasticity of substitution. In differentiated form, we get:

$$(11) \qquad \frac{dK}{K} = - \cfrac{1}{\cfrac{1 - \dfrac{\eta}{v}}{\sigma} - \dfrac{\eta}{v}\left(1 - \dfrac{1}{v}\right)} \; \frac{d\left(\dfrac{c}{p}\right)}{\left(\dfrac{c}{p}\right)} + \cfrac{\left(1 - \dfrac{v}{\eta}\right)}{1 - \cfrac{v}{\eta\left(1 + \sigma - \dfrac{\sigma}{v}\right)}} \left(\frac{dL}{L}\right)$$

β is the share of capital cost in output value, σ and v are elasticity of substitution and returns to scale.

d. A note on the "neoclassical model"

The model described as neoclassical in the literature was derived by Jorgenson [1963 and ff.] using the marginal condition:

$$(7a) \qquad \Pi'_{1K} = p^* \, f_K \; = \; c^*$$

and resolving optimal capital in terms of output and the real cost of capital:

$$K = K(Q, c^*/p^*)$$

As many authors (such as Coen [1969], Gould [1969] and Duharcourt [1970]) have pointed out, this model constitutes an erroneous specification of the "true neoclassical" or notional-demand model. On the other hand, it resembles the effective-demand model because of the decisive role of the accelerator effect (on the respective influence of the accelerator and user cost, see the controversies between Eisner and Nadiri [1968, 1970], Hall and Jorgenson [1967, 1969], Jorgenson and Stephenson [1969], and Bischoff [1969], as well as the discussions of these models in Muet [1979a]).

The distinction progressively established between the profit-maximization model and the model of cost minimization at given output (ex. Helliwell [1976] and Brechling [1973]) is basically informed by the distinction between notional and effective demand (first applied to investment by Grossman [1972]). From the empirical point of view, the notional-demand model was soon abandoned after the unsuccessful attempts by Gould and Waud [1973], Schramm [1972] and Brechling [1973], while the model combining accelerator effect and user-cost influence in the Jorgenson version (c/p) or effective demand (c/w) has gradually prevailed. Even today, it continues to serve as the basic specification of the major econometric models.

1.3. Putty-clay model

The hypothesis that capital and labor bundled together are substitutable is a poor description of the actual process of capital-labor substitution, which essentially involves replacing obsolete machinery by new equipment. As a result, the econometric studies that have elaborated on the Jorgenson approach have generally adopted the hypothesis of a putty-clay production function. The econometric results obtained for different countries confirm the model's relevance (Bischoff [1971], Ando, Modigliani, Rasche and Turnovsky [1974] for the USA; King [1972] for Britain; de Ménil and Yohn [1977] for France; Artus, Muet, Palinkas and Pauly [1981] for West Germany and France; Schiantarelli [1983] for Italy).In this hypothesis, substitution no longer involves capital as a whole, but investment alone, since production techniques rigidify when the equipment is installed. Optimization is accordingly applied to the equipment's profitable lifetime, and the user cost of capital is redefined by factoring in expected wage-cost changes (Ando, Modigliani, Rasche and Turnovsky [1974]).

The choice of production techniques is summed up by the *ex ante* production function linking the desired increase in production capacity ΔQ_t to investment I_t and to the quantity of labor ΔL_t required to implement it:

$$\Delta Q_t = f(\Delta L_t, I_t)$$

The *ex post* production function has fixed coefficients. Ignoring physical depreciation of capital and assuming that technical progress is entirely embodied in the equipment, installed production capacity at date t and the quantity of labor required to implement it remain constant in later periods:

$$\Delta L_{t+\theta} = \Delta L_t \quad , \quad \Delta Q_{t+\theta} = \Delta Q_t \qquad \forall\, \theta \geq 0$$

The net discounted profit on the investment expenditure becomes:

$$\int_0^T (p_{t+\theta} \cdot \Delta Q_t - w_{t+\theta} \cdot \Delta L_t) \, e^{-r\theta} \, d\theta - q_t \, I_t$$

where T is the equipment's profitable lifetime (determined by the growth rates of the technical progress embodied in the machinery and of real wages).

The different specifications of the investment function corresponding to expected disequilibrium configurations are studied in detail in Chapter 8. For the moment, let us confine ourselves to the case of an expected demand constraint. Installed production capacity then becomes exogenous, and the maximization of discounted net profit on investment expenditure is reduced to the minimization of discounted production cost:

$$\text{Min} \left\{ \int_0^T w_{t+\theta} \cdot \Delta L_t \, e^{-r\theta} \, d\theta + q_t \, I_t \right\}$$

constrained by the *ex ante* production function: $\Delta Q_t = f(\Delta L_t, I_t)$.

Writing the expected wage growth rate ω, we can express the objective function as:

$$w_t \cdot \frac{1 - e^{-(r-\omega)T}}{(r-\omega)} \, \Delta L_t + q_t \, I_t,$$

so that by defining the user cost of capital as:

$$c_t^* = q_t \cdot \frac{(r - \omega)}{1 - e^{-(r-\omega)T}} \quad ,$$

we are led to minimize the usual function:

$$w_t \, \Delta L_t + c_t^* \, I_t$$

The only changes with respect to the previous model concern: (a) the form of user cost; (b) the fact that the relative capital-labor cost involves only new investment and not total capital. Using the earlier approximations and notations, with ΔQ_t^* as expected output expansion, the putty-clay model is written:

$$I_t = k_0 \quad (\Delta Q_t^*)^{1/v} \quad (w_t / c_t^*)^{\beta \sigma}$$

b. The influence of taxation

The analyses set forth earlier disregard taxation. This factor entails a redefinition of the user cost of capital to incorporate the profit-tax rate (β), the tax life of equipment (T_f) and the rates of tax deduction (k). We distinguish between two rates: k_1 is the rate of tax deduction that is applied to the level of investment and that reduces both the tax due and the depreciation base ; k_2 is the rate of deduction applied to the tax itself, without altering the depreciation base. This section follows the general description in Avouyi-Dovi and Muet [1987 a].

As interest charges are tax-deductible, the rate at which the firm must discount its cash inflows and outflows is $(1-\beta)$ r if it uses these to reduce its debt, $(1-\tau)$ r if it uses them to pay dividends (τ is the rate of tax on stockholders). We shall use the first formulation later in our discussion.

If we additionally assume the tax depreciation rules to be exponential, the depreciation of equipment (q I) in period t is:

$$A_t = q I \; \frac{\alpha \, e^{-\alpha t}}{1 - e^{-\alpha T_f}}$$

Fitting the previous optimization with the new value of the discounting rate, and distinguishing between the two rates of tax deduction, we can write the user cost of capital as:

$$c = q \; FISC \; \frac{(1 - \beta) \, r - \omega}{1 - e^{- [(1-\beta)r-\omega]T}}$$

with

$$FISC = \frac{1}{1-\beta} \left[1 - k_1 - k_2 - (1 - k_1) \beta \frac{\alpha}{\alpha + (1-\beta) r} \frac{1 - e^{-[\alpha + (1-\beta)r]T_f}}{1 - e^{-\alpha T_f}} \right]$$

1.4. Uncertainty, profitability and the implicit approach

The previously adopted hypothesis of given expected changes in demand leads to an investment demand whose form varies considerably according to whether or not the expected constraint is binding. This is obviously a caricature, as firms' expectations are not certain variables, nor will the firm ever be assured of finding itself in one of the two situations. By taking this uncertainty into account, notably as regards demand changes, we can generate an intermediate model, as we shall demonstrate. When the irreversibility of the investment decision is factored in (with, for example, a complementary-factor model), this approach also effectively highlights the role of "profitability" in the investment decision (Malinvaud [1980]). We shall therefore assume in this section that price expectations are certain variables, while expected demand change is random. We characterize this random variable by its cumulative function $P(Q)$:

$$P(Q) = \text{Probability that } Q_{t+1} \leq Q$$

The limits of the probability distribution of demand are designated by Q_m and Q_M: $P(Q_m) = 0$ $P(Q_M) = 1$,
and we assume the firm determines its desired capital for $(t+1)$ by maximizing the mean of its profit net of user cost of capital, constrained by the production function:

$$(12) \quad \underset{(K_{t+1}, L_{t+1})}{\text{Max}} \int_{Q_m}^{Q_M} [p^*_{t+1} Q - c^*_{t+1} K_{t+1} - w^*_{t+1} L_{t+1}] \ d P(Q)$$

$$Q \leq F(K_{t+1}, L_{t+1})$$

By expressing profit, as earlier, in terms of (random) demand Q and of capital stock to be installed K_{t+1}, the preceding maximization is written:

$$(12\,b\,) \qquad \text{Max} \left\{ \int_{Q_m}^{Q_M} \Pi_2(Q\,,\,K_{t+1})\; d\,P\,(Q) - c_{t+1}^{*}\,K_{t+1} \right\}$$

Mean of profit E (Π) Cost of capital

If the function Π_2 is continuous and derivable with respect to K_{t+1}, we obtain the maximum from the marginal condition:

$$(7.\,d) \qquad \frac{\partial\,E\,(\Pi)}{\partial\,K_{t+1}} = E\left[\frac{\partial\,\Pi}{\partial\,K_{t+1}}\right] = c_{t+1}^{*}$$

This condition expresses the fact that optimal capital K_{t+1} is such that the expected marginal return on capital equals the capital's user cost.

The determination of capital demand is closely dependent on the production-function hypotheses for two reasons: (a) the existence of notional demand in the hypothesis of diminishing returns to scale; (b) the irreversibility of the investment decision when the production technique applicable to the installed equipment has fixed coefficients (complementary factors or putty-clay model). When substitutions are possible on installed equipment, demand uncertainty has little effect on the investment decision, since an expectation error can always be corrected by adjusting the variable factors (in this case, by adjusting labor). The resolution then depends exclusively on the situation of notional supply Q^s_{t+1} relative to expected demand ($Q_m \le Q \le Q_M$). The marginal condition is written:

$$(7.\,e) \qquad E\left(\frac{\partial\,L}{\partial\,K_{t+1}}\right) = -\frac{c^{*}_{t+1}}{w^{*}_{t+1}} \qquad \text{if} \qquad Q^s_{t+1} > Q_M$$

$$(7.\,f) \qquad \frac{\displaystyle\int_{Q_m}^{Q^s_{t+1}} \left(\frac{\partial L}{\partial\,K_{t+1}}\right) d\,P\,(Q)}{P\,(Q^s_{t+1})} = -\frac{c^{*}_{t+1}}{w^{*}_{t+1}} \quad \text{if } Q_m \le Q^s_{t+1} \le Q_M.$$

In the first case, effective capital demand depends on the probability distribution of demand and on the relative capital-labor cost. It can be shown

(Rothschild and Stiglitz [1971]) that if the elasticity of substitution is less than or equal to unity, an increase in output variability will increase optimal capital. As an example, using a Cobb-Douglas function, we get:

$$(13) \qquad K_{t+1} = A \left(\frac{c^*_{t+1}}{w^*_{t+1}} \right)^{-\frac{\beta}{\alpha+\beta}} [\, E(Q^{1/\beta})]^{\frac{\beta}{\alpha+\beta}}$$

In the second hypothesis, the resolution leads to a capital demand determined, as before, by the probability distribution of demand and by the relative capital-labor cost, but also by notional supply, and so by the cost of capital and labor. The model thus obtained stands halfway between effective demand in a certainty situation and notional demand. With a Cobb-Douglas function, we obtain:

$$(13\,b) \qquad K_{t+1} = A \left(\frac{c^*_{t+1}}{w^*_{t+1}} \right)^{-\frac{\beta}{\alpha+\beta}} \frac{\int_{Q_m}^{Q^s_{t+1}} Q^{\frac{1}{\beta}} \, dP\,(Q)}{P\,(Q^s_{t+1})}$$

This function expresses in a simple, continuous form the discontinuous model presented earlier.

The hypothesis of an absence of substitution on installed equipment allows an accurate expression of the effect of uncertainty on capital demand. It also permits the use of the implicit approach to investment demand (Tobin's q) without resorting to the notion of cost adjustment, as has generally been the case (see section 1.5 below). Thus, using a static formulation of the "putty-clay" hypothesis, Malinvaud [1983] has shown that the desired output capacity (here for the period t +1) could be connected to Tobin's q ratio. As earlier, P(Q) stands for the probability that demand in t +1 will be less than, or equal to, Q. The "putty-clay" hypothesis is reflected in the fact that the firm, at the date t, can choose the production techniques to be applied in t +1, but that once this choice is made, the short-term production function that describes the relationship between output capacity, labor and output for t +1 has fixed coefficients. We shall omit the index t +1 to simplify the notations; Q is output, Q^s output capacity, L labor, and k the coefficient of capital desired in t + 1. These values are linked together by the *ex post* production function:

$k = K/Q^s$

$L = Q \cdot g(k)$ $\qquad\qquad$ $g(k)$ being the *ex ante* function.

The profit net of capital cost is expressed in terms of actual output Q and production capacity Q^s :

$$\Delta V = [\, p^* - w^* \, g(k) \,] \, Q - c^* \, k \, Q^s$$

Its mean becomes:

$$E\,(\Delta V) = (p^* - w^* \; g(k)) \left[(1 - P(Q^s)) \, Q^s + \int_0^{Q^s} Q \; dP(Q) \right] - c^* \, k \, Q^s$$

The first term represents the profit related to the installation of capacity Q^s multiplied by the expected rate of utilization of this production capacity:

$$T\,(Q^s) = 1 - P\,(Q^s) + \int_0^{Q^s} \frac{1}{Q^s} \; Q \; d\,P\,(Q)$$

Corporate investment decisions therefore concern two variables:
- production capacity to be installed Q^s ;
- capital intensity k.

The necessary optimality conditions are therefore:

$$\frac{\partial E}{\partial Q^s} = [p^* - w^* \, g(k)] \, (1 - P(Q^s)) - c^* \, k = 0 \,;$$

$$\frac{\partial E}{\partial k} = - \, [w^* \, g'(k) \, T(Q^s) + c^*] \, Q^s = 0 \,;$$

or also:

(14) $\qquad [\, p^* - w^* \, g(k) \,] \; [\, 1 - P(Q^s) \,] = c^* \, k$

(15) $\qquad g'(k) \, T(\,Q^s\,) = - \; c^* \, / \, w^*$

The first equation indicates that, at the optimum, the cost of the capital required to produce one unit of good (c*k) is equal to the profit per unit produced multiplied by the probability of excess demand. The second equation shows that the marginal rate of capital/labor substitution adjusted by the expected capacity-utilization rate is equal to the relative price of capital and labor.

This static putty-clay model implies the assumption that identical conditions will prevail in later periods. If we also postulate equipment lifetime as infinite, the present value of profits generated by the equipment is:

$$V = \int_0^\infty [p^* - w^* g(k)] \cdot T(Q^s) \cdot e^{-rt} dt = \frac{[p^* - w^* g(k)] T(Q^s)}{r}$$

and the user cost is equal to $c^* = q_t \ r$.

Tobin's q ratio, defined as the ratio of discounted profits from the investment to the investment's value, is thus:

$$(16) \qquad q = \frac{V}{q_t k} = \frac{T(Q^s) [p^* - w^* g(k)]}{c^* k}$$

Substituting (16) into (14), we get:

$$q = T(Q^s) \ / \ [1 - P(Q)]$$

This equation determines capacity in terms of Tobin's q. If the expected distribution of demand has a lower limit Q_m, the left-hand term equals 0 when $Q^s = Q_m$ and tends to $+ \infty$ when $Q^s \rightarrow + \infty$. Malinvaud examines the case where the left-hand term is effectively increasing and monotonic, making capacity Q^s an increasing function of the q ratio. Artus [1984 a, Chapter 9 below] has adapted this model to the case of an explicitly intertemporal corporate optimization in the putty-clay hypothesis. The optimality conditions are more complex there, but yield a system of integratable differential equations that provide a single optimal path for firms' production capacity and labor force. The estimation of this model shows that corporate expectations of shifts in demand — embodied in probabilities P(Q) — greatly exceed those observed at the time of the investment decision.

1.5. Adjustment costs and implicit approach (Tobin's q): a simplified presentation

The inclusion of adjustment costs — originally introduced to justify lags in adjusting to desired capital (Eisner and Strotz [1963]; Lucas [1967]; Gould [1968]) — has led to a distinction between investment demand and capital demand. This method converges with the one introduced by Tobin (as in, for example, Abel [1980]). Before examining this approach in greater detail, we shall recall some results concerning adjustment costs.

a. Gradual adjustment to desired capital

The introduction of adjustment costs in the form of a function of net capital change ($K_{t+1} - K_t$) or gross capital change (I_t) has two consequences. First, it eliminates instant adjustment to desired capital. Second, it makes present and future decisions interdependent: by incorporating capital- or labor-adjustment costs, we can no longer decompose the maximization of the firm's value by period. The choice of K_{t+1} is no longer independent from that of K_{t+2} and therefore, recurrently, from the stock of optimal capital in all future periods. The impact on the adjustment of actual capital to desired capital can be shown by simply overlooking this intertemporal aspect. In our two-period model, this means disregarding the fact that K_{t+1} helps determine K_{t+2} . Let us, as earlier, define desired capital as the capital K^*_{t+1} that maximizes the profit net of capital cost in the absence of adjustment costs. This desired capital is determined by $\Pi'_K = c^*_{t+1}$. Since the profit net of capital cost is maximal for K^*_{t+1}, the choice of a non-optimum capital will entail a disadjustment cost that, in a first approximation, will be a quadratic function of the deviation ($K_{t+1} - K^*_{t+1}$). The adjustment cost of capital from t to t +1 (discounted in t +1) is a function of the difference $K_{t+1} - K_t$. This function is always positive, equaling zero when the capital does not vary. If we assume it to be continuous and differentiable up to the second order, we can approximate it by a quadratic function of ($K_{t+1} - K_t$).

Maximizing the net profit of costs is therefore the same as minimizing the sum of adjustment and disadjustment costs:

$$\text{Min } \{ \ a \ (K_{t+1} - K_t)^2 + b \ (K_{t+1} - K^*_{t+1})^2 \ \}$$

yielding:

$$K_{t+1} = \lambda \ K_t + (1-\lambda) \ K^*_{t+1} \qquad \text{with} \quad \lambda = a \ / \ (a+b)$$

The adjustment of optimal capital to desired capital is therefore a geometrical one, whose mean lag ($\theta = \lambda \ / \ (1-\lambda) = a \ / \ b$) is equal to the ratio of adjustment cost to disadjustment cost. More generally, when the production function comprises several factors, for example n factors of the x^i type, the total cost, in a first approximation, takes the quadratic form:

$$C(X_{t+1}) = (X_{t+1} - X^*_{t+1})' \ B \ (X_{t+1} - X^*_{t+1}) + (X_{t+1} - X_t)' \ A \ (X_{t+1} - X_t)$$

where B and A are symmetrical square matrices and X the production-factor vector. By minimizing total cost, we obtain a vectorial adjustment equation that generalizes the preceding relation:

$$X_{t+1} = \Lambda \ X_t + (1-\Lambda) \ X^*_{t+1}$$

with $\qquad A = [B+A]^{-1} \ A$

As a result, the adjustment functions can accommodate "cross-lags" of various factors such as capital and labor.

This cross-adjustment model, introduced by Nadiri and Rosen [1969, 1974], was estimated for France by Pouchain [1980] and Artus and Migus [1986, Chapter 6 below]. The non-diagonal terms, however, have generally proved non-significant.

b. Implicit approach (Tobin's q)

In treating the investment decision as a financial investment, Tobin [1969] suggested that the investment rate should be a function of the ratio of the firm's increase in value resulting from a new-equipment purchase to the equipment cost (ratio called q). More recently, Yoshikawa [1980] has shown that the optimal investment rate must be such as to make the marginal cost of installing the new equipment equal q - 1. Empirical studies on the subject — such as von Furstenberg [1977]; Malkiel, von Furstenberg and Watson [1979] — use average q, the ratio of the firms' market value to the capital replacement value. Conversely, the theoretical models show the link between investment and marginal q, calculated from a marginal — and non-observable — increase in capital.

We can adapt Hayashi's formulation [1982] of Tobin's marginal q to the two-period model set out earlier. By the introduction of a capital adjustment cost C (It), equation (3), expressed in real terms, becomes:

$$\Delta V = (p_t Q_t - w_t L_t) - q_t I_t - q_t C(I_t) + \frac{(p^*_{t+1} Q_{t+1} - w^*_{t+1} L_{t+1})}{1+r} + \frac{q^*_{t+1} K_{t+1}}{1+r} - q_t K_t + d$$

with C' > 0, C" > 0, and the constraints:

(1) $I_t = K_{t+1} (1+\delta) - K_t$
(2') $Q_t \leq F (K_t , L_t)$ (2") $Q_{t+1} \leq F (K_{t+1} , L_{t+1})$

Maximization, relative to I_t , K_{t+1} and L_{t+1} , presupposes the following optimality conditions:

$$- w^*_{t+1} + p^*_{t+1} f_L(K_{t+1}, L_{t+1}) = 0 ;$$

(17) $$\frac{p^*_{t+1} f_K(K_{t+1}, L_{t+1})}{(1+r)} + \frac{q^*_{t+1}}{(1+r)} - \mu (1 + \delta) = 0 ;$$

$$- q_t [1+C'(I_t)] + \mu = 0$$

μ is defined as the multiplier associated with the constraint (1).

The first condition is the usual condition that the marginal productivity of labor must equal real wages. The second equation enables us to calculate the ratio:

(18) $$q_t = \frac{\mu}{q_t} = \frac{p^*_{t+1} f_K + q^*_{t+1}}{q_t (1+ \delta) (1+r)}$$

This ratio represents the change in the firm's discounted value entailed by a marginal increase in the investment made at date t. Thus q_t is indeed Tobin's marginal q.

Consequently, the third condition provides the investment function through an inversion of function C':

(19) $I_t = C'(q_t - 1)$

This is an increasing function of marginal q 's difference from unity (as $C''>0$). It would be wrong, however, to use (19) in isolation for an econometric study of investment, since q_t is an endogenous variable whose value is obtained by resolving system (17) in its entirety. Nevertheless, if the production function f is homogeneous of degree one, we get:

$$p^*_{t+1} Q_{t+1} = p^*_{t+1} \ f'_K K_{t+1} + w^*_{t+1} L_{t+1}$$

and (18) can be written:

(20) $$q_t = \frac{p^*_{t+1} Q_{t+1} - w^*_{t+1} L_{t+1} + q^*_{t+1} K_{t+1}}{q_t (I_t + K_t) (1+r)}$$

q_t then becomes identical to the ratio of the firm's discounted value at the end of period t +1 to the value of its capital at the end of period t — i.e. to Tobin's average q. Only in this case of degree-one homogeneity are average q and marginal q identical.

One must also postulate fully competitive markets ensuring equality among productivities and prices. The hypothesis of given demand eliminates the relation between the "marginal" ratio and the firm's value, hence between the investment and the firm's value (Blanchard and Sachs [1982a,b]). Equation (18) accordingly becomes:

(18 b) $$q_t = \frac{w^*_{t+1} \dfrac{f'_K}{f'_L} + q^*_{t+1}}{q_t (1+\delta) (1+r)} \quad ,$$

while (19) remains unchanged.

In the expression of q , marginal productivity of capital is replaced by the cost reduction resulting from a shift along the isoquant ($w^*_{t+1} \cdot f'_K / f'_L$). A wage rise will increase, say, the *marginal q* ratio and investment, but diminish the firm's value and the *average q* ratio. This divorces investment from the *average q ratio* , which is alone observable.

1.6. Adjustment cost and implicit approach: complete modeling in continuous time with infinite horizon

The consequence of incorporating adjustment costs has been spelled out in the simplified context of the two-period model used to introduce the main investment models. In this section, we shall discuss those implications in the broader context of a continuous-time, infinite-horizon model. We have drawn on the articles by Blanchard and Sachs [1982 a,b] and d'Autume and Michel [1984].

Companies maximize their discounted value:

$$\text{Max } V = \int_0^x [\, pQ - wL - q\,I\,(1 + \phi(I/K))\,]\,e^{-rt}\,dt$$

where $\phi(I/K)$ is an investment installation cost, assumed to be convex in I/K.

The firm's production function is: Q=f(K,L)

The constraints are the same as before:

$f(K,L) \le \bar{Q}$ (demand constraint, multiplier: $p\,\lambda_Q\,e^{-rt}$)

$I \le \bar{I}$ (constraint on the investment, multiplier: $q\,\lambda_I\,e^{-rt}$,

resulting for example from a financial constraint)

$L \le \bar{L}$ (constraint on available labor, multiplier: $w\,\lambda_L\,e^{-rt}$)

$\overset{\circ}{K} \le I - \delta K$ (capital accumulation, multiplier: $q\,q\,e^{-rt}$)

Euler's conditions are written:

(21) $\dfrac{\partial \mathcal{H}}{\partial I} = 0 \;\Leftrightarrow\; \phi\!\left(\dfrac{I}{K}\right) + \dfrac{I}{K}\,\phi'\!\left(\dfrac{I}{K}\right) = q - 1 - \lambda_I$

(22) $\dfrac{\partial \mathcal{H}}{\partial L} = 0 \;\Leftrightarrow\; f'_L(K,L) = \dfrac{w\,(1+\lambda_L)}{p\,(1-\lambda_Q)}$

(23) $\dfrac{d(q\,qe^{-rt})}{dt} = -\dfrac{\partial \mathcal{H}}{\partial K} \;\Leftrightarrow\; \overset{\circ}{q} = (r+\delta-\rho)\,q - \dfrac{p}{q}\,f'_K\,(1-\lambda_Q) - \left(\dfrac{I}{K}\right)^2\phi'\!\left(\dfrac{I}{K}\right)$

where $\mathcal{H}$ is the Hamiltonian and ρ the investment-price growth rate. Since ϕ is convex, the left-hand member of the first condition is an increasing function of (I/K).

If the firm experiences no direct constraint on investment ($\lambda_I = 0$), the investment rate I/K is an increasing function of q - 1, where, as before, q is Tobin's marginal q (change in the firm's value due to change in available capital). Similarly, (22) shows that if the firm's demand or available labor are constrained (respectively $\lambda_Q > 0$ and $\lambda_L > 0$), the marginal productivity of labor quite logically exceeds real wages w/p.

If the firm experiences no constraint at all and if the production function exhibits constant returns to scale, then (22) is written:

$$f_L\left(1, \frac{L}{K}\right) = f_L (K, L) = \frac{w}{p}$$

from which we can deduce that the capital-labor ratio is determined exclusively by real wages.

We can therefore summarize the solution by:

$$I = \text{Min} \{\bar{I}, I^d\}$$

When $I = I^d$, then, removing ($1 - \lambda_Q$) between (22) and (23), we get:

$$(24) \quad \overset{\circ}{q} = (r + \delta - \rho)\, q \; - \frac{w}{q} \;\; (1+\lambda_L) \;\; \frac{f_K(1, L/K)}{f_L(1, L/K)} - \left(\frac{I}{K}\right)^2 \; \phi'\!\left(\frac{I}{K}\right)$$

The transversality condition — which, moreover, needs to be verified — is :

$$\lim_{t \to \infty} \; (q\; q\, e^{-rt}\, K) = 0$$

We see that q increases with $w\, f_K / q\, f_L$ (the gain in wage costs afforded by a capital increase along the isoquant) and $(I/K)^2 \phi'$ (the fall in installation cost made possible through a marginal increase in capital stock).

a) If the firm is totally unconstrained ($\lambda_Q = \lambda_L = \lambda_I = 0$), we have seen that, with constant returns to scale, N/K depends solely on real wages. As f_K is then exclusively determined by N/K, the ratio f_K / f_L is therefore solely dependent on real wages.The optimal investment rate, defined by:

(21) $\quad \dfrac{\partial \mathcal{H}}{\partial I} = 0 \quad \Leftrightarrow \quad \phi\!\left(\dfrac{I}{K}\right) + \dfrac{I}{K}\,\phi'\!\left(\dfrac{I}{K}\right) = q - 1$

therefore depends only on q.

The change in q (equation 24) therefore makes q dependent on $(r+\delta-\rho)$, w/q, w/p and q: by integrating, we see that q (and in particular q_0 at $t = 0$) depends only on expected exogenous variables, and not on existing capital stock K_0.

Tobin's *average q* is the ratio $V/q_0 K_0$; *marginal q* is $dV/q_0 dK_0$; if *marginal q* does not depend on K_0 , we see that V is a linear function of K_0, so that *average q and marginal q are identical* (result first established by Hayashi [1982]).

Another feature of this constraint-free situation is that, if wages w rise, f'_L must rise and L/K must consequently fall, since $f'_L(1,L/K)= w/p$ and $f''_{L^2}< 0$. If $f''_{LK} > 0$ (as occurs in a production function of the Cobb-Douglas or CES type), f'_K falls. Since q is a function of f'_K (equation 24), q drops too, implying a fall in the investment rate.

b) If the firm is demand-constrained ($\lambda_Q > 0$), I/K remains a function of q , but $f'_L > w/p$, and q no longer has a fixed relation to the firm's value V. Integrating (24) with $\lambda_L = 0$, we obtain:

$$q = \int_0^\infty \left(\frac{w}{q}\,\frac{f'_K}{f'_L} + \left(\frac{I}{K}\right)^2 \phi'\!\left(\frac{I}{K}\right) \right) e^{-(r+\delta-\rho)t}\, dt$$

If w increases, q rises for a given f'_K / f'_L , so the firm gradually augments its capital. But since $f(K,L) = Q$, L/K falls, as does f'_K (if $f''_{LK} > 0$). If initially wf'_K / qf'_L is certain to have increased, q 's later variation trend is uncertain.

In stationary equilibrium (assuming constant w, q, Q and p) *with demand constraint,* we get:

$$\frac{I}{K} = \delta$$

$$\bar{Q} = f\,(N,\,K)$$

Thus:

$$q = 1 + \phi(\delta) + \delta\,\phi'(\delta)$$

and

$$(r+\delta-\rho)\, q \; - \; \frac{w}{q}\, \frac{f'_K}{f'_L} \; - \; \delta^2\, \phi'(\delta) \; = 0$$

yielding:

$$\frac{f'_K}{f'_L} = \frac{q\,(r+\delta-\rho)}{w}\,(1 + \phi(\delta) + \delta\,\phi'(\delta)\,) - \frac{q}{w}\,\delta^2\phi'(\delta)$$

Only when $\phi(\delta) = \phi'(\delta) = 0$ do we once again encounter the usual condition: $f_K'/f_L' = w/c$, where c is the user cost of capital.

Without demand constraint:

$$f_L' = w/p$$
$$q = 1 + \phi(\delta) + \delta\,\phi'(\delta)$$

and as before:

$$\frac{f'_K}{f'_L} = \frac{q\,(r+\delta-\rho)}{w}\,(1 + \phi(\delta) + \delta\,\phi'(\delta)\,) - \frac{q}{w}\,\delta^2\phi'(\delta)$$

1.7. Financial constraints

Investment demand may be limited by financing conditions, in particular when credit is restricted. The credit supply then becomes a constraint, and self-financing resources and indebtedness opportunities determine the financially feasible investment. But other considerations, notably the solvency constraint, can lead firms to prefer self-financing to borrowing. Let us take, for example, the solvency constraint, that is, the obligation for a firm to pay interest on its debts and reimburse them at maturity. One can show (Malinvaud [1981]) that, when profits are random, this constraint imposes a maximum ratio of indebtedness (medium- and long-term debt to equity). This ratio is an increasing function of profit expectations, asset liquidity and debt maturity. By expressing financial constraints as an indebtedness ratio, we can give a very general description of the investment demand of a financially-constrained firm. Taking the balance of the corporate "equity and financial" account:

$$q_t \, I_t = A_t + B_{t+1} - B_t \quad ,$$

dividing by nominal capital ($q_t K_t$) and applying conventional approximations, we obtain an increasing relation between I_t / K_t and the indebtedness ratio for period t and t +1 ($R_t = B_t / q_t K_t$):

$$(21) \qquad \frac{I_t}{K_t} = \frac{A_t}{q_t K_t} + R_{t+1} \left(1 + \dot{q}_{t+1} - \delta + \frac{I_t}{K_t} \right) - R_t$$

The indebtedness ratio R_{t+1} must also comply with the constraint:

$$(22) \qquad R_{t+1} \leq R_m$$

in which R_m depends, as indicated before, on profit expectations, the debt structure and the degree of credit availability (credit rationing causes R_m to fall).

This enables us to distinguish between two regimes, depending on whether constraint (22) is binding or not. If inequality (22) is fulfilled, investment is determined by the models set out above, and (21) determines the indebtedness rate R_{t+1}. If, on the contrary, the investment demand studied earlier entails a rate exceeding R_m, (21) determines the investment that is financially feasible under the prevailing financial constraints. Investment (I/K) thus becomes an increasing function of expected and actual profits and a decreasing function of credit controls, the initial indebtedness ratio and the debt interest rate.

1.8. Investment models

a. Implicit and explicit approaches

The investment models derived earlier by and large offer an explicit approach to investment demand – in that they utilize an explicit treatment of:
- expectations about the different components of investment profitability;
- production-function parameters.

By contrast, in models based on the implicit approach, technical characteristics and expectations about the investment's future profitability are totally subsumed under variable q. The implicit approach has the advantage of integrating expectations directly, but it also has two drawbacks. The first is that formal derivation (such as equation (19)) does not provide an accurate specification for the model and so does not permit an economic interpretation of the coefficients. In fact, the econometric estimates of these models remain distinctively "empirical". The second drawback is that the conventional measure of q (average q) does not coincide with its theoretical value (marginal q) unless we assume competitive markets and constant returns to scale. The explicit approach is the only one to have been extensively applied to the French economy, in the form of effective-demand or general models.

b. Conventional specifications of investment demand

Assuming a production function where *ex ante* and *ex post* substitutions are identical , that is the hypothesis adopted earlier, the investment function can be directly deduced from the differentiated formulations of the various demands. Before looking at the resulting models, we must define the expectation specification.

Information on economic agents' expectations is seldom available. As a result, we are led in practice to equate this expectation process with the optimal forecast of a value based on available information (rational expectations in the broad sense). For lack of direct knowledge of agent information, we can choose between two solutions. The first is to assume that agents base their expectations about that value on past observations alone. The expectation then becomes the optimal autoregressive representation of the expected value. If the value grows in the long run at a constant rate, the autoregressive representation must integrate the trend or apply to the growth rate. In the case of demand, for example:

$$(23) \qquad \overset{o}{Q}{}^{*}_{t+1} = \Phi(L) \cdot \overset{o}{Q}_{t}$$

where L is the lag operator ($L \overset{o}{Q}_{t} = \overset{o}{Q}_{t-1}$) , $\overset{o}{Q}_{t}$ the growth rate of $\overset{o}{Q}_{t}$ and $\Phi(L)$ the lag distribution representing the stochastic process $\overset{o}{Q}_{t}$.

The alternative hypothesis postulates, on the contrary, that the agent is fully informed of the state of the economy (rational expectation in the conventional sense). It is rarely used in estimating the investment function alone, since it can be applied only in a complete model.

Therefore, if we choose a growth-rate specification and an expectation based on aggregate growth, the three models of section 1.2 above yield the following specifications:

- *notional demand (9)*

$$\frac{I}{K} = \Phi_1 \ (L) \left(\frac{\overset{o}{c}}{p} \right) + \Phi_2 \ (L) \left(\frac{\overset{o}{w}}{p} \right) + d$$

- *effective demand (14)*

$$\frac{I}{K} = \Phi_1 \ (L) \ \overset{o}{Q} + \Phi_3 \ (L) \left(\frac{\overset{o}{c}}{w} \right) + d$$

- *labor constraint (16)*

$$\frac{I}{K} = \Phi_1 \ (L) \left(\frac{\overset{o}{c}}{p} \right) + \Phi_2 \ (L) \ \overset{o}{N} + d$$

The long-term coefficients[3] are equal to the elasticities calculated earlier, for example for the effective-demand model:

$$\Phi_1(1) = \frac{1}{v} \qquad\qquad \Phi_2(1) = -\beta\sigma$$

When the production function is putty-clay, substitution no longer affects total capital but only investment. In addition, the discounted profit calculation must cover the equipment's profitable lifetime. We can then redefine the user cost of capital by incorporating the expected change in real wages and the equipment's profitable lifetime (see Ando, Modigliani, Rasche and Turnovsky [1974]). We can use different specifications for the putty-clay model:
   - non-linear model (Bischoff [1971]);
   - log-linearized model;
   - accumulation-rate model.
These specifications and their estimates for the effective-demand model are set out in section 2.3 below.

---

3 It will be recall that the long term coefficient of a distributed lag model $\Phi(L) = a_0 + a_1 L + \dots + a_n L^n$

is $\Phi \ (1) = (a_0 + a_1 + \dots a_n)$ and the mean lag $\dfrac{\Phi' \ (1)}{\Phi \ (1)}$.

c. Financial constraints and general models

Financially constrained investment is an increasing function of actual and expected profits, and a decreasing function of interest rates and indebtedness. A general specification can be written:

$$\frac{I_t}{K_t} = \Phi_1\,(L)\,\Pi_t + \Phi_2\,(L)\,r_t + \Phi_3\,(L)\,R_t + d$$

$$\qquad\quad > 0 \qquad\qquad < 0 \qquad\quad < 0$$

where Π = profit rate; r = interest rate; R = indebtedness rate. In fact, the model is most often restricted to the impact of profits.

The general models that incorporate the financial variables and the previous determinations are of three kinds:

1. Models that include all the variables additively. The theoretical basis for these models can be the aggregation of financially constrained and unconstrained firms. Let us, for example, adopt the profit model for financially constrained firms and the effective-demand model for unconstrained firms. Using the conventional restrictive conditions for aggregation (Chapter 2), we get:

$$\frac{I}{K} = (1-\rho)\left[\frac{1}{v}\,\Phi_1(L)\,\overset{o}{Q} + \beta\sigma\,\Phi_2(L)\left(\frac{\overset{o}{w}}{c}\right)\right] + \rho\,a\,\Phi_3(L)\,\Pi + d$$

The lag distributions are standardized ($\Phi_i(L)=1$) and the coefficient ρ stands for the proportion of financially constrained firms in terms of capital fractions. This model is a general version of the accelerator-profits model ($\sigma=0$) often used in empirical studies.

2. Models that incorporate financial variables into the adjustment lags of the acceleration model or effective-demand model. This implicitly assumes that financial constraints are transitory.

3. An estimation of a multi-regime model. If, for example, we emphasize demand constraints and financial constraints, the general model will be written:

$$I = \text{Min} \{\ I_e\ ,\ I_f\ \}$$

where I_e is the effective-demand model, I_f the financially-constrained model.

2. MAIN RESULTS ON FRENCH DATA

The econometric models of investment used in practice are far less numerous than the theories examined earlier suggest. Setting aside purely academic exercises, two models derived from the acceleration principle have been dominating empirical analysis for many years:
- the effective-demand or "neoclassical" model encountered in the literature of English-speaking countries;
- the accelerator-profits model.
Virtually all the studies oriented toward practical applications have produced a combination of the three explanatory factors - demand, relative cost, profits.

We shall begin by a brief analysis of the notional-demand model, whose few estimations are a good proof of its unrealistic character (the model is nevertheless the implicit basis of a great number of theoretical studies). Next, we shall turn to a fuller examination of the effective-demand model, distinguishing between the influence of demand and that of relative costs. The subsequent section discuss the incorporation of financial constraints. Finally, we present an estimate of multi-regime models.

The results yielded by the implicit approach (Tobin's q) will be examined in the last chapter of the book.

2.1. The notional-demand model

The notional-demand model has been estimated by Schramm [1972] and Muet [1979a; 1979c, Chapter 2 below] for investment, and by Villa, Muet and Boutillier [1980, Chapter 5 below] for labor and investment simultaneously. These estimates show that the model fails to provide a realistic picture of the investment process. The only significant elasticity is that of the user cost of capital, but its estimated value (-0.3 in the first two estimates) is far below its theoretical value (it ought to be considerably greater than unity in absolute value). Moreover, the simultaneous estimate shows a positive influence on labor and a negative one on investment. While this accurately reflects the substitution effect of the effective-demand model, it is incompatible with the notional-demand model, in which the elasticities must all be negative.

The integration of dynamic processes (Artus and Migus [1986, Chapter 6 below]) in the joint estimate of investment and labor does not alter our assessment: the relative-price variables are barely significant, and the estimated inertia of capital and labor is too high to be credible.

Lastly, when we estimate the general model — which is equal to the minimum for notional and effective demands — by applying the constraint that production-function parameters must be identical (Artus and Muet [1983, 1984a, Chapter 8 below]), the notional-demand regime never appears.

2.2.   Effective demand: the acceleration effect

Many estimates[4] have been calculated for the acceleration effect, either in the form of the simple flexible accelerator, or through a more general estimate of the effective-demand model (see Table 1). When the specification links the accumulation rate to distributed lags in the growth rate, the long-term coefficient represents the inverse of the production function's returns to scale (v). The same elasticity can be obtained in the estimate of the log-linearized putty-clay model:

$$\text{Log } I_t = \sum_i a_i \ \text{Log}[Q_{t-i} - (1 - \delta) \ Q_{t-i-1}] + \dots$$

Table 1 shows that this elasticity is generally less than   — but not significantly different from   — unity. Average lags vary between 1.5 to 5 years using annual data with infinite lag distributions (of the first or second order), while they are shorter using quarterly data, when lags are polynomial distributions (4 to 5 quarters). The lag structure peaks within one year using annual data; within four quarters using quarterly data. The only exception is the period following the first oil crisis, where the downward adjustment seems to have been more rapid. By contrast, the inclusion of more recent years shows up a return to pre-1974 distributions (see especially Bucher and Sterdyniak [1983]).

If we give the same weight to each estimate, the average distribution of the acceleration effect works out as follows:

- 6 % of the total effect occurs during the current quarter;

---

4. Apart from the estimates specified with accumulation rate given below, the flexible-accelerator model has been estimated on annual national-accounts series by Desplats-Redier [1971] and Brefort [1974] and on panel data by Echard and Henin [1970].

TABLE 1 :   Comparison of acceleration-effect estimates
(Standard deviation listed in parentheses)

Type of estimate		Data	Results			References
Model	Lag form		Elasticity 1/v	Mean Lag	Maximum	
Pure flexible accelerator with accumulation rate	First-order distribution	15 industries x 8 years	0.76	3.4 years	1 year	Thollon-Pommerol and Malinvaud [1971], p.105
		18 industries x 13 years	0.60	2.1 years	1 year	Muet [1978a], p. 81
		53-74, Annual	1.33 (0.3)	5.5 years (1.3)	1 year	Muet [1979c, Chapter 2 below]
		Equipment only 53-74, Annual	0.99 (0.2)	1.9 years (0.4)	1 year	
	Second-order	Equipment only 53-74, Annual	0.80 (0.2)	1.6 years (0.7)	0 years	
(I/K)	Finite distributions	8 industries x 12 years	0.67	1.3 years	1 year	Thollon-Pommerol and Malinvaud [1971], equation 20
		195 industries x 8 years	0.68(*)	1.1 years	0 years	Oudiz [1978], P. 523
	Polynomial distributions	Quarterly 67-78	0.60(**)	3.0 qrs (0.4)	3 qrs	Muet and Zagame [1976], p.115
		Quarterly 65-74	0.59 (0.11)	4 qrs	4 qrs	Le Marois [1979], p.138
Effective demand for investment	Accumulation-rate polynomial	Quarterly 67-78	0.93 (0.04)	5.0 qrs (0.3)	0 qrs	Artus and Muet [1980b, Chapter 3 below]
	Log-linear putty-clay polynomial	Quarterly 67-78	1.06 (0.08)	5.2 qrs (0.4)	0 qrs	Artus, Muet [1981], p. 14

* After correction for profit influence (see p. 524 of article cited).
** Calculated by dividing by capital coefficient

- 30 % during the current year;

- 60 % during the first two years.

Some models use not only the acceleration effect but also the influence of the production-capacity utilization rate (this is especially the case with the DMS *[Dynamique Multi-Sectoriel]* model). If firms adjust their capital to expected demand by seeking to attain normal utilization of their production capacity, then investment will indeed depend both on the expected growth in output (acceleration effect) and on the gap between the actual and average rates of capacity utilization (pressures on output capacities). Although that influence is indisputable, it is difficult to separate it in practice from the acceleration effect, owing to the strong correlation between output growth and the production-capacity utilization rate. As a result , the influence is often overlooked in econometric studies.

2.3. Effective demand: capital-labor substitution

In the effective-demand model, the elasticity of capital (or of investment in the putty-clay hypothesis) with respect to the relative capital-labor cost is equal to the product of the elasticity of substitution (σ) by the share of wage costs in total costs ($\beta = 0.7$). In general, only the relative capital-labor cost is included in investment-only or investment-and-labor estimates. When the estimate includes more than two factors, the property described earlier still applies: for a given output level, the demand elasticity of a factor relative to the price of another factor equals the product of the partial elasticity of substitution by the share of the variable-price factor's cost in the total output cost. The effective-demand model can therefore be enlarged to more than two factors.

If two factors are included, the conventional specifications of the investment function are:

-putty-putty in accumulation-rate form

$$\frac{I}{K} = \Phi_1(L)\ \overset{o}{Q} + \Phi_2(L)\ \left(\frac{\overset{o}{w}}{c}\right) + d$$

-log-linearized putty-putty

$$\text{LogK} = \Phi_1(L) \text{ Log}(Q) + \Phi_2(L) \text{ Log}\left(\frac{w}{c}\right) + d(t)$$

-putty-putty in accumulation-rate form

$$\frac{I}{K} = \Phi_1(L) \overset{o}{Q} + \Phi_3(L) \frac{(w/c)^b}{\text{trend } (w.c)^b} + d$$

-putty-clay in level form (Bischoff)

$$I = \Phi_1(L) \left(\frac{w}{c}\right)^b e^{\gamma t} [Q - (1 - \delta) Q_{-1}]$$

-log-linearized putty-clay

$$\text{Log I} = \Phi_1(L) \text{ Log} [Q - (1 - \delta) Q_{-1}] + \Phi_2(L) \text{ Log}\left(\frac{w}{c}\right) + d(t)$$

with $\Phi_1(1) = 1/v$ and $\Phi_2(1) = b = \beta\sigma$.

The results obtained for coefficient b estimates are reported in Table 2.

When a putty-clay model is used, the elasticity of substitution between capital and labor varies between 0.6 and unity. But when totally malleable putty-putty capital is assumed, the elasticity becomes very low (0.03-0.09), except when the estimate combines sectorial and time-series data (Artus and Bismut [1980]) or panel data (Dormont [1983]), which provide a better understanding of long-term substitution effects. The results based on time series using a putty-putty or putty-clay hypothesis diverge sharply as regards long-term substitution effects on capital stock. On the other hand, they provide comparable figures for the short-term impact of factor-cost changes on investment.

In the putty-putty hypothesis, total capital is affected, but with low elasticity. In the putty-clay hypothesis, only new equipment is concerned, but with a strong substitution effect. The discrepancy between these estimates can be explained by the fact that the econometric adjustment is quite probably based on short-term fluctuations. The time-series estimates show that changes in the relative capital-labor cost have a fairly limited impact on investment. In both hypotheses, a 10% fall in the relative cost boosts investment by about 3 to

TABLE 2 :   **Elasticity of capital (putty-putty) or investment (putty-clay) with respect to relative capital-labor cost.**
(Standard deviation listed in parentheses)

Model	relation estimated	Data	Value of b =βσ	Mean lag	References
Putty-clay	Investment (I)	Quarterly 63-75	0.4		de Menil, Yohn [1977]
	Investment (I)	Quarterly 67-78	0.17 and 0.35	2.3 qrs	Artus, Muet [1980b, Chapter 3 below]
time series	Investment (I/K)	Quarterly 67-78	0.17 (0.05)	1.0 qr	
	Investment (I)	Quarterly 67-78	0.45		INSEE [1981]
	Investment (Log I)	Quarterly 67-78	0.70 and 0.65 (0.11) (0.16)	2.5 and 2.8 qrs (0.6) (0.7)	Artus and Muet [1981]
Putty-putty	Investment (I/K)	57-74, Annual	0.02 (0.01)	0.5 years (0.1)	Muet [1979c, Chapter 2 below]
	Investment (I/K)	57-74, Annual	β=0.4 σ=0.08 (0.1) (0.01)	0.3 years (0.1)	Villa, Muet and Boutillier [Chapter 5 below]
time series	and employment (N)	Quarterly 58-74	β=0.6 σ=0.03 (0.1) (0.01)	6.6 qrs	
	Investment (I/K)	Quarterly 67-78	0.06 (0.015)	6.5 qrs (2.2)	Artus and Muet [1980b, Chapter 3 below]
	Capital (Log K)	50-65 Annual	0.9		Schramm [1972]
Putty-putty	Investment (I/K)	13 industries x 15 years 63-77, Annual	0.35 (0.07)		Artus and Bismut [1980]
Industry and panel data	Capital (Log K)	124 firms x 9 years 67-75, Annual	0.634 and 0.436 (0.077) (0.042)	0 by definition	Dormont [1983]

6%. This moderate influence can take the form of a high capital malleability and a low elasticity of substitution (putty-putty model), or a low malleability and high substitution at capital-replacement time (putty-clay model). Certain studies based on a time-distribution of the relative-prices effect show that reality approximates more closely to the putty-clay hypothesis (Chapter 3).

... and capital-energy substitution

The direct estimate of capital-energy-labor elasticities of substitution has generally been performed using a cost function. The results presented in Table 3 show that capital and labor are always substitutable, with partial Allen elasticity usually at about 0.6-0.7. By contrast, there is no overall result concerning capital and energy, which are at times complementary (negative Allen elasticity of substitution), at others substitutable (positive elasticity).

We can interpret the ambiguity of these capital-energy substitution findings by employing a more structural approach. When new equipment is installed, energy consumption generally increases. If only this effect is taken into account, higher energy prices necessarily lead to lower investment. However, firms can also invest in order to save energy. As this effect counteracts the first, the results obtained in the overall estimates set out in Table 3 owe their ambiguity to the fact that they measure only the sum total of the two effects.

Table 4, instead, presents estimates that separate the two influences. The first effect is reflected by an elasticity of substitution between labor on the one hand, capital and energy on the other; the second effect is reflected by the elasticity of substitution between capital and energy bundled together. When the second effect outweighs the first (as in West Germany and Britain), rising energy prices boost investment. In the three other countries, on the contrary, higher energy prices slow private investment. It is also worth noting the low elasticity of substitution of capital to labor in Britain.

TABLE 3 : **Influence of capital/labor and capital/energy prices on investment: partial Allen elasticities of substitution estimated for various countries (translog cost function)**

Period and country		Elasticity of substitution		References
		capital/labor	capital/energy	
France	1963-1978	0.65	-0.95	1
France	1959-1969	0.41	1.05	3
France	1959-1973	0.72	0.56	4
United States	1963-1978	0.79	-0.70	1
United States	1959-1973	1.41	1.77	1
United States	1955-1969	0.06	1.07	3
United States	1947-1971	1.01	-3.53	2
West Germany	1963-1978	0.93	-0.07	1
West Germany	1959-1969	0.50	1.03	3
West Germany	1959-1973	0.71	0.66	4
Britain	1963-1978	0.43	0.13	1
Britain	1959-1969	0.39	1.04	3
Britain	1959-1973	0.64	0.36	4
Japan	1959-1973	0.70	0.74	4

1. Artus and Peyroux [1981, Chapter 7 below]
2. Berndt and Wood [1975]
3. Griffin and Gregory [1976]
4. Pindyck [1979]

TABLE 4: **Estimates of the two substitution effects**

Annual data 1963-1979	Elasticity of substitution between labor and capital/energy bundled together	Elasticity of substitution within the capital/energy bundle	Overall, capital and energy are :
United States	1	0.26	Complementary
West Germany	0.50	0.60	substitutable
France	1	0.37	Complementary
Britain	0.20	0.41	substitutable
Japan	0.50	0.28	Complementary

Source : Artus and Peyroux [1981, Chapter 7 below]

2.4. General models

We have mentioned earlier three ways of simultaneously incorporating the influence of the different variables:
- aggregation of different models depending on constraints perceived by firms;
- influence of financial conditions on the desired-capital adjustment process;
- estimate of a multi-regime model.
The first model includes the different variables in additive form (with standardized distribution lags):

$$\frac{I}{K} = (1-\rho)\left[\frac{1}{v} \; \Phi_1(L)\overset{o}{Q} + \beta\sigma\,\Phi_2(L) \begin{pmatrix} \overset{o}{w} \\ c \end{pmatrix} \right] + \rho\,a\,\Phi_3(L) \; \Pi + d$$

It has been estimated on an annual time series with a constant ρ coefficient (Muet [1979c], Chapter 2 below), then with a temporal variation of the financial constraint (Muet and Zagame [1980]). The second of these estimates shows up a steady decrease of the ρ coefficient over the period 1957-1974.

This model also enables us to test the hypothesis that the influence of financial variables is transitory. If the hypothesis is verified, the influence of the profit rate on investment must be initially positive, then negative. This change of sign in the coefficients has been brought to light on a quarterly series (Artus and Muet [1981], pp. 16, 17) in the putty-clay and putty-putty specifications of effective demand, whereas it does not appear in the profit-accelerator model.

There are many estimates for the second type of model (Coen [1971]; Eisner [1978a]; Gardner and Sheldon [1975]; Sarantis [1979]; Artus, Muet, Palinkas and Pauly [1981]). For France, an estimate has been made using the base-1962 version of the METRIC model. The influence of profits is very weak on the long-term coefficient, but strong on the lag structure: the average lag rises from 3.5 quarters in the 1960s to more than 5 during the crisis.

These two types of models are highly inadequate for evaluating financial constraints. Indeed, these appear only when actual self-financing and the alternative-financing resources fall short of desired investment (as measured by the other expressions of effective demand). The only model capable of accommodating this constraint is the general expression of effective investment demand as a minimum of the different potential demands.

The estimate for the French economy of multi-regime models with a putty-clay production-function hypothesis yields the following results (Artus and Muet [1983, 1984a, Chapter 8 below]). Omitting a possible labor constraint, the general model can be estimated in the form:

$$I = \text{Min} \ \{ \ I_n \ , I_e \ , I_f \ \}$$

where I_n = notional demand; I_e = effective demand; I_f = financially constrained investment.

If we impose the constraint of identical production-function parameters in effective and notional demands, then notional demand never appears. If we abandon this hypothesis — a move that can be justified by incorporating adjustment costs — then notional demand and financially constrained investment appear with a non-zero probability at certain periods, but the effective-demand regime predominates (Graph 1).

If we assume the demand constraint to be always binding, we can estimate the model in the form:

$$I = \text{Min} \ \{ \ \text{Max} \ (\ I_{en} \ , I_e \ ) \ , \ I_f \ \}$$

where I_{en} = investment for given employment and demand.

Graph 2 shows the estimated probability of each of the three regimes.

GRAPH 1 : **Regime probabilities without labor constraint**

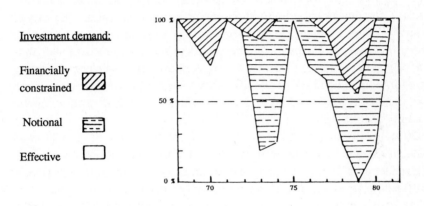

Investment demand:

Financially constrained

Notional

Effective

GRAPH 2 **Regime probabilities with demand constraint and, optionally, labor constraint**

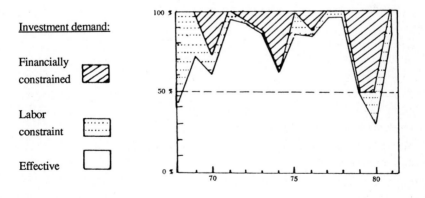

Investment demand:

Financially constrained

Labor constraint

Effective

Conclusion

The models and estimates summarized in this chapter are presented in detail in the chapters that follow. We begin by reexamining the relative influence of demand, cost and profit variables on the investment decision (Chapter 2). Next, we consider the choice of the best model (putty-putty or putty-clay) for describing possibilities of substitution of capital for labor (Chapter 3). These findings are then applied to a study of economic policies affecting investment (Chapter 4). The interdependent estimate of demand factors (Chapters 5 and 6) confirms the weak short-term influence of factor prices on investment and labor. We also show that capital and energy tend to be complementary, so that, in France, rising energy prices tend to slow investment (Chapter 7).

The most difficult problem is to assess the influence of profits and financial constraints. Estimates of models with rationings (Chapter 8) indicates that these factors play a transitory but sometimes major role in certain years. The influence of profitability is not necessarily linked to the presence of a financing constraint or to the absence of a demand constraint, but can result from uncertainty about future demand (Chapter 9).

CHAPTER 2
Econometric models of investment : a comparative study on annual data*
by
Pierre-Alain Muet

Introduction

The analysis of the theories on which econometric formalizations of investment demand are based usually distinguishes between three types of models: (a) acceleration models relying on the adjustment of capital to expected demand; (b) "neoclassical" models in which investment demand derives from the maximization of profit under a production-function constraint, with a hypothetically perfect financial market; (c) profit models — or, more generally, financial models — in which financing conditions play a decisive role.

This distinction, which rests mainly on the explanatory variables employed in the three types of models, is well suited for studying the variables' influence. However, it is not the most adequate from the theoretical standpoint. For example, the profit model can represent either (a) the influence of expected profitability on the investment decision assuming perfect inter-industry mobility of capital or (b) the influence of available self-financing on the converse assumption of constraints on the loan-fund market. Similarly, the models labeled as "neoclassical" in the literature most often correspond to highly divergent models of investment: some, which we describe as "true neoclassical models," apply the standard assumptions of neoclassical general equilibrium (competitive markets, Say's law); the others — in fact, the majority of empirical models — actually resemble what we shall call "effective investment demand," determined in particular by expected demand changes.

When corporate behavior is reduced to the maximization of pure profit, we can successively describe the various investment models (accelerator, "neoclassical," profits) in terms of the hypotheses chosen for the functioning of the markets involved in the investment decision (neoclassical equilibrium, or

---

* Originally published as "Modèles économetriques de l'investissement: une étude comparative sur données annuelles," *Annales de l'INSEE* 35:85-133, 1979.

equilibriums with rationing). With perfect competition and unrationed markets, corporate investment demand is solely determined by expected prices and costs.

This model, which we refer to as "notional investment" demand or "true neoclassical model," is defined only under the restrictive assumption of diminishing returns to scale.

When firms perceive or expect a constraint on changes in demand for their output (the traditional Keynesian hypothesis), investment demand becomes a function of expected output growth (acceleration effect) and — depending on the value of the production function's elasticity of substitution — a function of the relative capital-labor cost. The "effective demand" model thus defined corresponds to what is generally called the "neoclassical" model.

Lastly, when the firm's indebtedness capability is limited, either because the credit supply itself is limited (credit-restriction period) or because the solvency constraint puts a ceiling on new debt, investment demand depends on the financing capability — particularly on cash-flow resources. If we set aside the "true neoclassical model," which rests on largely unrealistic hypotheses, we are therefore led to two opposing determinations of investment based on:

- the growth of demand and relative costs in the absence of financial constraints;

- financing conditions on the contrary assumption.

If we consider that financing constraints do not affect all firms, we can propose a macroeconomic model that simultaneously incorporates the acceleration effect, the relative capital-labor cost and the influence of profits. This general model subsumes, as special cases, the main econometric models of investment through variations in the magnitude of the financial constraint (represented by the number of constrained firms in terms of a fraction of total capital) and in the magnitude of the capital-labor substitution (elasticity of substitution).

The first part of the chapter makes a detailed study of the theoretical foundations of investment models. The second part presents an estimate of the models on annual time series from 1950 to 1974 and analyzes the influence of growth, interest rates (cost of capital) and profits on the fixed investment of non-financial enterprises.

1. THEORETICAL FOUNDATIONS

1.1.   A typology of investment models: notional demand and

effective demands

Corporate investment decisions involve four markets: the product market, whose changes determine firms' capital and labor requirements; the capital-goods market; the financial market (or loan-funds market); and, indirectly, the labor market. For simplicity's sake, we shall equate investment demand with capital demand by using a purely static model.[1] Investment demand I^d during the period will be simply deduced from capital demand K^d by :

$$I^d = K^d - (1-\delta) K_{-1}$$

K_{-1} is the capital at the end of the previous period; δ is the equipment replacement rate. Capital demand K , labor demand N and supply of goods Q^s are linked by the production function:

(1) $Q^s = f (K^d , N^d)$

Capital demand is matched by a demand for goods I^d on the capital-goods market and a demand for loan funds on the financial market, which, in a first approximation, we equate with the corporate financing requirement:

(2) $B^d = q\, I^d - Aut$

Aut is corporate cash flow, q the price of capital goods.
We assume that the firm maximizes its expected profit:

(3) $\Pi = pQ - w\, N - c\, K$

---

1. These notions are formulated in a dynamic context in Zagamé [1977]. When adjustment costs q(I) are present, desired capital and adjustment lags are determined by the same optimization process (discounted profit):

$$\int_0^\infty e^{-rt} [\, pQ - wN - q(I)\, I\,]\, dt$$

The equations for desired capital are identical to those obtained with our static model, provided the user cost of capital is suitably defined.

under the constraint of the production function (1). Parameter c is the user cost of capital. Intuitively, if r is the discount rate (or interest rate), the user cost represents what the firm could have gained by investing money capital (qK) at the interest rate r. If δ is the capital depreciation rate, this opportunity cost is equal to $(r + \delta)(qK)$, which gives us $c = (r + \delta)$ q. Many authors, including Jorgenson [1963], have developed a more rigorous proof for this equation, using the optimization set out in note 1. Suffice it to say that user cost c subsumes in a single variable the two price variables of the financial and capital-goods markets (respectively r and q).

We shall confine our study to three particularly significant regimes:
- neoclassical equilibrium (competitive markets) ;
- product-demand constraint (Keynesian hypothesis) ;
- loan-fund supply constraint .

In keeping with Clower's definitions, investment demand will be called "notional" in the first case, "effective" in the other two.

a. Notional demand: the "true neoclassical model"

When markets are totally unconstrained and function competitively, corporate investment demand depends only on expected prices and costs (p*, w*, q* and r*).

If the production function has decreasing returns to scale, the optimization determines a goods supply Q^s and factor demands N^d and K^d that are solely dependent on expected real costs:

$$\frac{\partial f}{\partial K} = \frac{c^*}{p^*} \qquad\qquad Q^s = Q^s\left(\frac{c^*}{p^*}, \frac{w^*}{p^*}\right)$$

$$\frac{\partial f}{\partial N} = \frac{w^*}{p^*} \qquad \Rightarrow \qquad N^d = N^d\left(\frac{c^*}{p^*}, \frac{w^*}{p^*}\right)$$

$$Q = f(K,N) \qquad\qquad K^d = K^d\left(\frac{c^*}{p^*}, \frac{w^*}{p^*}\right)$$

The investment model thus defined corresponds to what we shall call the "true neoclassical model." As in the neoclassical general equilibrium, the demand for capital or investment depends only on market prices. Assuming a Cobb-Douglas production function:

$$Q = A \, K^\alpha \, N^\beta \, e^{\gamma t} \, , \qquad \alpha + \beta < 1$$

notional demand for capital is equal, for example, to:

(4)
$$K^d = C \left(\frac{w^*}{p^*} \right)^{-\frac{\beta}{1-(\alpha+\beta)}} \left(\frac{c^*}{p^*} \right)^{\frac{\beta-1}{1-(\alpha+\beta)}} e^{\frac{\gamma}{1-(\alpha+\beta)} t}$$

where C is a constant determined by production-function parameters.

b. *Goods-market constraint*

When the goods market is in a "disequilibrium" of the Keynesian type that is, when the notional supply of goods exceeds effective demand for goods (we assume fixed prices) the investment and labor demands derived from profit maximization depend on the expected constraint Q^* and, if the production function has substitutable factors, on the relative capital-labor cost (c^*/w^*) :

$$f(K, N) = Q^* \qquad\qquad N^d = N \left(Q^*, \frac{c^*}{w^*} \right)$$

$$\Rightarrow$$

$$\frac{\dfrac{\partial f}{\partial K}}{\dfrac{\partial f}{\partial N}} = \frac{c^*}{w^*} \qquad\qquad K^d = K \left(Q^*, \frac{c^*}{w^*} \right)$$

Assuming a Cobb-Douglas function, effective capital demand is, for example:

(5a)
$$K^d = C \, (Q^*)^{\frac{1}{\alpha+\beta}} \left(\frac{w^*}{c^*} \right)^{\frac{\beta}{\alpha+\beta}} e^{-\frac{\gamma}{\alpha+\beta} t}$$

Lastly, on the broader assumption of a constant-elasticity-of-substitution (CES) production function :

$$Q = [aK^{-\rho} + bN^{-\rho}]^{-\frac{v}{\rho}}, \qquad \sigma = \frac{1}{1+\rho},$$

effective capital demand takes a slightly more complex form :

(5b)
$$K^d = \frac{1}{a}(Q^*)^{\frac{1}{v}} \left[a^{\sigma-1} + b^\sigma \left(\frac{c^*}{w^*}\right)^{\sigma-1} \right]^{\frac{1}{\sigma-1}}$$

Our first comment is that, insofar as the level of capital demand is fixed by the demand constraint Q* , no returns-to-scale hypotheses are required to obtain a maximum profit — unlike the notional-demand model, which supposes diminishing returns to scale. Secondly, capital elasticity with respect to output (demand) is equal to the inverse of returns to scale $(1/(\alpha+\beta)$ or $1/v$). It is therefore usually rather close to unity, and somewhat smaller if as production-function estimates show — returns to scale are increasing.

Finally, the sensitivity of capital demand to the relative capital-labor cost depends on the production function's elasticity of substitution σ . When σ equals zero, the relative costs cease to influence capital demand, and we get an accelerator investment model. This response is an increasing function of the elasticity of substitution, but the functional form is simple only when the elasticity equals unity (Cobb-Douglas function).

However, we can demonstrate that, whatever the form of the production function, capital-demand elasticity with respect to relative capital-labor cost equals the product of the share of wages in output (β) multiplied by the elasticity of substitution (σ). When technical progress is Harrod-neutral and the real wages grow in the long term at the same rate as technical progress, coefficient β is constant in the long term but is determined, in the short term, by variations in the relative capital-labor cost $(\beta = w\,N\,/\,(wN+cK)\,)$.

c. Credit-supply constraint

The last case we shall examine is that of restricted credit. Credit supply becomes a constraint B ; indebtedness capability and cash-flow resources (Aut) determine the financially feasible investment, to borrow the terms of the

"FIFI" model of the French economy. Goods supply Q^s and labor demand N^d are accordingly expressed in terms of the financially feasible investment and the real wage rate (these are obtained by maximizing profit under the constraint of the production function and feasible capital):

$$\bar{I} = \frac{1}{q} \left(Aut + \bar{B} \right)$$

$$Q^s = Q^s \left(Aut + \bar{B}, \frac{w*}{p*} \right)$$

$$N^d = N^d \left(Aut + \bar{B}, \frac{w*}{p*} \right)$$

The reader will observe that this hypothesis is exactly identical to the Scandinavian model (Courbis [1973]). In the "traded-goods sector," the cash-flow constraint is binding, for the price is set by the foreign competition; this is not the case in the "non-traded-goods sector," which can adjust its cash-flow through pricing.

Again using the Cobb-Douglas production function as an example, we get the financially feasible investment, capital and output from:

$$\bar{I} = \frac{1}{q} \left(Aut + \bar{B} \right)$$

$$\bar{K} = \frac{1}{q} (Aut + \bar{B}) + K_{-1} (1 - \delta)$$

$$Q^s = C \left(\bar{K} \right)^{\frac{\alpha}{1-\beta}} \left(\frac{\omega*}{p*} \right)^{-\frac{\beta}{1-\beta}}$$

C, as before, is a constant determined by production-function parameters.

Our simplified model omits time periodization and the difference between (a) the production function applicable to installed equipment and (b) the production function representing *ex ante* available investment choices. In this model, cash-flow resources ought to be endogenous variables of optimization and should not necessarily constitute a constraint (I^d should depend solely on B). The constraint may, however, appear if we incorporate the two factors omitted from our simplified model.

The explanation is that the financing constraint uses the available profit realized with all the equipment, while the investment decision concerns future profits and profits generated by new equipment only. Available profit (cash flow) is therefore predetermined for the firm when it makes its investment choice. This profit can represent a constraint if the firm cannot exceed a certain level of indebtedness B because of credit controls or — as we shall see later — solvency requirements.

The static model just examined has enabled us to furnish a simple description of the main determinants of business fixed investment. For a better fit with the econometric models we must, however, take account of the intertemporal dynamics and examine some aspects of investment decision-making that lie outside this simplified typology. Accordingly, we shall now return to a more conventional classification of investment models.

1.2. Investment models

In the first model examined (notional demand or "true neoclassical model"), the investment decision depends only on expected real costs (real cost of labor w/p, real cost of capital c/p). The definition of such a function is based on highly restrictive hypotheses: diminishing returns to scale[2] , unconstrained demand for the firm's output. Consequently, its usefulness is purely "educational."

If we therefore set aside this model, the preceding analysis leads us to two conflicting determinations of investment:
- a determination based on relative costs and growth, in the absence of financial constraints;
- a determination based on financing conditions under the contrary assumption.

---

2. We can nevertheless ease these conditions by allowing for uncertainty (see Malinvaud [1982], p. 227) and by observing that returns can be diminishing at firm level and increasing at the overall level.

In reality, the situation is less clearcut when viewed in a macroeconomic context. The constraints affecting firms at any given moment are not uniform, and it is entirely possible for the two influences to be jointly observable at the overall level. The macroeconomic investment function ought therefore to depend simultaneously on all these explanatory variables. By positing a few simple hypotheses on the individual functions, we can offer an aggregate model — a general model — that incorporates all the variables.

We shall successively examine:
- the flexible accelerator and effective-demand model;
- the profit model;
- the general model (accelerator + profits).

a. Flexible accelerator and effective-demand model

Earlier, we equated investment demand with capital demand by showing how the latter developed from information perceived by the firm — namely, in this case, from expected demand and relative cost. To go from capital demand (or desired capital) to actual investment, we must specify the expectation formation and the time required to effect the investment (Muet and Zagamé [1976]). This is necessary because investment decisions involve a time span that is all the longer as the capital is fixed (for demand expectations) or as the production function applicable to installed plant is less substitutable (for relative-cost expectations affecting the choice of production techniques). As it happens, the concept of permanent value allows us to describe precisely this type of long-term expectation provided, of course, that we adapt it to the context of a growth-referenced economy. This can be done in particular by substituting the notion of permanent growth of value x_t for that of permanent value. The firm's decision will then be informed by the expected permanent growth for the future period $(t, ..., t + \theta, ...)$:

$$\overset{0}{x_t}{}^* = ... = \overset{0}{x}{}^*_{t+\theta} = ... = \sum_{i=0}^{\infty} (1-\lambda)\lambda^i \overset{0}{x}_{t+i}$$

In addition, this specification is well suited to that of the effective-demand function owing to the log-linear form of the equations that define desired capital. Assuming a Cobb-Douglas function, desired capital K^* becomes a linear function of expected growth rates of demand (Q^*) and relative costs $(c/w)^*$: As Q^* and $(c/w)^*$ are distributed-lag functions of observed growth rates, and as actual investment is itself a distributed-lag function of desired investment, we deduce the overall investment function by combining the different lags:

(7) $$\frac{I}{K} = \Phi_1(L)\overset{o}{Q} + \Phi_2(L)(\overset{o}{c/w}) + d$$

$\phi_1(L)$ and $\phi_2(L)$ are the distributed-lag functions that we can represent in a general form by polynomials of the lag operator L defined by $Lx_t = x_{t-1}$. If the expectation lag distribution is geometrical (permanent demand), and if the function of adjustment to desired capital is geometrical too (for example, when adjustment costs grow at the adjustment speed of capital), functions $\phi_1(L)$ and $\phi_2(L)$ must be second-order distributions. In practice, however, we shall see that first-order lag distributions suffice to represent distributed lags in these models.

When the production function is of the Cobb-Douglas type, the long-term coefficient of the demand growth rate equals the inverse of returns to scale $1/(\alpha+\beta)$, and the long-term coefficient of the relative-cost growth rate equals $\beta/(\alpha+\beta)$. When the elasticity of substitution differs from unity, the second of these coefficients ceases to be strictly constant. It is equal to the product of the share of wages in output β by the elasticity of substitution σ. Coefficient β in turn depends on the relative cost c/w, but the coefficient's variations are totally negligible in comparison to those of c/w's growth rate. For practical purposes, therefore, β can be regarded as constant. Finally, if the production function has fixed coefficients, the model is reduced to the flexible accelerator:

(8) $$\frac{I}{K} = \Phi(L)\overset{o}{Q} + d$$

The effective-demand model just studied is in fact a fairly close approximation, in formal terms, of what the literature improperly refers to as "neoclassical investment models" (on this point, see Muet [1979a]).

b. Profit models

We have seen that credit controls were an initial reason for positing the influence of cash flow on corporate investment; other considerations too can lead firms to prefer self-financing to borrowing. Accordingly, if we allow for a financial risk that grows in proportion to indebtedness (Kalecki [1937]), or for a solvency constraint on businesses (Courbis [1968]), we obtain an optimal financial structure that can constrain the amount of the actual investment.

As an example, let us take solvency behavior, that is, the need for a firm to pay the interest on its debts and reimburse them when they fall due. It can be shown (Malinvaud [1982], pp. 186 ff.) that the incorporation of the solvency constraint thus defined imposes — when profits are random — a maximum indebtedness ratio (medium- and long-term debt to net assets) that is an increasing function of profit expectations, asset liquidity and debt maturity. Assuming steady growth and slightly more restrictive hypotheses, the same solvency behavior can justify a minimum proportion of internally-financed investment (Courbis [1968, 1973]). This will be all the lower as the nominal investment growth is faster and the mean duration of indebtedness is greater.

These considerations enable us to substantiate the influence of cash flow on corporate investment expenditures. Such influence can be represented by the connection between the accumulation rate I/K and the ratio of cash flow to nominal capital (Aut/qK or ratio of retained earnings to capital). The investment's responsiveness to cash flow should be particularly high when credit controls prevail — assuming, that is, the "desired" investment exceeds the firm's available finance.

The "imperfection" of the capital market is thus the keystone for demonstrations of cash-flow behavior, but the influence of profits on investment may also be attributable to diametrically opposite causes involving capital mobility. The reason is that financial investments are motivated by the expected profitability of different industries and eventually equalize industry profit rates. Such leveling is continually thwarted by overall economic change (especially in wages) and by developments in industry production techniques — which explains the permanent disequilibrium among industry profit rates. The feedback of industry profitability on capital accumulation therefore proves to be a major mechanism in inter-sectorial dynamics.

This last factor should not, however, affect the macroeconomic level, where the influence of profit should normally reflect purely financial considerations. For the econometric estimate, we shall use the simplest formulation of the profit model, linking the investment rate to the non-distributed profit rate, that is, the ratio of retained earnings to gross capital at replacement cost :

(9) $\qquad \dfrac{I}{K} = \Phi\,(L)\,\pi + d \qquad\qquad \left(\pi = \dfrac{Aut}{qK}\right)$

c. A general model

Our earlier analysis yielded two conflicting determinations of investment:

- the effective-demand model, which, in the general form

(7) $\qquad \dfrac{I}{K} = \Phi_1(L)\,\overset{o}{Q} + \Phi_2\,(L)\,(\overset{o}{c/w}) + d$

incorporates the flexible accelerator ($\Phi_2 = 0$);

- the profit model

(9) $\qquad \dfrac{I}{K} = \Phi\,(L)\,\pi + d$

whose theoretical basis we have just outlined.

Indeed, looking at the individual firm, we can consider that the investment actually decided upon is shaped by one of these two models depending on the importance of perceived constraints on demand and financing:

$$\dfrac{I}{K} = \text{Min}\left\{\dfrac{I_1}{K}\left[\overset{o}{Q^*},\left(\dfrac{\overset{o}{c^*}}{w^*}\right)\right],\dfrac{I_2}{K}[\Pi^*]\right\}$$

By making a few simple assumptions on the nature of constraints perceived by firms, we can *offer a macroeconomic model that takes these two aspects into account simultaneously.*

Beforehand, it will be useful to give some details on the aggregation of our two models. We shall characterize firms by the index i and, to avoid secondary complications, we shall focus exclusively on the investment decision I*/K and its relation to the expected values Q*, c*/w* and π*. The distribution of firms will be characterized by their capital size, that is, by the ratio of the firm's capital to total capital:

$$v_i = \frac{K_i}{K} \quad \text{with} \quad \sum_i v_i = 1$$

Let us first examine the effective-demand model. Firm i's investment decision rests on its expected growth $\overset{\circ}{Q}_i{}^*$ and on the expected change in the relative capital-labor cost (c^*/w^* identical for all firms). The model is easily aggregated, for total growth $\overset{\circ}{Q}{}^*$ is then exactly equal to the weighted sum of the individual growth rates:[3]

$$\overset{\circ}{Q}{}^* = \sum_i v_i \overset{\circ}{Q}{}^*_i$$

When production functions differ among firms, investment functions can still be aggregated if we assume that expected growth $\overset{\circ}{Q}_i{}^*$ is identical for all firms, in other words, if we assume that firms base their investment decisions on the general movement of the market for their product, and not on their own situation. This hypothesis is admittedly restrictive, but may be fairly close to actual corporate practice. We shall use it to define the general model.

The aggregation of the profit model assumes the same restrictive hypotheses, that is, either identical model coefficients or identical expected profit rates. While the second hypothesis is admissible for a profitability rate, it is more arguable for the ratio of cash flow to capital. We shall therefore assume that the profit-model coefficients are identical for all firms.

The firm's investment is defined by the function:

$$\left(\frac{I_i}{K_i}\right) = \text{Min} \begin{cases} \left(\dfrac{I_i}{K_i}\right)^1 = \dfrac{1}{v_i}\overset{\circ}{Q}{}^* - \beta_i\,\sigma_i\,(c/w)^* + d_i \\[4mm] \left(\dfrac{I_i}{K_i}\right)^2 = a\,\pi^*_i + b_i \quad \text{with} \quad \pi^*_i = \dfrac{\text{Aut}_i}{qK_i} \end{cases}$$

---

3. As we assume production functions and the relative capital-labor cost to be identical for all firms, the capital coefficient too is identical in all firms. Consequently, the distribution of firms as fractions of total capital is identical to their distribution in terms of production:

$$v_i = \frac{K_i}{K} = \frac{Q_i}{Q} \quad \Rightarrow \quad \overset{\circ}{Q}{}^* = \sum_i v_i \overset{\circ}{Q}{}^*_i$$

We can thus divide firms into two categories, depending on whether their investment is determined by the first or second model — in other words, on whether the financial constraint is binding or not:

$$i \in I \text{ if } \quad I_i^* = I_i^1 < I_i^2 \quad \text{ no financial constraint}$$

$$i \in II \text{ if } \quad I_i^* = I_i^2 < I_i^1 \quad \text{ financial constraint}$$

v is the number of firms (in terms of share of total capital) that are financially constrained:

$$1 - v = \sum_{i \in I} v_i \qquad\qquad v = \sum_{i \in II} v_i$$

Assuming a sufficiently stable time-distribution of firms, we can adopt a fixed-coefficient model, that is, by reintroducing distributed lags:

$$(10) \qquad\qquad \frac{I}{K} = \Phi_1 (L) \overset{o}{Q} + \Phi_2 (L) (c/w) + \Phi_3 (L) \pi + d$$

with the long-term coefficients:

$$\Phi_1(1) = \frac{1 - v}{v} ; \ \ \Phi_2(1) = - \beta \, \sigma \, (1 - v) ; \ \ \Phi_3(1) = v \, a$$

Parameters v , β and σ characterize the "macroeconomic" production function of firms in sector I:

$$\frac{1}{v} \sum_{i \in I} \frac{v_i}{v_i}, \quad \beta \, \sigma = \sum_{i \in I} \beta_i \, \sigma_i \, v_i$$

A less restrictive hypothesis would be to admit that the distribution of constrained firms varies. This calls for a model in which v is a function of a financial-constraint indicator such as credit control, while the other coefficients remain fixed.

1.3. Conclusion : from simple models to the general model

The general formulation defined earlier subsumes as special cases the different models we have examined. Table 1 summarizes this presentation of the models according to production-function form — that is, elasticity of substitution σ — and to the size of the financial constraint ν.

To examine effective demand, we can — in the general case of a function with constant elasticity of substitution σ and non-zero financial constraint ν define the most general model (10) dependent on all factors (growth, relative, profits). When all firms are financially constrained with ν = 1, we get the profit model (9). If, on the contrary, the financial constraint is zero, the investment model is the effective-demand model (7). Finally, if the elasticity of substitution is zero, the general model reduces to the accelerator-profits model (11), and the effective-demand model to the flexible accelerator (8).

The last model, notional demand (12), is of purely theoretical interest.

TABLE 1 Investment models in brief

I. Effective demand

Financial constraint	Production function	
	Fixed coefficients	Substitutable factors
$\nu = 0$	Flexible accelerator (8) $I/K = \Phi_1 (L) \overset{\circ}{Q} + d$	Effective-demand model (7) $I/K = \Phi_1 (L) \overset{\circ}{Q} + \Phi_2 (L) (\overset{\circ}{c/w}) + d$
$0 < \nu < 1$	Accelerator-profits (11) $I/K = \Phi_1 (L) \overset{\circ}{Q} + \Phi_3 (L) \pi + d$	General model (10) $I/K = \Phi_1 (L) \overset{\circ}{Q} + \Phi_2 (L) (\overset{\circ}{c/w}) + d$ $\quad\quad + \Phi_3 (L) \pi + d$
$\nu = 1$	Profit model (9) $\quad I/K = \Phi_3 (L) \pi + d$	

II. Notional demand

Notional demand or "true neoclassical model" (12)
$$I/K = \Phi_4 (L) (\overset{\circ}{c/p}) + \Phi_5 (L) (\overset{\circ}{w/p}) + d$$

2.   AN ECONOMETRIC ESTIMATE ON ANNUAL DATA

We shall successively examine the earlier-defined models principally by means of the annual time series of French national accounts (base 1962). Our estimates distinguish between structures, equipment, and total investment. The series used (described in Appendix 1) are:

I: Gross fixed capital formation of non-financial firms. 1949-1974 series at 1959 prices: structures, equipment and total.

K: Fixed capital of non-financial firms. Mairesse [1972] series updated by H. Delestre. 1949-1974 at 1959 prices: structures, equipment and total.

p: Prices of gross domestic product (base 1962, DMS-model data bank).

Q: Gross domestic product at 1963 prices (base 1962, DMS-model data bank).

c: User cost of capital 1954-1975. Series compiled by Malinvaud [1971], updated from 1969 on:

$$c = q \cdot FISC \cdot (r\text{-}p)$$

q: Prices of gross fixed capital formation of non-financial firms (buildings, equipment and total). National accounts, base 1962.

FISC: Taxation index. Malinvaud [1971] series, updated from 1969 on.

(r-p) : Discounting effect (real interest rate). Malinvaud [1971] series, updated by the INSEE.

w: Nominal-wage index. Ratio of gross salaries (including social-security contributions) in the national accounts to salaried employment.

π = (Aut / q K) : Profit rate: ratio of gross cash-flow to total capital at replacement cost.

2.1. The accelerator effect: a decisive influence and long reaction times

The many econometric studies of investment performed in France and the United States have consistently shown up the importance of the adjustment of capital to demand — in other words, the acceleration effect — as well as the considerable length of these adjustment lags. The estimates on annual data and using specifications linking the accumulation rate (I/K) to the output growth rate (ex. Thollon-Pommerol and Malinvaud [1971]; Muet and Zagamé [1976]) have shown that the lag distribution generally reached a maximum for a one-year-lagged growth rate and could be adequately represented by a first-order distribution:

$$\Phi\,(L) = \frac{a_0 + a_1\,L}{1 - \lambda\,L} = a_0 + (a_1 + \lambda\,a_0)\,L + \dots + \lambda^{n-1}\,(a_1 + \lambda a_0)\,L^n + \dots$$

This, however, is not the only function that can be envisaged a priori for describing the distributed lags of the flexible accelerator. If we admit that the investment decision rests on permanent growth (represented by a geometrical distribution) and that the adjustment to desired capital can also be represented by a geometrical distribution (adjustment costs), the total lag distribution is of the second order:

$$\Phi\,(L) = \frac{a}{1 - b\,L - c\,L^2}$$

These two distributions are estimated in autoregressive form, in particular if we admit that the errors of these autoregressive forms are independent:

$$(8\text{ a}) \qquad \frac{I}{K} = \lambda\left(\frac{I}{K}\right)_{-1} + a_0\,\overset{o}{Q} + a_1\,\overset{o}{Q}_1 + d$$

$$(8\text{ b}) \qquad \frac{I}{K} = b\left(\frac{I}{K}\right)_{-1} + c\left(\frac{I}{K}\right)_{-2} + a\,\overset{o}{Q} + d$$

The first distribution is convergent and has positive coefficients if λ lies between zero and one. For the second, the roots λ_1 and λ_2 of the characteristic equation must be real, positive and smaller than one:

$$\lambda^2 - b\lambda - c = 0$$

The lag distribution is then expressed in terms of the two roots λ_1 and λ_2, which are the parameters of the geometrical distributions composing the second-order distribution:

$$\Phi(L) = \frac{a}{(1 - bL - cL^2)} = \frac{a}{(1 - \lambda_1 L)(1 - \lambda_2 L)} = \sum_{n=0}^{\infty} a \frac{(\lambda_1^{n+1} - \lambda_2^{n+1})}{(\lambda_1 - \lambda_2)} L^n$$

The acceptable values for b and c must correspond to a point located inside the shaded area on Graph 1.

Table 2 presents estimates for the different models over the years 1953-1974. Student t values for the estimated coefficients are given in parentheses. Standard deviations, calculated by linearizing the equations, provide only an approximate indication of the confidence interval[4]. Table 2a compares the adjustments obtained with a first-order distribution for total investment and equipment investment. The figures are identical to the difference between the adjustment lags of total investment and equipment investment already reported in many estimates on annual data (respectively 5.5 and 1.9 years)[5]. In addition, the econometric adjustment is far more accurate for equipment investment: the estimated coefficients are all significantly different from zero; the long-term coefficient and the mean lag are estimated more accurately than for overall investment.

Lastly, for equipment investment, we have compared the estimates obtained with a first-order and second-order distribution (Table 2b). For the second of these, in which the estimate of ordinary least squares exhibits a negative autocorrelation of errors, we have indicated two estimates theoretically free of asymptotic biases: the estimate using instrumental variables $\overset{\circ}{Q}_{-1}$ and $\overset{\circ}{Q}_{-2}$, and the estimate using the Cochrane-Orcutt method.

---

4. Fieller has advanced a more rigorous method for constructing a confidence interval (see, for example, Muet [1978b], p. 37).

5. See, for example, the investment functions of the DMS model in Fouquet et al. [1978], pp. 97, 104.

TABLE 2

Flexible accelerator : comparison of first-and second-order distributions

	Coefficients and Student ts			Long-term coefficient	Mean lag	R² DW	Estimation method*
	$\hat{a_0}$	$\hat{a_1}$	$\hat{\lambda}$				
a. First-order distributions							
Total gross fixed capital formation......	0.150 (4.6)	0.066 (1.9)	0.838 (23.0)	1.33 (4.6)	5.5 years (4.2)	0.98 2.6	OLS (1953-1974)
Equipment investment......	0.260 (6.7)	0.127 (2.7)	0.610 (8.9)	0.99 (6.6)	1.9 years (4.8)	0.94 2.2	OLS (1953-1974)
	Coefficients and Student ts			Long-term coefficient	Mean lag	R² DW	Estimation method*
	$\hat{a}$	$\hat{b}$	$\hat{c}$				
b. Second-order distributions (equipment)							
Equipment investment......	0.246 (5.7)	0.896 (8.9)	- 2.202 (2.0)	0.80 (4.0)	1.6 years (2.3)	0.93 2.7	OLS (1953-1974)
	0.233 (5.1)	0.994 (7.1)	- 0.269 (1.5)	0.84	1.6 years	0.93 2.8	IV (1953-1974)
	0.259 (4.6)	0.997 (10.1)	- 0.298 (3.4)	0.86	1.3 years	0.92 2.2	CORC (1954-1974)

* OLS : Ordinary least squares ; CORC : Cochrane-Orcutt method ; IV : Instrumental-variables method.

GRAPH 1: Comparison of two specifications for flexible-accelerator distributed lags: 95% confidence interval and lag pattern

a. First-order distribution

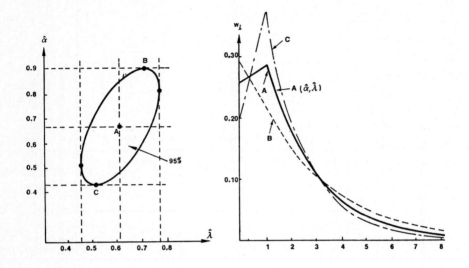

b. Second-order distribution

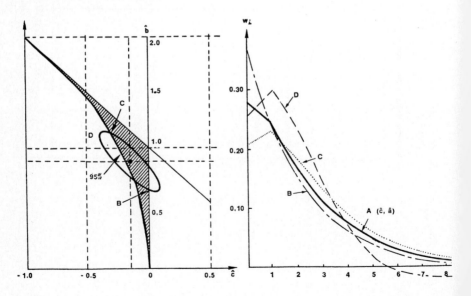

A comparison of these with the least-squares estimate can give an idea of the asymptotic bias: b is apparently underestimated by 0.10, and the absolute value of c by slightly less (0.07 / 0.10). For these two coefficients, the difference is of the order of the standard deviation and therefore negligible. Thus, despite an obvious error autocorrelation (ρ significantly different from zero), the bias remains smaller than the estimation accuracy. It will be noted that the accuracy of the instrumental variables is inferior to that of the least squares, and that the Cochrane-Orcutt method gives the more accurate estimate for coefficients b and c.

The long-term coefficients and the average lags of the two distributions do not differ significantly, but the estimates are more accurate with a first-order distribution. Lastly, we observe that in neither estimate does the long-term coefficient differ greatly from unity. When we constrain this coefficient to be equal to one, the lag distributions becomes dependent on only two coefficients, which we can estimate by the least-squares method applied to non-linear models (NLLS). Under the standard stochastic hypotheses, this method is equivalent to the maximum-likelihood method. The iterative program employed (TSP : Time Series Processor) yields the following values for the coefficients and their standard deviation:

$$\hat{\alpha} = 0,672 \quad \hat{\lambda} = 0,612 \quad \Phi(L) = \frac{(1 - \lambda)\,[\alpha + (1 - \alpha)\,L]}{(1 - \lambda L)} \quad \text{1st order}$$
$$\underset{(0,086)}{} \quad \underset{(0,053)}{}$$

$$\hat{b} = 0,901 \quad \hat{c} = 0,167 \quad \Phi(L) = \frac{1 - b - c}{1 - bL - cL^2} \quad \text{2d order}$$
$$\underset{(0,099)}{} \quad \underset{(0,090)}{}$$

While greater accuracy of the coefficient estimates is obtained, the improvement is fairly minimal for the second-order distribution; more important, the decrease in absolute value of coefficient c makes its estimated value not significantly different from zero. To assess the accuracy of the two estimates and compare their distributed-lag patterns, we have plotted the confidence intervals of the pairs (α, λ) and (b, c); in addition, we have shown on Graph 1 the lag pattern of the estimated distributions (solid-line curves) as well as the pattern of different lag distributions for points B, C, D, etc. located at the limit of the 95% confidence interval (dotted-line curves). The comparison between the two estimated distributions (solid-line A curves) shows, first, that the lag pattern is practically the same, whether the distribution is first- or second-order. This is corroborated by the mean-lag values: 1.9 years for the first-order distribution, 2.4 for the second-order distribution. By contrast, the first-order distribution exhibits far greater accuracy: if we plot the lag distributions for the two outermost points of its confidence interval (B and C), we obtain curves that are fairly close to the estimated distribution, with maximum uncertainty for a one-year lag. In particular, the fact that the confidence interval does not intersect the straight line $\alpha = 1$ shows that this distribution differs significantly from a geometrical one.[6]

The same analysis shows that the lag distribution is estimated less accurately in the second-order distribution. The confidence interval does not lie entirely inside the acceptable-value area (shaded on the graph). In other words, it includes lag distributions with positive, then negative coefficients. Examples are point D, which corresponds to complex roots λ_1 and λ_2, and points to the right of point B. We also observe that the estimated distribution does not differ significantly from the geometrical distribution (point B) or from the second-order Pascal distribution (point C). The three distributions B, C and D located at the confidence-interval limit clearly illustrate the uncertainty that affects the estimate of distributed lags using a second-order distribution.[7]

These two specifications for the distributed lags of the flexible accelerator yield mean lags of about two years for the acceleration effect. These lags are shorter than those estimated for total investment (5.5 years) — the reason being that adjustment lags for capital in structures are considerably longer than those for equipment investment, which is the only factor taken into account here.

2.2. Capital-labor substitution and influence of the interest rate: a disputed effect

The so-called "neoclassical" models incorporate the influence of the interest rate on investment through the user cost of capital. Earlier, we defined two investment models based on this approach:

---

6. The test corresponding to a 95% confidence interval is stricter than the conventional Student test at the 5% level.

7. This analysis draws on Griliches [1967]. See especially pp. 30-32 of that article for the identical graphs corresponding to the Griliches-Wallace investment function.

- "Notional" demand or "true neoclassical model":

$$(12) \qquad \frac{I}{K} = \Phi_1 (L) \; (\overset{o}{c/p}) + \Phi_2 (L) \; (\overset{o}{w/p}) + d$$

- Effective investment demand:

$$(7) \qquad \frac{I}{K} = \Phi_1(L) \overset{o}{Q} + \Phi_2 (L) \, (\overset{o}{c/w}) + d$$

We have already mentioned the largely unrealistic character of the first model, whose econometric estimate amply corroborates our opinion. By contrast, the estimate of the effective-demand model shows that the real interest rate exerts a tangible influence on investment, although to a lesser extent than the acceleration effect. As with the flexible accelerator, we shall focus on equipment investment, which predictably entails the most significant adjustments.

a. "Notional" demand or "true neoclassical model": an unrealistic model

To represent lags in adjustment to factor-cost variations, we use first-order distributions:

$$(12) \qquad \frac{I}{K} = \frac{a_0 + a_1 L}{1 - \lambda_1 L} \, (\overset{o}{w/p}) + \frac{b_0 + b_1 L}{1 - \lambda_2 L} \, (\overset{o}{c/p}) + d$$

If we posited the more constraining hypothesis that parameters λ_1 and λ_2 are equal in each distribution, we could estimate the model in autoregressive form using ordinary least squares. More generally, we must estimate a model in which the coefficients are constrained:

$$\frac{I}{K} = (\lambda_1 + \lambda_2) \left(\frac{I}{K} \right)_{-1} - \lambda_1 \lambda_2 \left(\frac{I}{K} \right)_{-2} + a_0 \, (\overset{o}{w/p}) + (a_1 - \lambda_2 a_0) \, (\overset{o}{w/p})_{-1}$$

$$- \lambda_2 a_1 \, (\overset{o}{w/p})_{-2} + b_0 \, (\overset{o}{c/p}) + (b_1 - \lambda_1 b_0) \, (\overset{o}{c/p})_{-1} - \lambda_1 b_1 \, (\overset{o}{c/p})_{-2} + d'$$

We calculate the residual-variance minimum by iterations (Gauss method). Table 3 gives the estimate of this model on 1957-1974 time series. The long-term coefficient of the real cost of capital is approximately 0.3; the mean adjustment lag about four years for equipment investment and eight years for total investment. But, as the Student t values for these parameters show, none of them differs significantly from zero. Long-term coefficients and mean lags for labor cost are negligible. Therefore — if we exclude the influence of user cost of capital, to which we shall return in the effective-demand model, — it appears that the notional-demand model does not provide a plausible explanation of corporate investment behavior.

b. *Effective demand: a low elasticity of substitution ...*

As with the preceding model, we use two different first-order distributions for the acceleration effect $(\overset{\circ}{Q})$ and the relative capital-labor cost:

$$(7a) \qquad \frac{I}{K} = \frac{a_0 + a_1 L}{1 - \lambda_1 L} \overset{\circ}{Q} + \frac{b_0 + b_1 L}{1 - \lambda_2 L} \overset{\circ}{(c/w)} + d$$

and we estimate the model by minimizing the residual variance on the autoregressive form. The estimates of this model for total investment and equipment investment are reported in Table 4.

The two explanatory variables have coefficients significantly different from zero. The value of the acceleration effect's long-term coefficient is less than unity for equipment investment, reflecting increasing returns to scale (an approximate confidence interval at the standard level is 0.62 ± 0.30). For total investment, the value does not differ significantly from unity.

The user-cost-of-capital coefficient is indeed negative and differs significantly from zero, but is well below the value corresponding to a Cobb-Douglas production function. Under this hypothesis, it should be equal to $-\beta/(\alpha + \beta)$, that is, close to 0.6 or 0.7 in absolute value. In fact the coefficient is equal to -0.017 for total investment and -0.022 for equipment investment.

TABLE 3 : "Notional" demand or "true neoclassical model" : autoregressive estimate for 1957-1974

	Labor cost (w/p)					Capital cost (ċ/p)					Adjustment characteristics
	$\hat{a}_0$	$\hat{a}_1$	$\hat{\lambda}_1$	LTC	ML	$\hat{b}_0$	$\hat{b}_1$	$\hat{\lambda}_2$	LTC	ML	
Total gross fixed capital formation......	0.033	-0.07	0.15	0.031	-0.07	-0.014	-0.025	0.89	-0.36	8.9	NLLS (GAUSS) R^2 = 0.968 DW = 2.1 S = 0.213 10^{-2}
	(0.7)	(0.1)	(0.5)	(0.4)	(0.03)	(1.9)	(3.0)	(11.0)	(1.1)	(1.3)	
Equipment investment............	0.057	-0.031	0.21	0.032	-0.90	-0.022	-0.043	0.77	-0.29	4.1	NLLS (GAUSS) R^2 = 0.805 DW = 1.9 S = 0.260 10^{-2}
	(0.9)	(0.4)	(0.7)	(0.3)	(0.1)	(2.5)	(4.1)	(3.6)	(0.3)	(0.9)	

LTC = long-term coefficient ; ML = mean lag ; NLLS : non linear least squares ; S is the regression's standard deviation. Values in parentheses are t statistics.

TABLE 4 :   Effective demand : autoregressive estimate for 1957-1974
Equipment investment and total investment

	Acceleration effect $\overset{\circ}{Q}$					Relative cost ($\overset{\circ}{c}$/w)					Adjustment characteristics
	$\hat{a}_0$	$\hat{a}_1$	$\hat{\lambda}_1$	LTC	ML	$\hat{b}_0$	$\hat{b}_1$	$\hat{\lambda}_2$	LTC	ML	
Total gross fixed capital formation......	0.084	0.105	0.80	0.95	4.6	- 0.006	- 0.014	- 0.17	- 0.017	0.5	NLLS (GAUSS) R^2 = 0.980 DW = 2.5 S = 0.167 10^{-2}
	(2.1)	(2.5)	(21.9)	(3.5)	(5.1)	(1.6)	(2.7)	(0.8)	(2.1)	(3.2)	
Equipment investment...............	0.143	0.164	0.50	0.62	1.5	- 0.008	- 0.019	- 0.22	- 0.022	0.5	NLLS (GAUSS) R^2 = 0.885 DW = 2.2 S = 0.197 10^{-2}
	(2.9)	(3.5)	(6.3)	(4.6)	(4.6)	(1.5)	(2.5)	(1.0)	(2.0)	(3.5)	

If we compare these elasticities to their theoretical value (-β σ), we can represent the production function by means of a CES function with low elasticity of substitution (σ close to 0.03). In addition, and contrary to what one might expect, user-cost-of-capital adjustment lags are very short, whereas in the realistic hypothesis of a putty-clay production function, the lags should be much longer than demand adjustment lags. Despite this, our specification does not provide a proper interpretation of the putty-clay model, whose validity has, however, been amply illustrated by the quarterly-data estimates by de Ménil and Yohn [1977]. Nevertheless, by estimating an approximation of the putty-clay effective-demand model, one can verify that our estimate is not incompatible with the putty-clay hypothesis and an *ex ante* elasticity of substitution equal to unity.

c. ...or a putty-clay production function

The putty-clay investment model is precisely characterized by the absence of an acceleration effect for the relative capital-labor cost. The capital-labor substitution no longer affects total equipment but only new equipment. If k_t^* stands for the marginal coefficient of expected capital, k_t^* the average coefficient and Q_t^* expected demand, desired gross investment is, in the putty-clay hypothesis:

$$I_t = k_t^* [Q_t^* - (1 - \delta) \overset{\circ}{Q}_{t-1}]$$

instead of:

$$I_t = \bar{k}_t^* Q_t^* - (1 - \delta) \bar{k}^*_{t-1} Q_{t-1}^*$$

in the putty-putty hypothesis.

Returning to our accumulation-rate specification, and assuming unit returns to scale, we get :

(7a)
$$\left(\frac{I}{K}\right)_t = \overset{\circ}{Q}_t^* - \sigma \beta (\overset{\circ}{c_t^*/w_t^*}) + d$$

in the putty-putty hypothesis with a CES production function, and:

(7b)
$$\left(\frac{I}{K}\right)_t = \overset{o}{Q}_t{}^* + (g + \delta)\left(\frac{k_t{}^*}{\bar{k}_t{}^*}\right) + d$$

$$k^*_t = A\left(\frac{c_t{}^*}{w_t{}^*}\right)^{-\beta} e^{-\gamma t} \text{ and } \bar{k}_t{}^* = \sum_{i=0}^{T} a_i\, k^*_{t-i}$$

in the putty-clay hypothesis with a Cobb-Douglas function; g is the growth rate of the economy, δ the replacement rate and T equipment lifetime. The mean coefficient k* is a lag distribution of the marginal coefficient k*. *In steady-state growth at rate* g, the lag distribution (a_i) is a geometrical distribution with a common ratio of $1/(1+g)$. We can therefore replace k* by the trend of the marginal capital coefficient and use the model:

$$\left(\frac{I}{K}\right) = \overset{o}{Q}{}^* + (g + \delta)\ \frac{(c^*/w^*)^{-\beta}}{(\tilde{c}^*/\tilde{w}^*)^{-\beta}} + d$$

where $\tilde{c}^*/\tilde{w}^*$ is the trend of the relative capital-labor cost. Taking first-order distributions for each explanatory variable and positing $\beta = 0.7$, we shall estimate the model:

(7b)
$$\left(\frac{I}{K}\right) = \frac{a_0 + a_1 L}{1 - \lambda_1 L}\overset{o}{Q} + \frac{b_0 + b_1 L}{1 - \lambda_2 L} \cdot \frac{(c/w)^{-0.7}}{(\tilde{c}/\tilde{w})^{-0.7}} + d$$

Table 5 presents the estimate of this model — for corporate investment in equipment — obtained by minimizing the residual variance of the autoregressive form.

The result of this estimation is not very different from the preceding estimate. The long-term demand coefficient is identical, and that of the user cost of capital is of the same magnitude (0.04). If we eliminate the parameter λ_2, which does not differ significantly from zero, the latter coefficient becomes equal to 0.05 — which, given the standard deviation of 0.015, puts it fairly close to its theoretical value $(g+\delta = 0.10)$.

TABLE 5 : **Effective demand : putty-clay model estimate equipment investment**

Accelerator effect					Relative cost					Adjustment
λ_1	a_0	a_1	LTC	ML	λ_2	b_0	b_1	LTC	ML	characteristics
0.67	0.14	0.06	0.62	2.4	- 0.30	0.02	0.03	0.04	0.3	$R^2 = 0.870$
										DW = 1.7
(6.7)	(2.7)	(1.2)	(2.9)	(2.6)	(1.2)	(2.2)	(2.2)	(2.7)	(2.4)	$S = 0.21 \ 10^{-2}$
										MCNL 1957 - 1974

The estimate of the effective demand model thus shows up a low user-cost-of-capital coefficient. This is compatible with a production function possessing a low elasticity of substitution ($\sigma \approx 0.03$), or with a putty-clay production function and an *ex ante* elasticity of the order of unity (our estimate is based on a Cobb-Douglas function). In both cases, the response times to changes in the user cost of capital are very short and the autoregressive term of the first-order distribution is never significantly different from zero.

d. Responsiveness of results to stochastic hypotheses

Our results totally corroborate the findings of Eisner and Nadiri [1968, 1970]. Turning to the controversies on these very findings between Eisner and Nadiri on the one hand and Jorgenson and Stephenson [1969] and Bischoff [1969] on the other, it appears that the prior assumptions about error, and consequently the estimation methods, go a long way to explaining these authors' contradictory results. This emerges from our estimation of the effective-demand model in autoregressive form — a valid approach if the errors of this form are independent, that is, if the errors of the distributed-lag model already exhibit a positive autocorrelation. As the standard Durbin and Watson statistic does not enable us to test the hypothesis of a potential autocorrelation of errors in the autoregressive form, we cannot be certain, despite the satisfactory value of this statistic (1.9), that our hypothesis is correct a priori. To study the responsiveness of our results to this hypothesis, we shall directly estimate the distributed-lag model with a putty-putty specification. The chief constraint on the estimate of this model is series shortness, particularly with regard to the user-cost-of-capital series. As an approximation of the preceding distributed lags, we shall therefore use a truncated geometrical distribution for Q and a distribution without prior constraints for user cost, estimating :

$$(7c) \qquad \left(\frac{I}{K}\right) = \left[a_0 \overset{o}{Q} + \sum_{i=1}^{4} (a_0 + a_1 \lambda) \lambda^{i-1} \overset{o}{Q}_{-i} \right] + \sum_{i=0}^{2} b_i \overset{o}{(c/w)}_{-i} + d$$

The estimate of this model yields virtually the same results as the autoregressive-model estimate. The coefficients a_0, a_1, λ , b_0 and b_1 have practically the same values as before; b_2 is positive and not significantly different from zero. This is exactly what we get by developing the first-order function previously estimated for user cost.

The accuracy of the coefficients estimated for user cost is very poor :

$$\hat{b}_0 = -0.009 \quad , \quad \hat{b}_1 = -0.016 \quad , \quad \hat{b}_2 = +0.007$$
$$\text{(T)} \qquad (1.3) \qquad\qquad (1.8) \qquad\qquad (0,9)$$

but it improves if we eliminate coefficient b_2, which has no empirical or theoretical significance (it should be negative).

Lastly, the value of the Durbin and Watson statistic (DW = 1.3) shows that the distributed-lag model exhibits positive autocorrelation ($\rho = 1 - DW / 2 = 0.4$), which is the very justification for the autoregressive estimate of this model (one of the main reasons for this autocorrelation of residuals is the incomplete specification of acceleration lags in the direct estimate). In conclusion, we shall therefore use a discrete distribution for user cost $(b_0 + b_1 L)$ and a first-order distribution $(a_0 + a_1 L)/(1 - \lambda L)$ for the accelerator effect. We shall use the simulations of the latter model to study the influence of the explanatory variables on investment changes.

e. Influence of expected growth and of the interest rate: a simulation of the effective-demand model

We have chosen the model :

(7d) $$\frac{I}{K} = \frac{a_0 + a_1 L}{1 - \lambda L} \overset{o}{Q} + (b_0 + b_1 L)\,(\overset{o}{c/w}) + d$$

Table 6 gives two estimates of this model for the period 1957-1973:
-   an estimate in autoregressive form;
-   an estimate in developed form, with acceleration lags limited to four years:

$$\left[a_0 \overset{o}{Q} + \sum_{i=1}^{4} (a_0 + a_1 \lambda)\,\lambda^{i-1}\, \overset{o}{Q}_{-i} \right]$$

While the coefficients estimated by the two methods do not differ significantly, the estimates are more accurate in the autoregressive form. The long-term coefficient of user cost of capital, equal to -0.03, is thus very different from the value that would be obtained by assuming a Cobb-Douglas production function.

However, as Graph 2 shows, the influence of user cost on investment fluctuations is far from negligible. The upper part of the graph represents (a) observed and simulated accumulation rates (respectively I/K and $\hat{I/K}$); (b) the influence of growth ($\overset{o}{Q}$) and the relative capital-labor cost ($\overset{o}{c/w}$).

For this simulation, we use the estimate of the developed-form model, which directly spells out the impact of each of the explanatory variables. We can see that growth variations (acceleration efect) account for nearly two-thirds of the accumulation-rate changes (I/K). The relative capital-labor cost encapsulates the influence of four explanatory variables: real interest rate ($r - \overset{o}{p}$), taxation changes (FISC), the relative price of capital (q/p) and the relative price of labor (real wage rate w/p). We can use the multiplicative form of relative cost:

$$\frac{c}{w} = \frac{c/p}{w/p} = \frac{(r - \overset{o}{p}) \cdot \text{FISC} \cdot (q/p)}{w/p}$$

TABLE 6 : Effective demand : autoregressive and developed estimates for 1957-1974
Equipment investment

	Acceleration effect $\overset{\circ}{Q}$					Relative cost $(\overset{\circ}{c/w})$				Adjustment characteristics
	$\hat{a}_0$	$\hat{a}_1$	$\hat{\lambda}$	LTC	ML	$\hat{b}_0$	$\hat{b}_1$	LTC	ML	
Developed form..............	0.162 (2.8)	0.122 (2.1)	0.662 (5.4)	0.84 (3.8)	2.3 (2.2)	- 0.011 (1.6)	- 0.018 (2.0)	- 0.03 (2.0)	0.6 (4.5)	NLLS (GAUSS) $R^2 = 0.833$ DW $= 1.0$ S $= 0.227 . 10^{-2}$
Autoregressive form..............	0.143 (2.9)	0.136 (3.3)	0.504 (5.3)	0.56 (3.8)	1.5 (3.8)	- 0.010 (2.0)	- 0.019 (2.8)	- 0.03 (2.9)	0.7 (6.9)	NLLS (GAUSS) $R^2 = 0.882$ DW $= 2.5$ S $= 0.194 . 10^{-2}$

GRAPH 2 Simulation of the effective-demand model

a. Influence of growth and of changes in relative capital-labor cost

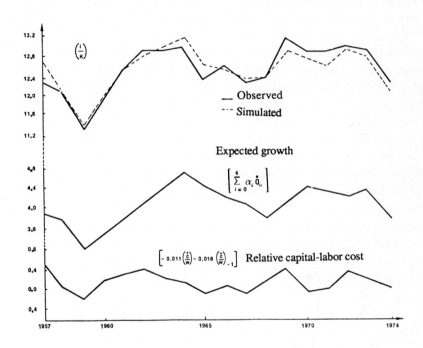

b. Breakdown of the "relative capital-labor cost" effect

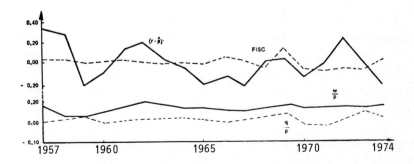

to divide the influence of the annual growth rate (c/w) into four components:

$$(\overset{o}{c/w}) = (\overset{o}{r} - \overset{o}{p}) + \overset{o}{FISC} + (\overset{o}{q/p}) - (\overset{o}{w/p})$$

This breakdown of the influence of relative capital-labor cost shows that the main variable affecting changes in that cost is the real interest rate. The breakdown directly reflects the method used to calculate user cost (Malinvaud [1971]), which overestimates the influence of the real interest rate while underestimating the effect of taxation changes (Bernard [1977]). In actual fact, though, taxation changes seem to have a stronger impact than the model suggests, for the investment recovery of 1966 and the investment level of 1969 would be more adequately described if taxation changes had a greater influence on the calculation of the user cost of capital.

Finally, we note that changes in the real interest rate are due more to variations in the expected growth rate of prices than to fluctuations in the nominal interest rate, the latter being relatively narrower than the former. This stability of the nominal interest rate with respect to prices implies that the long-term trend of the real interest rate largely reproduces — but in the opposite direction — the change in the growth of expected prices. While in no way disproving the potential influence of the real interest rate, this connection does show that past nominal-interest-rate fluctuations were too weak to have an undisputable influence on investment expenditures.

2.3.   The accelerator-profits model: a difficult estimate on time series, but accurate on panel data

Before examining the general model defined in the first part of this chapter, we shall study the restriction constituted by the accelerator-profits model, for which there are many estimates based on panel data and time series.[8] These estimates show considerable differences in lag distributions for acceleration and profit variables: the influence of profits becomes insignificant after two years, while the distributed lags of acceleration variables are comparable to those estimated earlier for the flexible accelerator. The estimates using annual time series (ex. Muet [1978a], chap. 4) or even quarterly series (Le Marois [1979]) are imprecise, and involve difficulties in

---

8. The adjustments yielded by the profit model are distinctly inferior to those of all other models (accelerator, effective demand, etc.). Its estimate is given in Appendix 2a.

separating profit and acceleration variables notably because of the correlation of the two time series. By contrast, panel data (Eisner [1978b]; Oudiz [1978]) or longitudinal data (Muet [1978a], chap. 5) yield accurate coefficient estimates and permit a clear distinction between the respective influence of profits and growth. The estimates clearly demonstrate the influence of "permanent" variations in demand and the more "transitory" impact of profits. Also, the influence of profit is shown to be stronger in France than in the United States owing to the imperfection of the French capital market. However, this situation has changed considerably over the last twenty years, as shown in particular by the time-series estimate of the accelerator-profits model.

Table 7 presents the estimate of this model for total fixed investment[9] of non-financial firms for the periods 1952-1974 and 1957-1974 and, for total investment in manufacturing industries, for a cross-section of 18 industries x 9 years (1961-1969). The model estimated is:

(11)
$$\frac{I}{K} = \frac{a_0 + a_1 L}{1 - \lambda L} \overset{o}{Q} + (b_0 + b_1 L) \pi + d$$

The estimate was obtained, as before, using non-linear least squares applied to the model's autoregressive form.

It will be noted that the long-term coefficient of the acceleration variables approximates unity in time-series estimates, whereas it differs considerably from unity in longitudinal data (0.42). The long-term coefficient of the profit rate is correspondingly higher in the longitudinal (cross-section) data estimates than in the time-series estimates. This may be due in particular to the fact that the influence of financing constraints is concentrated at the sector level and is much more diffuse at the macroeconomic level. But the low value of the long-term coefficient of the acceleration variables is also attributable to the fact that the estimate on longitudinal data includes only those industries in which returns to scale are generally increasing; moreover, the upward trend of returns to scale is more easily measured on this type of data than on time series. If we take account of the standard deviations of the coefficients, we can conclude that the long-term coefficient of the acceleration effect is of a magnitude comparable to the long-term coefficient of the profit rate.

---

9. The influence of profit on equipment investment is much weaker than on overall investment (see Appendix 2b), as financing conditions mainly affect total investment expenditure.

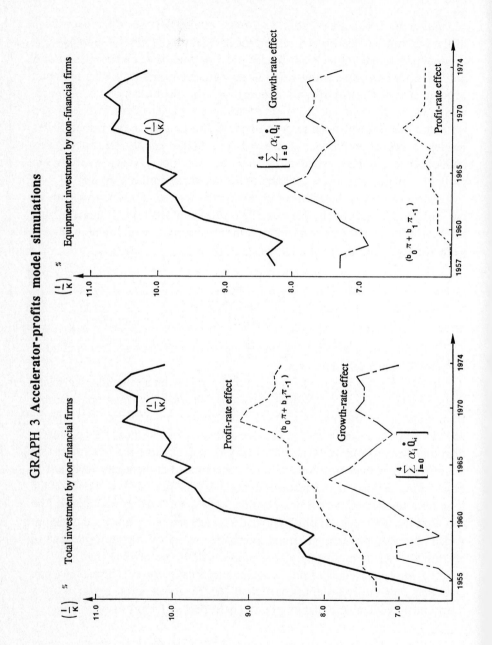

GRAPH 3 Accelerator-profits model simulations

This result tallies well with the estimates on panel data by Oudiz [1978] (the coefficients are respectively 0.49 and 0.38 for an estimate concerning 195 firms and 8 years) and on quarterly data by Le Marois [1979]). To gain an accurate idea of the influence of these two variables, however, we must simulate the model over its estimation period.

The influence of acceleration and profit variables is shown in Graph 3. For the acceleration effect, we have confined the distributed-lag development to the first five years:

$$\frac{a_0 + a_1 L}{1 - \lambda L} \overset{o}{Q}_t \approx a_0 \overset{o}{Q}_t + \sum_{i=1}^{4} (a_1 + \lambda a_0) \lambda^{i-1} \overset{o}{Q}_{t-i}$$

The left side of Graph 3 represents the influence of demand and profits in the model estimate for 1952-1974, the right side the same simulation for the model estimated for 1957-1974. For the whole period 1952-1974, the influence of profit nearly matches that of the acceleration variables. The long-term changes in the profit rate provide a clear explanation in particular of the rise in the accumulation rate, which then leveled off and decreased from 1969 on. In the estimate for 1957-1974, the influence of the profit rate is instead much weaker and largely insignificant, as corroborated by the Student t values of the estimated coefficients. This result accurately reflects the influence of internal financing of investment during the 1950s, at a time when restrictions on access to financial markets limited corporate investment opportunities. These constraints seem to have eased during 1960-1974, owing to the development of the financial market and rising corporate profits. One ought, no doubt, to distinguish between restricted-credit and "liberal" periods, but the limited number of observations does not permit such an analysis using the time series. On the longitudinal data we can, however, verify that investment is more responsive to cash-flow resources when credit controls are in force (see, for example, Muet [1978a], pp. 265-266).

TABLE 7 :   Accelerator-profits' model estimates for total investment Longitudinal data

	Acceleration effect					Relative cost				Adjustment characteristics
	$\hat{a}_0$	$\hat{a}_1$	$\hat{\lambda}_1$	LTC	ML	$\hat{b}_0$	$\hat{b}_1$	LTC	ML	
Longitudinal data............	0.04 (1.5)	0.06 (2.0)	0.75 (13.0)	0.42 (2.5)	3.5 (3.8)	0.40 (4.3)	0.31 (2.4)	0.72 (4.2)	0.4 (4.0)	NLLS (GAUSS) R^2 = 0.740 N = 18 x 9 = 162
Time series 1952-1974............	0.14 (3.0)	0.09 (1.7)	0.78 (8.3)	1.04 (2.2)	3.9 (2.1)	0.43 (2.1)	0.17 (1.1)	0.60 (2.1)	0.3 (1.5)	NLLS (GAUSS) R^2 = 0.977 N = 23 DW = 2.1
Time series 1957-1974............	0.12 (2.7)	0.09 (1.7)	0.77 (10.7)	0.92 (2.5)	3.8 (2.9)	0.27 (1.5)	- 0.03 (0.2)	0.23 (0.9)	-	NLLS (GAUSS) R^2 = 0.969 N = 19 DW = 2.4

2.4. The general model and the impact of the interest rate, growth and profits on investment

The study of the effective-demand and accelerator-profits models has enabled us to describe the influence and form of the variables' distributed lags. We can therefore apply our earlier findings to produce an accurate specification of the general model before estimating it for the period 1957-1974. The brevity of the series and the correlation of explanatory variables impose a limit on the number of parameters to be estimated.

We shall therefore use a first-order distribution, pre-set for the acceleration variables:

$$\Phi(L) = \frac{\alpha + (1 - \alpha) L}{1 - \lambda L} (1 - \lambda) = (1 - \lambda) \{ [\alpha + (1 - \alpha) L] + \dots$$

$$+ \dots + \lambda^n [\alpha + (1 - \alpha) L] L^n + \dots \}$$

The earlier estimates lead us to values for α close to 0.5 and values for λ of about 0.5 for equipment investment and 0.8 for total investment. By limiting the acceleration-variable lags to the first six years and standardizing the resulting distributions, we can directly estimate the model in its developed form using ordinary least squares.

Instead of pre-setting the value of α and λ , we shall determine the optimal values and use the adjustment that entails the least residual variance. For different values of α and λ, we shall therefore estimate the model:

(10) $\qquad \dfrac{I}{K} = a \ ACCT + b_0 \ (\overset{o}{c/w}) + b_1 \ (\overset{o}{c/w})_{-1} + c_0 \ \pi + c_1 \ \pi_{-1} + d$

with:

$$ACCT = \frac{\alpha \overset{o}{Q} + [\alpha\lambda + (1 - \alpha)] \overset{o}{Q}_1 + \dots + \lambda^4 [\alpha\lambda + (1 - \alpha)] \overset{o}{Q}_5}{\alpha + [\alpha\lambda + (1 - \alpha)] + \dots + \lambda^4 [\alpha\lambda + (1 - \alpha)]}$$

Investment and Factor Demand

Appendix 3 indicates the value of the residual variance of the model estimates for different values of α and λ.

The minimum variance corresponds to $\alpha = 0.4$ and $\lambda = 0.5$ for equipment investment, and we have chosen the values $\alpha = 0.2$ and $\lambda = 0.8$ for total investment.[10] The long-term coefficients of the explanatory variables are largely unaffected by variations of parameter α but are more responsive to those of parameter λ . For example, when λ rises from 0.6 to 0.9 for total investment, the long-term coefficient for profit falls from 0.9 to 0.75, while the coefficients for growth and relative costs increase respectively from 0.45 to 0.65 and 0.018 to 0.032 (in absolute value for the second of these coefficients, which is negative). These changes, however, show that the estimates obtained are fairly solid.

The models used are listed below (the full set of estimates is given in Appendix 4).

Equipment investment

$$\frac{I}{K} = 0.504 \, ACCT - 0.011 \, (\overset{o}{c/w}) - 0.019 \, (\overset{o}{c/w})_{-1} + 0.210 \, \pi + 0.007 \, \pi_{-1} + 0.076$$
$$\quad\ (5.4) \qquad\qquad (2.6) \qquad\qquad (3.7) \qquad\qquad (1.7) \qquad (0.5) \qquad\quad (15.0)$$

$$R^2 = 0.920 \quad DW = 2.2 \quad \Sigma \, e^2 = 0.305 \, . \, 10^{-4} \quad S = 0.159 \, . \, 10^{-2}$$

with, for $\lambda = 0.5$ and $\alpha = 0.4$:

$$ACCT = 0.205 \, \overset{o}{Q} + 0.410 \, \overset{o}{Q}_1 + 0.205 \, \overset{o}{Q}_2 + 0.102 \, \overset{o}{Q}_3 + 0.051 \, \overset{o}{Q}_4 + 0.026 \, \overset{o}{Q}_5$$

---

10. The minimum of 0.360 corresponds to an α close to 0.1, but a confidence interval for α at the standard level (5%) comprises 0 and 0.3. Accordingly, we have chosen the value 0.2, which tallies more closely with the usual estimates of acceleration lags.

Total investment

$$\frac{I}{K} = \underset{(4.7)}{0.614} \text{ ACCT} - \underset{(2.6)}{0.013} \overset{o}{(c/w)} - \underset{(3.2)}{0.016} \overset{o}{(c/w)}_{-1} + \underset{(3.5)}{0.440} \pi + \underset{(2.8)}{0.360} \pi_{-1} - \underset{(1.1)}{0.006}$$

$$R^2 = 0.976 \quad DW = 1.7 \quad \Sigma e^2 = 0.373 \ 10^{-4} \quad S = 0.176 \ 10^{-2}$$

with, for $\lambda = 0.8$ and $\alpha = 0.2$:

$$\text{ACCT} = 0.058 \overset{o}{Q} + 0.280 \overset{o}{Q}_{-1} + 0.224 \overset{o}{Q}_{2} + 0.179 \overset{o}{Q}_{3} + 0.143 \overset{o}{Q}_{4} + 0.115 \overset{o}{Q}_{5}$$

The long-term coefficients of the three explanatory variables differ significantly from zero in both estimates. Their value is listed in Table 8. These two estimates, together with their simulations (Graphs 4), yield the same results calculated earlier. The influence of profits is stronger on total investment than on equipment investment, while the latter is more responsive to variations in acceleration and relative cost.

TABLE 8 : **Long-term coefficients of the three explanatory variables**

	Accelerator a	Relative cost $b_0 + b_1$	Profits $c_0 + c_1$
Total investment.................	0.614 (4.7)	- 0.029 (3.7)	0.800 (10.4)
Equipment investment..........	0.504 (5.4)	- 0.030 (4.3)	0.218 (3.7)

The order of importance of the explanatory variables is reversed between total investment and equipment investment except for the acceleration effect, which predominates in both simulations. Fluctuations in equipment investment are mainly due to the acceleration effect and, to a lesser degree, to the relative capital-labor cost. Profits and acceleration effect, on the other hand, have roughly the same impact on total investment, which is less affected by relative cost.

GRAPH 4 Simulations of general model

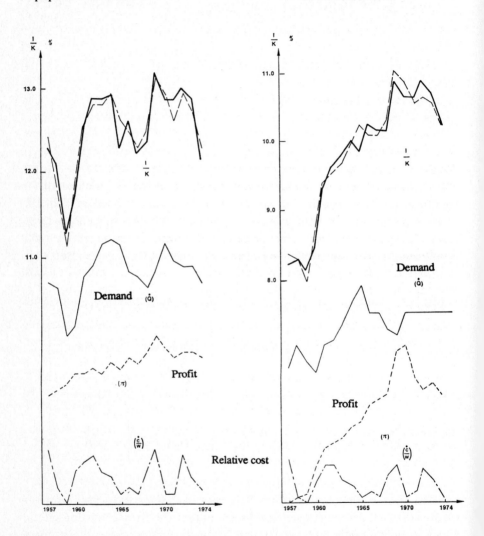

Equipment investment   *Total investment*

Nota: the curves showing the influence of explanatory variables have been shifted upward.

Conclusion

The general model developed in the first part of this chapter has allowed us to take simultaneous account of the influence of growth, profits and relative capital-labor cost in a single model that nevertheless includes as special cases the main econometric models of investment. We have put forward a model typology based on the financial constraint (υ) and on the value of the overall production function's elasticity of substitution (σ).

The estimation and comparison of these models showed that the acceleration effect remained a determining factor in corporate investment decisions, with adjustment lags spreading over many years (on average, 1.5 years for equipment investment, 3.5 years for total investment). The relative capital-labor cost also has a tangible influence on firms' equipment investment, but its elasticity stays well below the value corresponding to a Cobb-Douglas function (0.03 compared to 0.5-0.6); furthermore, the adjustment lags are very short (less than one year). The adjustments obtained correspond either to a production function with a low elasticity of substitution or to a putty-clay Cobb-Douglas function. Both models yield virtually equivalent adjustments.

The breakdown of the relative capital-labor cost also shows that the real interest rate remains the main explanatory factor for changes in this cost. The influence of the real interest rate on investment therefore proves significant, but because the changes in nominal interest rate are so minimal compared to fluctuations in expected prices, it is hard to be certain about the influence of the nominal interest rate.

Total investment was influenced to a rather large extent by the mass of realized profits, but this influence waned considerably during the 1960s. The estimates on longitudinal data nevertheless show its continuing importance during periods when credit controls were in force. Lastly, investments adjusted rapidly to profit changes: the influence of profits did not extend beyond the first two years, the mean lag being about six months.

The estimate of the general model has enabled us to define the influence of each of these variables on total investment and equipment investment. The model's simulation allows us to rank the explanatory variables in order of importance: demand, relative cost and profits for equipment investment; demand and profit, followed by relative cost, for total investment. This general model is very useful for studying economic policy measures of a fiscal, taxation or monetary nature. Theoretical analyses of the Keynesian or classical nature of under-employment (ex. Malinvaud [1978]) and studies of

economic policy using macroeconomic-model simulation (ex. Guillaume and
Muet [1979] for the DMS model) show the special role played by the influence
of demand and profits in determining business fixed investment. To take a
simple example, an *ex ante* increase in wages produces contradictory effects on
the general model's three explanatory variables:

(a) a revival of consumption and demand, and consequently a recovery of
investment through the acceleration effect;

(b) an increase in capital intensity and therefore in investment through a
fall in the relative capital-labor cost;

(c) a shrinking of corporate profits (all other factors being equal) that
tends to reduce investment.

The relative fragility of results obtained from annual time series shows
that much progress remains to be accomplished before macroeconomic theory
can be assured of a solid empirical foundation.

APPENDIX 1 Statistical sources for annual time-series estimates (1949-1974)

Years	Growth rate $\dot{Q}$	Profit rate π	Accumulation rate I/K Equipment	Accumulation rate I/K Total	Real cost of capital c/p Equipment	Real cost of capital c/p Total	Real cost of wages w/p
1949	–	8.50	–	–	–	–	–
1950	8.20	7.59	–	–	–	–	–
1951	5.60	6.74	11.96	7.50	–	–	–
1952	2.40	6.45	10.18	6.54	–	–	–
1953	2.70	6.91	9.81	6.55	–	–	–
1954	5.10	6.71	9.99	6.57	181	178.7	77.8
1955	5.75	6.83	10.98	7.25	144	142.0	83.0
1956	5.70	7.19	11.67	7.75	123	121.4	87.7
1957	6.40	7.02	12.32	8.30	114	113.3	90.7
1958	3.30	7.31	12.11	8.40	132	130.0	92.3
1959	3.10	7.38	11.32	8.22	126	124.2	95.0
1960	7.59	8.10	11.78	8.54	123	120.7	100.0
1961	5.53	7.90	12.55	9.34	106	104.7	107.6
1962	7.04	8.21	12.90	9.63	108	107.1	114.6
1963	6.28	8.15	12.88	9.71	100	100.0	120.3
1964	7.01	8.60	12.91	9.98	110	110.5	126.3
1965	4.81	8.39	12.30	9.80	110	110.5	132.2
1966	5.84	8.93	12.62	10.17	115	116.5	136.9
1967	5.38	8.68	12.27	10.12	123	124.3	142.9
1968	4.82	9.14	12.38	10.13	104	107.7	151.8
1969	7.95	9.99	13.15	10.71	104	107.4	159.9
1970	5.72	9.49	12.85	10.55	119	122.3	166.6
1971	5.65	8.94	12.87	10.56	106	111.1	176.7
1972	5.87	9.05	12.98	10.74	103	107.2	184.2
1973	6.05	9.07	12.90	10.63	103	108.2	194.7
1974	3.58	8.83	12.21	10.20	117	122.3	204.1

I/K, $\dot{Q}$ and π are given in %, c/p and w/p as an index (100 = 1963 and 1960 respectively).

APPENDIX 2   Additional econometric data
on the profit and accelerator-profits models

a. Profit model (OLS)

		λ	c_0	c_1	d	Estimate characteristics
TOTAL	1952-1974	0.641 (3.9)	0.596 (2.9)	- 0.100 (0.4)	0.007 (1.0)	$R^2 = 0.953$ DW = 1.0 S = $0.334.10^{-2}$
	1957-1974	0.482 (3.0)	0.414 (2.6)	0.086 (0.4)	0.009 (1.4)	$R^2 = 0.940$ DW = 1.7 S = $0.232\ 10^{-2}$
EQUIPMENT	1952-1974	0.519 (2.8)	0.687 (2.3)	- 0.270 (0.8)	0.024 (1.7)	$R^2 = 0.759$ DW = 0.8 S = $0.524\ 10^{-2}$
	1957-1974	0.330 (1.2)	0.362 (1.4)	- 0.106 (0.3)	0.062 (2.3)	$R^2 = 0.453$ DW = 1.3 S = $0.386\ 10^{-2}$

t statistics are given in parentheses.

b. Accelerator-profits model : equipment investment

Estimates period	Accelerator effect			Profits		Adjustment characteristic
	a_0	a_1	λ	b_0	b_1	
1957-1974	0.193 (2.7)	0.180 (4.1)	0.378 (3.0)	0.345 (2.0)	- 0.232 (1.4)	$R^2 = 0.977$ DW = 2.0 S = $0.125\ 10^{-2}$
1952-1974	0.259 (4.6)	0.179 (2.5)	0.450 (3.5)	0.431 (2.0)	- 0.088 (0.4)	$R^2 = 0.926$ DW = 1.4 S = $0.308\ 10^{-2}$

APPENDIX 3 Search for optimal pattern of accelerator lags
(residual variance of adjustment x 10⁻⁴)

TOTAL INVESTMENT					EQUIPMENT INVESTMENT				
α \ λ	0.6	0.7	0.8	0.9	α \ λ	0.4	0.5	0.6	0.7
0.2..............	0.531	0.434	0.373	0.387	0.2..............	0.330	0.317	0.353	0.447
0.3..............	0.562	0.461	0.392	0.397	0.3..............	0.322	0.305	0.334	0.424
0.4..............	0.606	0.500	0.421	0.414	0.4..............	0.346	0.317	0.335	0.413
0.5..............	0.660	0.549	0.459	0.438	0.5..............	0.400	0.355	0.354	0.416
0.6..............	0.722	0.561	0.506	0.468	0.6..............	0.475	0.413	0.391	0.431

APPENDIX 4 Responsiveness of general-model coefficients
to the specification of acceleration-effect lags

a. LONG-TERM COEFFICIENT OF THE ACCELERATION EFFECT (â)

Total ($\sigma_{\hat{a}} = 0.15$)					Equipment ($\sigma_{\hat{a}} = 0.09$)				
α \ λ	0.6	0.7	0.8	0.9	α \ λ	0.4	0.5	0.6	0.7
0.2..........	0.443	0.535	0.614	0.642	0.3.........	0.441	0.485	0.522	0.536
0.3..........	0.440	0.541	0.624	0.655	0.4.........	0.458	0.503	0.542	0.559
0.4..........	0.437	0.536	0.624	0.661	0.5.........	0.456	0.505	0.548	0.571
0.5..........	0.416	0.518	0.614	0.659	0.6........	0.434	0.489	0.540	0.572

b. LONG-TERM COEFFICIENT OF RELATIVE COST ($b_0 + b_1$)

	Total ($\sigma_{b0+b1} = 0.008$)					Equipment ($\sigma_{b0+b1}) = 0.007$)			
α \ λ	0.6	0.7	0.8	0.9	α \ λ	0.4	0.5	0.6	0.7
0.2.........	- 0.017	- 0.022	- 0.029	- 0.034	0.3....	- 0.029	- 0.029	- 0.039	- 0.045
0.3.........	- 0.014	- 0.020	- 0.026	- 0.032	0.4.....	- 0.025	- 0.030	- 0.035	- 0.042
0.4.........	- 0.011	- 0.017	- 0.023	- 0.030	0.5.....	- 0.022	- 0.026	- 0.032	- 0.039
0.5.........	- 0.009	- 0.014	- 0.021	- 0.028	0.6....	- 0.019	- 0.023	- 0.029	- 0.036

c. LONG-TERM COEFFICIENT OF PROFITS ($c_0 + c_1$)

	Total ($\sigma_{c0+c1} = 0.08$)					Equipment ($\sigma_{c0+c1} = 0.08$)			
α \ λ	0.6	0.7	0.8	0.9	α \ λ	0.4	0.5	0.6	0.7
0.2.........	0.899	0.851	0.800	0.762	0.3.......	0.249	0.230	0.208	0.188
0.3.........	0.894	0.846	0.793	0.756	0.4.......	0.235	0.218	0.195	0.176
0.4.........	0.893	0.844	0.791	0.750	0.5.......	0.028	0.210	0.188	0.210
0.5.........	0.895	0.846	0.792	0.750	0.6.......	0.229	0.229	0.186	0.164

CHAPTER 3
A reconsideration of the comparison between putty-putty and putty-clay hypotheses in the estimation of effective demands for investment*

by

Patrick Artus and Pierre-Alain Muet

Introduction

The modeling and estimation of investment functions have long since brought to light the links between (a) the elasticities of investment demand with respect to quantities and prices and (b) the parameters of the production function from which the demand derives. Indeed, estimating investment demand has become one of the choice methods for assessing and testing hypotheses about production-function forms.

However, while the specification of investment functions is informed by production-function hypotheses, it also rests on assumptions about the economic environment (competitive or rationed markets) and firms' behavior. In this chapter — as, for that matter, in the great majority of econometric studies on investment — we focus on effective demand for investment. In other words, we assume that firms determine their investment according to the expected pattern of demand growth by choosing the optimal production technique, that is, the one that will minimize the total discounted cost of production. The responsiveness of investment to the relative capital-labor cost therefore depends, in this model, on the production function's elasticity of substitution and on the degree of capital malleability. Most important, if production techniques on installed equipment are fixed (putty-clay model) the responsiveness of investment to the relative capital-labor cost will — for an identical elasticity of substitution — be nearly ten times lower than in the full-substitution putty-putty model[1].

---

* Originally published as "Un retour sur la comparaison des hypotheses 'putty-putty' et 'putty-clay' dans l'estimation des demandes effectives d'investissement," *Annales de l'INSEE* 38-39:193-206, 1980.

1. Substitution affects only investment rather than total capital. The ratio between the two effects is therefore I/K.

In addition, investment will no longer depend on changes in the relative capital-labor cost but only on its level. In other words, the relative cost will not exert an acceleration effect on investment if the production function is putty-clay. Most of the comparisons between the two models since Bischoff [1971] have been based on these two properties.

This chapter aims to show that while the putty-clay model has been adequately verified by econometric estimates — notably owing to the low response of investment to changes in user cost — the choice between a putty-putty model with low elasticity of substitution and a putty-clay model is less clearcut.

We begin by describing the specification of the two models and go on to examine the results yielded by Bischoff's approach. In the third part, we present an estimate of the two models based on an accumulation-rate specification that spells out the significance of each coefficient and allows a more meaningful comparison between the two hypotheses.

1. EFFECTIVE DEMAND FOR INVESTMENT AND THE FORM OF THE PRODUCTION FUNCTION

We assume that firms adjust to expected changes in demand (desired production capacity Q^*) by choosing the optimal production technique, namely, the capital coefficient k that minimizes the production cost, for a given expected relative capital-labor cost (c^*/w^*). Let σ be the elasticity of substitution and β the ratio of wage costs to total costs [$\beta = w^* N/(c^*K + w^*N)$]. In a first approximation, we obtain:

$$(1) \qquad \hat{k}^* = e^{-\gamma t}\left(\frac{w^*}{c^*}\right)^b$$

with $b = \beta \sigma$. [2]

The distinction between the putty-putty and putty-clay models is simple. In the first, the choice concerns total capital and consequently the mean capital coefficient. If δ stands for the capital replacement rate (here assumed constant, which is the same as assuming constant equipment lifetime), desired gross investment is:

$$(2) \qquad I^d = [\hat{k}^* Q^* - \hat{k}_{-1}^* (1-\delta) Q_{-1}^*]$$

In the putty-clay model, the choice of capital coefficient concerns only new investment, in other words, the marginal coefficient of capital. Investment here is:

$$(3) \qquad I^d = \hat{k}* \, [Q^* - (1 - \delta) \, Q^*_1]$$

By linearizing the two models, we can easily verify that investment in the putty-clay model depends on the level of the marginal coefficient of capital, whereas in the putty-putty model it depends on changes in the mean coefficient. That is the basis of Bischoff's comparison. We introduce two distributed-lag functions to represent investment expectations and actual investment-completion times. We also distinguish between relative-cost and demand expectations:

$$(4) \qquad \text{demand expectations}^3 \qquad Q_t^* = \sum_j a_j \, Q_{t-j}$$

$$(5) \qquad \text{expectations about } \hat{k}_t = e^{-\gamma t} \left(\frac{c}{w} \right)_t^b \qquad \hat{k}_t^* = \sum_i b_i \, \hat{k}_{t-i}$$

$$(6) \qquad \text{completion time} \qquad I_t = \sum_k c_k \, I^d_{t-k}$$

The total investment function results from the combination of the different lag patterns. We get:

$$(7) \qquad I_t = \sum_{(i,j,k)} c_k b_i a_j \, (\hat{k}_{t-k-i} Q_{t-j-k} - (1 - \delta) \, \hat{k}_{t-k-i-1} Q_{t-j-k-1}) \qquad \text{\textit{«putty-putty»}}$$

$$(8) \qquad I_t = \sum_{(i,j,k)} c_k b_i a_j \, \hat{k}_{t-k-i} \, (Q_{t-j-k} - (1 - \delta) \, Q_{t-j-k-1}) \qquad \text{\textit{«putty-clay»}}$$

---

2. b is strictly constant only in a Cobb-Douglas function ($\sigma = 1$). On this approximation, see also Villa, Muet and Boutillier [1980, Chapter 5 below].

3. We have kept Bischoff's specification, which omits demand growth. The latter should entail a discounting of expectations by the growth rate.

2. BISCHOFF'S ESTIMATE REVISITED

Bischoff's analysis rests on the fact that the putty-putty and putty-clay specifications — equations (7) and (8) respectively — are special cases of the general model :

$$(9) \qquad I_t = \sum_{(i,j)} \beta_i^j \, \hat{k}_{t-i} \, Q_{t-j}$$

The margins of the matrix β_i^j do indeed represent the lag pattern of demand Q_{t-j} and of the relative capital-labor cost (described by k_{t-i}) in the linearized model. Now while that pattern is identical for demand in both hypotheses:

$$(10) \qquad \beta^j = \sum_i \beta_i^j = \left(\sum_i b_i \right) \cdot \left[\sum_{k=0}^{j} c_k \left(a_{j-k} - (1 - \delta) \, a_{j-k-1} \right) \right]$$

it differs for the capital coefficient. The putty-putty model accommodates the acceleration effect:

$$(11) \qquad \beta_i = \sum_j \beta_i^j = \left(\sum_j a_j \right) \cdot \left[\sum_{k=0}^{i} c_k \left(b_{i-k} - (1 - \delta) \, b_{i-k-1} \right) \right]$$

whereas this distribution is monotonic in the putty-clay model:

$$(12) \qquad \beta_i = \sum_j \beta_i^j = \left(\sum_j a_j \right) \cdot \left[\sum_{k=0}^{i} \delta \, c_k b_{i-k} \right]$$

Bischoff reduces the estimation of the coefficients of this matrix to that of the two diagonals β_i^i and β_i^{i+1} . In calculating the margins, he accordingly finds a positive, then a negative distribution for β_j. This reflects the acceleration effect of demand,[4] whereas the distribution β_i is monotonic: the putty-clay hypothesis is therefore validated.
Using the same procedure, we find a similar result. The model, restricted

---

4. β^i becomes negative when the b_i coefficients eventually decrease at a rate exceeding δ . This supposes that the demand expectation is formed over a shorter period of time than the capital's lifetime — an entirely realistic hypothesis.

to the two diagonals, is not linear with respect to b and γ :

(13) $\qquad I_t = \sum_{i=0}^{15} \beta_i^{\,i} \, \hat{k}_{t-i} \, Q_{-i} + \sum_{i=0}^{15} \beta_i^{\,i+1} \, \hat{k}_{t-i} \, Q_{t-i-l} + \sum_{j=0}^{4} \lambda_j \, RES_{-j} + d$

with:

$$\hat{k}_t = \left(\frac{w_t}{c_t}\right) e^{-\gamma t}$$

RES stands for the intensity of credit restrictions.

We estimate coefficients $\beta_i^{\,i}$, $\beta_i^{\,i+1}$ and λ_i using Almon's method,[5] by looking for the values of b and γ that minimize the estimates' residual variance. We obtain :

$b = 0.17 \qquad$ and $\qquad \gamma = 0.012$

The values of coefficients $\beta_i^{\,i}$ and $\beta_i^{\,i+1}$ and of parameters β_i, β_j are listed in Table 1. These confirm the existence of an acceleration effect for demand, while the β_i coefficients are all positive. This result is found whatever the value set for coefficient b (we have caused b to vary in the [0.05 ; 0.5] interval). Two comments, however, are in order. First, the β_i coefficients are of the same magnitude as the standard deviation of the estimated coefficients $\beta_i^{\,i}$ and $\beta_i^{\,i+1}$, so that the test has little significance. Second, the $\beta_i^{\,j}$ matrix is reduced to the two estimated diagonals in only two cases:

- putty-clay model without expectation lags ($a_i = b_i = 0$) ;
- putty-putty model without expectation lags on the relative capital-labor cost ($b_i = 0$) and expectation lags limited to one period for demand (a_0 , a_1).

These restrictive assumptions greatly diminish the validity of the comparison. In particular, if the acceleration effect of demand largely outweighs the influence of relative cost (as is the case here) the finding of β_i coefficients that are all positive may be due to the fact that the estimate of the two diagonals accurately describes the acceleration effect of demand without yielding meaningful results for the influence of relative cost. For in the case of

---

5. The estimates reported here use second-degree polynomials equal to zero at the point $\underline{i} = 16$. We have checked that the absence of constraints and the use of a higher degree do not significantly alter our results.

the accelerator effect:

$$(14) \qquad I_t = \sum_i \alpha^i \, \bar{k} \, [Q_{t-i} - (1 - \delta)\, Q_{t-i-1}] + d$$

the two diagonals' coefficients are respectively α^i and $- (1-\delta)\,\alpha^i$ and the distribution β_i is nothing other than $\delta\,\alpha^i$. Indeed, one can verify that in all the estimates, and therefore whatever the value of b, the β_i coefficients are — at least for the first terms, which are the only significant ones — approximately proportional to the $\beta_i{}^i$ coefficients. Thus the approximation that consists in estimating two diagonals imposes constraints on relative-cost expectation lags that are too restrictive to constitute a valid test for deciding between the putty-putty and putty-clay hypotheses. Of course, it would be impossible to estimate all $\beta_i{}^j$ coefficients. However, a direct estimate of the margins — that is, an estimate of the linearized model — is possible and does not set such rigid constraints on lag patterns, since it is compatible with all specifications. Moreover, in this estimate, we can allow for the fact that the demand lag pattern is of the accelerator type by specifying the model as[6] :

$$(15) \quad I_t = \sum_{j=0}^{m} \bar{k}\,\alpha^j \, [Q_{t-j} - (1 - \delta)\, Q_{t-j-1}] + \sum_{i=0}^{n} (g + \delta)\, \bar{Q}\, \beta_i \hat{k}_{t-i} + \sum_{j=0}^{p} \lambda_j \, RES_{t-j} + d$$

As before, we estimate the model by determining the optimal values of b and γ, and using polynomial distributions for α^j and λ_i . All the α^j coefficients are indeed positive and represent the resultant of the compounding of demand expectation lags (a_j) and completion times (c_k):

$$\alpha^j = \sum_{k=0}^{j} c_k a_{j-k} \qquad \beta^j = \alpha^j - (1 - \delta)\,\alpha^{j-1}$$

The β_i coefficients too are always positive whatever the chosen length of the relative-cost lags . However, as these coefficients cease to differ significantly from zero after eight quarters, we have limited the number of lags to the first

---

6. Q and k stand respectively for the mean values of value added and of the capital coefficient. Unlike Bischoff, we take demand growth (rate g) into account in the linearization:

$$Q_{t-j} - (1 - \delta)\, Q_{t-j-1} \,\#\, [(1 + g) - (1 - \delta)]\, Q_{t-j-1} = (g + \delta)\, \bar{Q}$$

seven quarters.The optimal value of b is 0.35; accordingly, the direct estimate of the margins validates the hypothesis of a putty-clay production function with an *ex ante* elasticity of substitution of approximately 0.5 (b=β σ).

This linearization of the model nevertheless has the disadvantage of not yielding economically meaningful β_i and α_i coefficients which greatly limits the interpretation of our results. For example, one can assume that a fall in coefficient b may be offset by an increase in the sum of the β_i coefficients; but since we cannot interpret that sum, we cannot conclude that the optimal value found for coefficient b (0.35) effectively corresponds to the theoretical putty-clay model.

3. ACCUMULATION-RATE SPECIFICATIONS

When the two models are specified in terms of accumulation rate (I/K), the long-term coefficients represent the production-function parameters (see Chapter 2 above). In the putty-putty model, they are expressed in terms of returns to scale (v), elasticity of substitution (σ) and share of wages in total cost (β):

(16)
$$\frac{I}{K} = \sum_j \alpha^j \overset{o}{Q}_j + \sum_i \alpha_i \, (\overset{o}{w/c})_{-i} + \sum_{i=0}^{4} \lambda_i \, RES_{-i} + d$$

with:

$$\sum_j \alpha^j = \frac{1}{v} \qquad \sum_i \alpha_i = b = \beta \, \sigma$$

$\overset{o}{Q}$ stands for the growth rate of value added, $(\overset{o}{c/w})$ the growth rate of the relative capital-labor cost. The model estimate yields returns to scale close to unity and an elasticity of substitution on the order of 0.1 (Table 1).

The putty-clay hypothesis also comprises a close specification of the investment function. Let k* be the desired marginal coefficient of capital and k the mean coefficient of capital. (3) becomes:

(17)
$$\left(\frac{I}{K_{-1}}\right)^d = \frac{k^*}{\overline{k}} \, \frac{Q^*}{\overline{Q}^*_1} - \frac{k^*}{\overline{k}} (1 - \delta)$$

Linearizing with respect to Q and k , and introducing expectation and completion lags, we get:

$$(18) \qquad \left(\frac{I}{K_{-1}}\right) = \sum_j \alpha^j \overset{o}{Q}_j + (\delta + g) \sum_i \beta_i \frac{k_{-i}}{\overline{\overline{k}}}$$

with

$$k = k_0 \left(\frac{w}{c}\right)^b e^{-\gamma t}$$

Parameter g stands for the mean value of the growth rate of value added. To carry out the estimate, we need a second approximation, for the mean coefficient is a function of the marginal coefficients of the different vintages of equipment. Let μ be the average growth rate of the relative cost over the lapsed period and $\overline{T}$ the average age of capital (whose value can be set with reference to that of δ). The mean coefficient approximately equals:

$$(19) \qquad \overline{\overline{k}} = \exp\left[(-\gamma + \mu b)(t - \overline{T})\right]$$

Substituting this value into (18), we get:

$$(20) \qquad \frac{I_t}{K_{t-1}} = \sum_{j=0}^{n} \alpha^j \overset{o}{Q}_{t-j} + (\delta + g) e^{(-\gamma + \mu b)\overline{T}} \sum_{j=0}^{n} \beta_i e^{-\mu b t} \left(\frac{w}{c}\right)^b_{t-i} + d$$

The I/K ratio is therefore a linear function of (a) the growth rate of value added and (b) the ratio of relative cost to its trend. The complete model also incorporates credit restrictions. The inclusion of the term $e^{(-\gamma + \mu b)T}$ complicates the estimate somewhat. First, we set the known values g, μ and T . Next, we estimate the model for different values of b and γ , thereby determining the form of the distributions (β_i and α^j). We can then set the lag distributions and estimate b using non-linear least squares. We repeat the procedure until we obtain convergence on b. The lag patterns are reported in Table 1. The value of b is low (0.17) and comparable to that obtained from level estimates. The simulation study of the influence of growth and user cost shows that the putty-putty and putty-clay specifications yield the same results.

In both cases, the influence of relative cost is weak compared to the acceleration effect of demand (Graphs 1 and 2).

GRAPH 1
Contribution to the explanation of the putty-clay accumulation rate

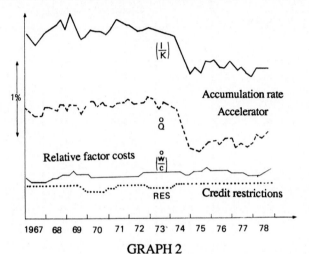

GRAPH 2
Contribution to the explanation of the putty-putty accumulation rate

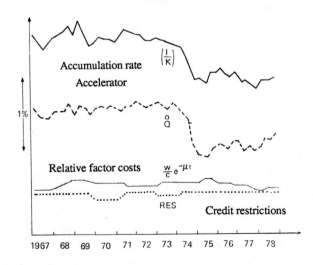

Investment and Factor Demand

TABLE 1 **Lag coefficients for the estimates (1967.I , 1978.IV)**

i or j quarters	Investment in level form			
	Estimate of 2 diagonals (13)			
	$\widehat{\beta_i^i}$	$\widehat{\beta_i^{i+1}}$	β_i	β^j
0................................	2.410	- 2.132	0.278	2.410
1................................	2.015	- 1.763	0.252	- 0.117
2................................	1.652	- 1.426	0.226	- 0.111
3................................	1.322	- 1.120	0.202	- 0.104
4................................	1.025	- 0.845	0.180	- 0.095
5................................	0.760	- 0.602	0.158	- 0.085
6................................	0.528	- 0.390	0.138	- 0.074
7................................	0.328	- 0.210	0.118	- 0.062
8................................	0.161	- 0.061	0.100	- 0.049
9................................	0.027	0.056	0.083	- 0.034
10.............................	- 0.075	0.143	0.068	- 0.018
11	- 0.144	0.197	0.053	- 0.001
12	- 0.180	0.221	0.040	0.017
13.............................	- 0.184	0.212	0.028	0.037
14.............................	- 0.155	0.173	0.018	0.057
15	- 0.094	0.102	0.008	0.079
Mean value* τ_i	4.7	3.9	-	-
Number of $\tau_i \geqslant 2$	9	10	-	-
Long-term coefficient	9.39	- 7.44		
(Standard deviation).......	(2.09)	(2.09)		
Mean lag	-	-	-	-
(Standard deviation)........	-	-	-	-
Structural parameters........	b = 0.17 $\qquad$ $\gamma=0.012$			
Estimate characteristics.....	Constrained 2nd degree Almon $R^2 = 0.982$ $\quad$ S/M = 2.3 % $\quad$ DW = 1.5			
* τ_i denotes the t statistics of coefficients				

The subscript index (i) relates to user cost ; the superscript index (j) to demand

$(I = 14\,954)$		Accumulation rate $I/K(\overline{I/K} = 0.035)$			
Direct estimate (15)		Putty-putty model (16)		Putty-clay model (20)	
$(g+\delta)\cdot\dot{Q}\cdot 10^{-5}$ $\hat{\beta}_i$	$\hat{k}\,\hat{\alpha}^j$	$\hat{\alpha}_i$	$\hat{\alpha}^j$	$A\cdot\hat{\alpha}_i$	$\hat{\alpha}^j$
0.495	0.350	0.0034	0.111	0.0108	0.107
0.434	0.330	0.0039	0.104	0.0081	0.101
0.371	0.309	0.0043	0.097	0.0054	0.095
0.309	0.288	0.0045	0.089	0.0027	0.089
0.248	0.268	0.0047	0.082	-	0.083
0.186	0.247	0.0048	0.075	-	0.077
0.124	0.225	0.0049	0.068	-	0.071
0.062	0.203	0.0048	0.061	-	0.064
-	0.182	0.0046	0.054	-	0.057
-	0.160	0.0044	0.047	-	0.051
-	0.138	0.0040	0.040	-	0.044
-	0.115	0.0036	0.033	-	0.039
-	0.093	0.0030	0.027	-	0.030
-	0.069	0.0024	0.020	-	0.022
-	0.046	0.0017	0.013	-	0.015
-	0.023	0.0009	0.006	-	0.008
5.4	15.4	3.3	14.5	-	16.1
8	16	16	16	-	16
2.38	3.04	0.060	0.93	0.027	0.95
(0.44)	(0.12)	(0.015)	(0.04)	-	(0.04)
2.33	5.07	6.54	4.96	1.0	5.14
(0.43)	(0.32)	(2.42)	(0.31)	-	(0.29)
$b = 0.35$ $\gamma = 0.005$ $\delta = 0.027$		$\hat{b} = 0.060$		$\hat{b} = 0.17$ $\hat{\gamma} = 0.005$	
		(0.015)		(0.05)	
Constrained 2nd degree Almon $R^2 = 0.980$ S/M = 2.4 % $DW = 1.4$		Constrained 2nd degree Almon $R^2 = 0.955$ S/M = 1.8 % $DW = 1.0$		Constrained 2nd degree Almon $R^2 = 0.950$ S/M = 2 % $DW = 0.9$	

CONCLUSION

The set of estimates performed shows that the influence of the relative capital-labor cost on investment is weak compared to the acceleration effect of demand. This finding — along with the fact that the estimate of a model without prior constraints on lag patterns does not suggest an acceleration effect on relative cost — is consistent with the putty-clay hypothesis, which postulates the absence of substitution on installed equipment. However, the estimate of the two specifications imposed a priori shows that both models describe a virtually identical influence of the relative capital-labor cost. In our view, this result reflects the fact that a time-series estimate of an investment function provides a good insight into the influence of interest-rate or, more generally, relative-cost changes. But we also conclude that it is hard to draw any lessons from the result as to long-term substitution effects. The elasticity of substitution would seem to be on the order of 0.1 in the putty-putty specification and in the 0.3-0.6 range in the various putty-clay specifications. Lastly, the estimation period (1967-1978) is strongly affected by the crisis: the comparison with estimates performed on earlier periods shows that the chief explanatory factor for investment fluctuations during 1967-1978 is demand growth.

CHAPTER 4
Economic policy and investment in the 1970s*
by
Patrick Artus and Pierre-Alain Muet

Introduction

This chapter aims to assess the impact of the main economic-policy measures affecting investment from 1973 to 1980. Since the first oil crisis in 1973, the Western economies have experienced a rapid succession of slumps and recoveries that have made it more difficult to implement cyclical adjustment policies. The analysis of the impact of economic policies applied since 1973 can therefore provide useful insights for future decisions. However, the complexity and interdependence of economic phenomena greatly restrict the lessons to be learned from a straightforward reading of past trends. For a proper assessment of the often very diverse effects of simultaneous policy measures, we can resort to the quantified, formalized representation of economic interrelationships supplied by a macroeconomic model. We can then evaluate the influence of policy measures on output levels, inflation and the external balance, and estimate their cost to the state budget. Such an analysis obviously requires a formalization of behaviors. It also rests on the implicit assumption of their stability during the period.

Cyclical fluctuations and long-term growth are closely shaped by corporate investment decisions. Taxation, monetary and fiscal policies have also influenced investment either deliberately or through various economic mechanisms. Graph 1 reports a wide variety of trends for the main components of total investment over the period. The slowdown in growth consecutive to the first oil crisis led to a sharp fall in private business investment, which — despite two short recoveries in 1975 and 1979 — had not recovered its end-1973 level by 1980. Personal investment, which remained stable on average for the entire period, nevertheless experienced two sharp surges in 1973-1974 and 1978-1979. These were partly due to investments in housing as a hedge against the prevailing inflation. The most significant phenomenon was the very strong growth in investment of the larger

---

* Originally published as "Politique conjoncturelle et investissement dans les années 70," *Observations et Diagnostics Economiques* 1: 61-90, June 1982.

GRAPH 1 **Real changes in main components of investment (in billions of 1970 francs)**

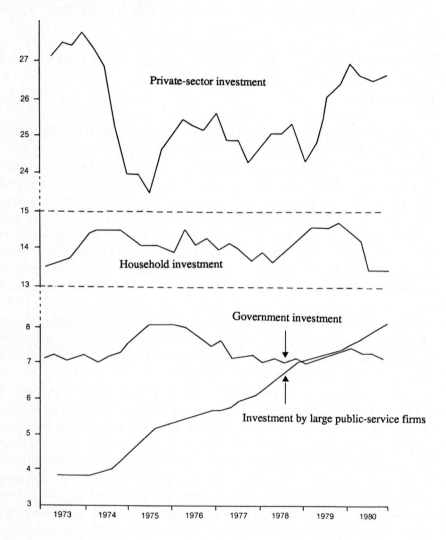

public-service firms[1] that began in mid-1974 and continued at an average pace exceeding 10% a year throughout the period. This acceleration, which was particularly marked during spells of private-investment slowdown, had a highly stabilizing effect — as we shall see.

To quantify the effect of economic policies on investment, we must first define the explanatory factors. In Chapter 1, we presented an assessment of French econometric studies of investment. Before looking at the fiscal, taxation and monetary policies that affected investment and evaluating their impact with the aid of the METRIC model simulations, let us summarize the main findings that led to the specification chosen in this chapter. The preceding chapters have shown the predominant influence of demand variations on investment decisions (acceleration effect). In Chapter 3, we also demonstrated that the substitution of capital for labor is properly described by the hypothesis of low capital malleability (putty-clay model) combined with an elasticity of substitution slightly below unity. Moreover, recent studies suggest that capital and energy are by and large complementary (Chapter 7) and that profits chiefly influence the speed of investment-project implementation — although the last two findings, it should be emphasized, are more arguable.

These findings are illustrated in Graph 2: 2a shows the influence of demand, factor costs and credit restrictions in an energy-inclusive model. The influence of factor costs is in turn broken down into effects of the real interest rate, taxation and relative prices of capital, labor and energy. The influence of demand is effectively predominant, both on short-term fluctuations and medium-term movements. Tax changes and credit restrictions have only limited, short-term, effects. The influence of real-interest-rate fluctuations, while not negligible, is smaller than that of relative prices. We can also observe a partial canceling-out of substitution effects among the three factors: investment is buoyed by real-wage rises but damped by energy-price increases. The influence of energy prices is particularly clearcut in 1974, when, according to this model, investment was driven down as much by rising energy prices as by falling demand.

---

1. Charbonnages de France (coal), Electricite de France (electricity), Gaz de France (gas), SNCF (railroads), RATP (Paris municipal transportation), Air France (domestic and international airline), Air Inter (domestic airline) and PTT (posts and telecommunications).

The METRIC model, used to produce the simulations set out below, includes a simpler investment-determination equation than the final equation described above, since the energy factor is left out and energy-price changes do not play a direct role. On the other hand, the model incorporates the effect of profits on the speed of investment completion.

Graph 2b charts the influence of demand, factor costs (relative prices, interest rate, taxation), and profits in this equation. As before, the influence of demand predominates. The graph gives only a very limited indication of profit influence, since this mainly affects adjustment lags. The mean adjustment lag expands, for example, from less than four quarters in the high-activity years to five and a half quarters after the first oil crisis. In the METRIC model, the rise in energy prices therefore has an indirect damping effect on investment. Apart from this, the effects of economic policies on labor or investment costs are charted in a very similar manner in both equations. Preserving the initial equation in the METRIC simulations therefore does not affect the analysis of economic policies given in the final section of this chapter.

GRAPH 2 **Influence of explanatory factors on investment**

a) Model with energy-prices effect   *b) METRIC model investment equation*

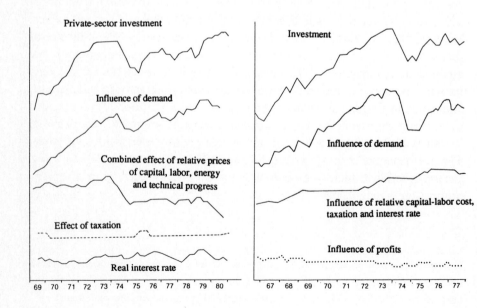

1. DESCRIPTION OF POLICIES AFFECTING INVESTMENT

The following section examines the major taxation, monetary and fiscal measures that have affected investment over the past ten or, in some cases, twenty years. The analysis of the macroeconomic consequences of the economic policies given in section 2 is confined to the period 1973-1980. However, the quantification of the behaviors on which it is based derives from an observation of the past two decades. We have therefore judged it important to extend the description of certain specific measures (taxation and credit restrictions) to the entire period.

1.1. Tax measures

Four tax measures directly or indirectly affected corporate investment decisions:

- Changes in the rules for deducting VAT on investments;
- Changes in the corporation profit-tax rate and in depreciation rules;
- Introduction of tax deductions for investments;
- Increases in employers' social-security contributions, with an impact on the relative capital-labor cost.

These measures often influence investment in different ways. It will be noted that they all affect corporate profits and therefore, in our model, the scheduling of investment-project completions. Some measures, however, exert a more direct influence through the changes they entail in the cost of capital (tax deductions, changes in deduction and depreciation rules) or the cost of labor (rate of employers' social-security contribution).

*The changes in the deduction system for VAT on investments are, in the new national-accounts system, directly included in the investment price, which is assessed net of deductible VAT. The most significant change simply concerned the model's estimation period: the extension of VAT deductibility to the economy as a whole in 1969, which at the time led to an across-the-board drop in investment prices of about 4%.

* The corporation profit-tax rate remained unchanged from the 50% level set by decree in 1958, except for temporary measures. During the period studied (1973-1980), the only such exceptional provisions were enacted in

1974. These comprised an 18% increase in corporation tax, the establishment of a mandatory minimum liability of 3,000 FFr whatever the company's fiscal-year results, and a change in the accelerated depreciation schedule (abolished the following year). Other temporary measures concerning the collection of corporation tax were enacted in 1975 and 1976. The payment of the installment due on 15 September 1975 was deferred to 15 April 1976; the payment of one half of the February 1976 installment to December. These lags briefly improved corporate cash flow and may have altered capital-goods delivery schedules by a few months. But these effects were too transient to be covered meaningfully in our study.

* The new depreciation system had a twofold effect on investment by modifying both the implicit cost of capital and corporate self-financing. The changes that occurred during 1973-1980 were either too cyclical (the 1974 measures) or too limited (depreciation allowances for specific kinds of firms and investments) to be included in the measurement of total cost of capital. All of these measures, even the most limited, automatically bear on the explanation of investment fluctuations via the actual-profit factor (self-financing). However, our analysis includes only the 1974 measures, amounting to approximately 5 billion FFr.

* Special investment incentives were implemented on several occasions in the form of tax deductions. Five such measures were successively enacted between 1965 and 1980:

- Law of 18 May 1966;
- Law of 9 October 1968;
- Laws of 29 May and 13 September 1975;
- 1981 budget, with effect from October 1980.

The first three measures were of a very distinctly cyclical nature, as they applied only to equipment purchased or ordered during relatively brief periods:[2]

Orders:
- 30 April-4 September 1969.
- 15 February-31 December 1966.

---

2. For a detailed study of these tax incentives, see Coutière and Nizet [1981].

- 30 April 1975-7 January 1976.

Deliveries:
- 15 February 1966-1 January 1968.
- 1 December 1968-31 March 1970.
- Delivery times: within three years of order.

The 1966 deduction (10% of purchase price) was chargeable only against corporation profit tax or income tax and therefore applied exclusively to profitable companies (the deduction could be used for five consecutive years). The 1968 deduction, on the other hand, was also chargeable against VAT. In this case, the deduction amounted to only 5% of the equipment price compared to the earlier 10%. The tax credit of 1975 (also 10% of purchase price) was chargeable against VAT and, if unchargeable in practice, could take the form of a refund. This measure was therefore analyzed as an investment subsidy through a tax provision.

The tax deduction introduced by the law of 3 July 1979 had a less pronounced cyclical character. Unlike its predecessors, this two-year provision applied not to the actual investment total, but to the nominal increase in investment (10% of the 1979-on-1978 and 1980-on-1979 increases).

The last incentive was introduced for a five-year period and represented 10% of the price of the subsidized investments net of VAT. The only eligible firms were those taxed on their actual profits (rather than at a standard rate). The firm's fiscal-year earnings were reduced by an amount corresponding to the deduction entitlement. This provision was enacted in October 1980 and therefore affected the last quarter of the period studied.

The influence of all these measures is summed up by an index reflecting the reduction in capital-acquisition cost (Graph 3). There are two possible approaches for assessing this cut. We can take into account all the deductions allowed by law, whether or not the firm was aware of the deduction at the time it decided to invest. This method yields a measurement of effective cost. But the index we are trying to construct is intended to reflect the conditions that explain corporate investments. Accordingly, we incorporate the deduction only if the firm utilized it when ordering. In this case, we include it in the order period, not the delivery period.

GRAPH 3 **Tax policy measures**

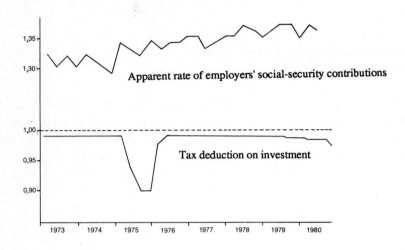

For the first three measures, which concern the investment's total value, the tax cut is not particularly hard to assess.[3] The calculation becomes trickier for the 1979 tax deduction, which applied only to the increase in investment. For this period, we have had to rely on assessment of its yield (0.4% in 1979 and 0.6% in 1980), which probably underestimates its influence.

* From 1973 to 1980, employers' social-security contributions rose uninterruptedly (see Graph 3). From an average of 28.2% in 1973, the apparent rate grew to 32.5% in 1977 and 34.1% in 1980. This led to an increase in labor costs and thus to a faster reorganization of production through productivity investments.

While the direct effect on investment is indeed positive (partly offset by the negative influence of higher contribution rates on profits), the total effect — after adjustment of the various macroeconomic factors — may be negative. The main reason for this is the fall in demand brought about by the higher unemployment resulting from the measure. The rise in unemployment partly undermines the desired goal — a balanced social-security — budget since it increases benefit payments while reducing the number of contributors.

---

3. For a detailed analysis of the assessment principle, see Malinvaud [1971]; Avouyi-Dovi and Muet [1987 a] and appendix p. 279-286.

1.2. Monetary policy: the real interest rate...

The real interest rate is the prime component of user cost of capital. Graph 4 shows its curve from 1973 to 1980, broken down into its two elements: nominal long-term interest-rate changes and inflation-expectation changes (calculated from the differentials in stock-market prices of standard bonds and price-indexed bonds). The graph shows that the nominal interest rate was high in 1974 (reflecting credit restrictions and rising world rates), during the winter of 1977-1978, and from late 1980 on, for the upswing that began in early 1979 lagged behind that of the international capital markets.

GRAPH 4 **Monetary policy : changes in nominal and real interest rates**

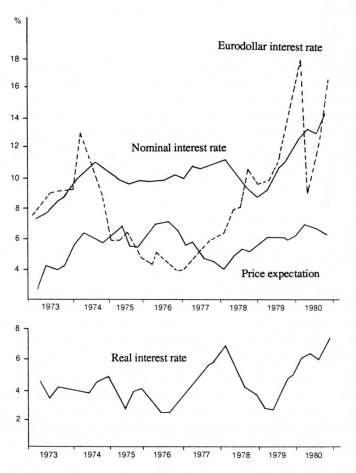

The resulting expected interest rate was high in 1977-1978 (when high nominal interest rates combined with a slowdown in inflation after the first oil crisis) and in 1980, with the final upsurge of nominal rates. In 1974, nominal rates and inflation moved in parallel without noticeably affecting real rates.

... and credit rationing

Credit rationing was used during the "Giscard Plan" from 1963 to 1965, and again from 1969 on. After the August 1969 devaluation, the authorized increase in loans was restricted and consumer credit regulations tightened (in the second half of 1969, loans to the economy remained nearly stable). Rationing was stiffened in February 1970 (from September to March, loans to the economy rose at an annual rate of only 6%) before being relaxed in April and June, with loans by then rising at a rate of 12%.

In October 1970, all credit controls were lifted and the increase in loans accelerated, totaling 7% for the last quarter of 1970. This expansion continued unimpeded until September and — more decisively — December 1972, when the government imposed credit controls requiring banks to set aside extra reserves. These were determined by a steeply graduated schedule based on the increase in loans issued. The increase was initially limited to 17% from June 1972 to July 1973, with a planned cut to 14% from September 1972 to September 1973, and 11% from March 1973 to March 1974. Loans to households were severely curtailed: personal loans were frozen at current levels, while access to mortages was restricted. In March and again in June 1974, credit controls were renewed.

However, from 1975 to 1977, falling demand made it easy for the banks to comply with the prevailing guidelines. The only tensions in the credit market appeared during the economic upturn of early 1976 and in mid-1977. In 1978, and even more so in 1979, the credit-control policy perceptibly hardened. Previously unrestricted sectors such as exports and housing were gradually reintroduced into the control calculations, in a proportion rising from 15% in 1978 to 20% then 30% in 1979, 40% in early 1980 and 50% by May of that year. In April 1979, the government imposed restrictions on consumer credit. After April 1980, supplementary savings-based housing loans came under control. During the second half of 1980, the ceilings for credit expansion were lowered even further, reaching 3.5% annually for the largest banks known as "class-one."

The present analysis required the choice of a synthetic variable to represent the degree of credit control. We chose the "banks" component of the Banque de France's control indicator.[4] The changes in this variable do in fact match the preceding description of monetary policy: active controls in 1973, transitory controls in 1977, and increasing tightness from 1979 on.

1.3. Post-1973 changes in investment by government and major public-service firms

Graph 1, which charts the changes in major investment components, vividly demonstrates the countercyclical role of investment by government and by the major state-owned firms during the recession consecutive to the first oil crisis. While in 1975 real private investment shrank by 11% compared to 1974, government investment rose by 10.4% and that of the big state-owned firms by 23%. Subsequently, even during the years of private-investment recession (1977-1978), government investment fell back or stagnated, with a growth rate on average below that of the earlier period (Table 1).

TABLE 1 Annual growth rate of public and private investment

Annual growth rate	Average 1968-1973	Average 1974-1980	1973	1974	1975	1976	1977	1978	1979	1980
Real private-sector investment (volume)........................	8.3	0.3	4.5	-1.8	- 11.1	6.5	- 0.2	1.3	1.3	5.9
Real government investment (volume)........................	1.8	0.5	2.4	0.3	10.4	- 0.8	- 6.3	- 2.9	1.5	1.4
Real investment by large public-service firms (volume)........................	0.1	10.5	5.9	4.8	23.3	9.4	6.9	12.4	9.0	7.6

---

4. The indicator comprises two elements: a "banks" component, representing the opinion of credit distributors on control stringency, and a "credit users" component. The latter is contingent on factors such as demand and firms' financial position. Because of this undoubtedly lesser resemblance to a pure economic-policy variable, we have chosen the "banks" component instead.

Investment by the major state-owned firms, on the other hand, continued to expand briskly over the entire period (10% a year on average from 1974 to 1980), whereas it had stagnated during 1968-1973. Of course, it would be wrong to regard investment by these firms as purely an instrument of cyclical economic policy. The rise was due to the launching of massive capital-investment programs such as the modernization of the telecommunications network (heavy spending from 1975 to 1978, with subsequent reduction), the building of nuclear power stations, and investments by the SNCF (TGV high-speed train) and Air France. In addition, certain projects such as the nuclear power stations were linked to the first oil crisis. Nevertheless, the economic downturn undoubtedly spurred planners to accelerate the implementation schedule of these programs.

2.   THE IMPACT OF PUBLIC POLICY MEASURES : AN ASSESSMENT BASED ON THE "METRIC" MODEL

The influence of each policy measure was assessed by means of METRIC model simulations. For this purpose, we compared: (a) the economic changes described by the model from 1973 to 1980, incorporating the economic policy measures effectively enacted; (b) the paths obtained by modifying each of these measures in succession.

Table 2 sets out the impact on investment and market gross domestic product of the various policies described earlier.

2.1.   A tax policy dominated by the depressive effect of social-security contributions

The three measures analyzed are tax deductions (in particular those of 1975-1976), the 1974 rise in corporation tax, and the progresssive increase in employers' social-security contributions.

The tax deduction of 1975-1976

By temporarily reducing the cost of capital, this deduction triggered an investment recovery. The resulting increase fed through to the economy as a whole via the distribution of additional income (the classic multiplier effect), which, by stimulating demand, helped to boost investment still further. The sum total of these effects put a slight brake on the 1975 fall in investment and intensified the 1976 rise (+1.1%). When the tax incentive expired, investment

TABLE 2 : **Influence of policy measures on GDP and investment**

	1973	1974	1975	1976	1977	1978	1979	1980
Real market GDP (1970 francs)								
Annual growth rate (%)..................	5.8	3.5	0.0	5.1	3.2	3.9	3.6	1.2
Influence of tax policy....................								
Tax deductions......................................			+ 0.1	+ 0.1	- 0.2	0.0	0.0	0.0
1974 tax increase..................................		- 0.1	- 0.1	- 0.3	0.0	+ 0.1	0.0	0.0
Employers' social-security contributions.........	0.0	0.0	- 0.1	- 0.3	- 0.5	- 0.2	- 0.4	- 0.1
Total..	**0.0**	**- 0.1**	**- 0.1**	**- 0.5**	**- 0.7**	**- 0.1**	**- 0.4**	**- 0.1**
Influence of monetary policy								
Real interest rate.....................................	0.0	- 0.1	+ 0.2	+ 0.1	- 0.1	+ 0.1	0.0	- 0.1
Credit restrictions...................................	- 0.2	- 0.5	- 0.9	+ 0.5	0.0	0.0	+ 0.4	0.0
Total..	**- 0.2**	**- 0.6**	**- 0.7**	**+ 0.6**	**- 0.1**	**+ 0.1**	**+ 0.4**	**- 0.1**
Influence of government and public-service firms' investment								
Government investment............................	+ 0.1	+ 0.1	+ 0.6	0.0	- 0.4	- 0.2	+ 0.1	+ 0.1
Investment by large public-service firms'.........	0.0	+ 0.1	+ 0.2	+ 0.1	+ 0.3	+ 0.4	+ 0.7	+ 0.3
Total..	**+ 0.1**	**+ 0.2**	**+ 0.8**	**+ 0.1**	**- 0.1**	**+ 0.2**	**+ 0.8**	**+ 0.4**
Investment in volume by firms' (1970 francs)								
Annual growth rate (%).....................	5.1	- 1.1	- 6.0	5.8	0.3	3.3	2.7	6.1
Influence of tax policy......................								
Tax deductions......................................			+ 0.5	+ 1.1	- 1.0	- 0.1	- 0.4	- 0.1
1974 tax increase..................................		- 0.5	- 0.1	- 0.3	+ 0.4	0.0	0.0	0.0
Employers' social-security contributions........	0.0	0.0	- 0.3	- 1.3	- 0.3	+ 0.9	- 0.7	+ 0.2
Total..	**0.0**	**- 0.5**	**+ 0.1**	**- 0.5**	**- 0.9**	**+ 0.8**	**- 1.1**	**+ 0.1**
Influence of monetary policy								
Real interest rate.....................................	- 0.2	- 0.6	+ 0.8	+ 2.0	- 1.7	- 0.5	+ 1.3	+ 0.3
Credit restrictions...................................	- 1.4	- 0.8	- 2.6	+ 1.8	+ 0.2	+ 1.5	+ 0.8	- 0.6
Total..	**- 1.6**	**- 1.4**	**- 1.8**	**+ 3.8**	**- 1.5**	**+ 1.0**	**+ 2.1**	**- 0.3**
Influence of government and public-service firms' investment								
Government investment............................	+ 0.3	+ 0.2	+ 1.3	+ 0.2	- 1.7	- 1.2	+ 0.3	+ 0.6
Investment by large public-service firms'......	+ 0.4	+ 0.2	+ 4.5	- 0.8	+ 3.0	+ 2.5	+ 3.0	+ 1.3
Total..	**+ 0.7**	**+ 0.4**	**+ 5.8**	**- 0.6**	**+ 1.3**	**+ 1.3**	**+ 3.3**	**+ 1.9**

gradually returned to its spontaneous level, aggravating the cyclical slowdown in 1977. The impact of these measures was moderate on GDP and negligible on prices and unemployment. All in all, despite the scope of the measure (10% deduction on investment), the macroeconomic consequences were limited and short-lived and, if anything, they accentuated the 1976-1977 cycle.

The tax increase of June 1974

The 1974 rise in corporation tax ate into profits. Firms responded by postponing investments and cutting overall costs through lower inventory build-ups, fewer hirings and slower wage increases. GDP slowed continuously from 1974 to 1976. This effect of profits on investment was itself modulated by demand growth: the stronger the growth, the greater the effect. In 1976, for instance, the year of growth recovery, the depressive effect on investment was greater than in 1975. Lastly, the impact on prices was, here again, negligible.

The increase in employers' social-security contributions

To measure the influence of successive rises in employers' social-security contributions as a percentage of the total wage bill, we conducted a simulation in which the percentage was kept at its 1973 level. We implicitly assume the social-security deficit to have been met from the general-government budget and financed by monetary creation. The effects of these increases are complex. In the long term, the increase in labor costs leads to productivity investments and a reduced workforce, hence to lower wage incomes and consumption. The overall effect on demand is therefore ambiguous. Moreover, the inflationary pressures generated by the feedthrough of costs to product prices increase the external deficit and amplify the consumption downturn. This is due to the rebuilding of monetary holdings. All told, the predominant effect is depressive not only on demand, but even on investment through the accelerator mechanism. The fall in employment — on the order of 3% by the end of the period — is attributable in roughly equal measure to the fall in demand and to the substitution effect. Of all the tax measures studied, the increase in employers' social-security contributions is the one that most affected output and employment.[5]

---

5. For a more detailed study of this measure and of alternative policies, see Artus, Sterdyniak and Villa [1980].

2.2. Monetary policy accentuated fluctuations

The impact of changes in the real interest rate...

The controlled variable is the money-market interest rate, whose changes determine those of short-term, long-term and bond rates, charted in Graph 4. On average, during 1973-1980, the real money-market interest rate was approximately zero. We have therefore chosen as a "neutral" policy the hypothesis of a constantly zero real interest rate. Observed real interest rate fluctuations are reflected in investment changes. The rate increases of 1973-1974 and 1977-1978 considerably reduced investment, while the opposite phenomenon occurred in 1975-1976 and 1979. The effects on GDP were slight for two reasons: (a) the changes were transitory and failed to trigger lasting multiplier effects; (b) the depressive effect was attenuated by interest transfers from government and businesses to households — with the growth in these transfers boosting the economy's propensity to spend.

... and credit restrictions

We have assessed the influence of credit restrictions through a simulation in which the variable representing credit-restriction intensity is set at its minimum value, that is, the value corresponding to maximum credit-distribution freedom. Credit was strictly controlled in 1973-1974 and again from 1979 on. This time profile is reproduced, with lags, in the investment curve. On two occasions, 1974-1975 and 1976, credit controls therefore accentuated the economic cycle, downward during the first period and upward during the 1976 recovery. In 1980, while domestic production slowed, investment soared. Credit restrictions therefore played a countercyclical role if we consider investment alone, pro-cyclical if we look at the entire economy.

The lag between control stringency and its maximum effect on economic activity is very clear during the first oil crisis: credit restrictions were discontinued in mid-1974, but it was in 1975 that their depressive effect was sharpest. In the medium term, according to the model, the control policy enacted made production capacity fall 0.8 points from 1973 to 1977, that is, by nearly 0.2 points a year. The model also suggests an adverse effect on inflation, with the restrictions triggering an additional 0.5-point rise in prices in 1974 and 1975. Specifically, we were able to identify the following behavior and include it in the METRIC model equations: when firms see their external resources rationed, they make only partial cuts in their projected expenditures while raising their sale prices to boost their self-financing capacity. Thus credit controls are initially inflationist even if they eventually succeed in slowing prices through a downturn in activity.

2.3. Government investment: a stabilizing role in 1974-1975

The role of government investment was assessed by comparing the historical change to that simulated by the model, assuming such investment to be constant throughout the period. This hypothesis modifies only the investment profile, without affecting its average change during the period. The strong growth of public-sector investment in 1974-1975 and its subsequent drop produced a change comparable to the GDP curve (+0.6 points in 1975, -0.4 points in 1977). Unlike tax and monetary policies, whose effects require fairly long time spans, public-spending policies have a very prompt impact. Higher state spending boosts output almost immediately, while direct or indirect incentive policies require changes in corporate decisions and therefore a certain response and implementation time.

When production capacity is under-used, higher public investment revives private investment via the acceleration effect despite the interest-rate rise observed in the case of financing through borrowing. The only instances where public spending would crowd out private spending would be: (a) if production capacities came under very heavy strain; (b) if the credit market were strictly rationed. In the first case, the crowding-out would result from the inability of capital-goods production to meet investment demand; in the second case, from an inadequate supply of credit. It is clear that such an effect cannot occur when private demand is tumbling. Quite to the contrary, by stimulating total demand, public investment revives private investment through the accelerator effect. The importance that some economists attribute to the crowding-out effect stems from the fact that conventional analysis tends to isolate certain phenomena generated by investment expenditure. In particular, such analysis omits the multiplier effect and its influence on private investment via the accelerator mechanism.

2.4. Investment by the major state-owned firms: a support for growth

We have measured the effect generated since 1974 by the massive expansion in investment by the major state-owned firms. For this, we compared the historical curve to the change that would have resulted from an annual 4% real growth of such investment. Any definition of a "neutral" policy is bound to be largely arbitrary. We could have chosen, for example, the growth in investment by these firms for 1968-1973 — which on average was slightly negative. We preferred to adopt a reference situation in which the growth of this investment would have been comparable in the long-term rise in private investment and would not have affected the change in total investment for 1968-1980. Our choice of a 4% reference growth has therefore, if anything, underestimated the impact of the nationalized sector.

Table 2 brings out the sizable support for growth provided by nationalized-sector investment. With respect to the reference defined above, the gains in output and employment levels were 2.1 and 1.2 points respectively by the end of 1980, representing the creation of 160,000 jobs and an 80,000-person reduction in unemployment.[6] As with government investment, this recovery is induced by the conventional mechanisms of the multiplier; initial rise in output, employment and incomes in the construction and capital-goods industries, with subsequent effects on consumption, then on private business investment, and so on. The inflationist impact is weak in the early years on account of the productivity gains entailed by the recovery: these cut production costs and offset demand pressures on prices and wages (this is known as the productivity-cycle phenomenon). In the longer term, demand pressure increases prices and wages, adding an average 0.25 points of inflation from 1973 to 1980. This assessment does not take into account a possible effect in the form of product-price increases, needed to maintain an adequate level of self-financing for investment projects. On total investment, the nationalized sector exerted a constantly stabilizing effect — from a very strong support in 1975 and 1977 to a damping effect in 1976. This is indeed an example of a deliberately or accidentally anti-cyclical "policy."

---

6. Job creation generates an extra demand that dampens its impact on recorded unemployment (this is known as the "discouraged-worker phenomenon").

CONCLUSION

The first conclusion we can draw from a study of the years 1973-1980 is that tax and monetary policies affecting investment did not help to stabilize the cyclical movements during the period.

This was mainly due to their slow impact. Although usually enacted at the time when the cycle seemed to call for them, these policies often produced their effects at the wrong moment. For example, the credit restrictions of 1973-1974, imposed as part of an anti-inflation plan, slowed investment from 1973 to 1975 and contributed heavily to the 1975 recession by cutting growth by 0.9 points just at the time when the government was implementing a recovery plan.

The tax deduction enacted as part of that recovery package yielded its maximum effect in 1976, when the upturn in growth and investment was already a certainty. Its abolition in January 1976 (decided on in 1975, when the measure came into effect) slowed investment growth (-1 point) and output growth (-0.2 points) at a time when a new cyclical slowdown was in the offing.

Response times do not alone explain the ineffectiveness of investment incentives. Investment basically depends on the expected growth in demand. If the incentives do not alter these expectations, their effect can well be purely transitory. Boosting supply without boosting demand only serves to accelerate investment temporarily. This is particularly true of tax deductions on investment, frequently used as instruments of cyclical policy. Such deductions can be effective in modifying production methods in the medium term, provided they are lasting and selective, such as the allowances aimed to promote energy-saving or job-creating investments. On the other hand, they are not very effective as cyclical measures compared with direct demand stimulation.

Because of its prompt effect, the increase in public investment is a suitable tools for cyclical stabilization. Furthermore, in a depression, demand stimulation is probably the surest way to revive private investment owing to the size of the accelerator effect. In this respect, the very rapid growth in investment by major state-owned firms since the onset of the crisis helped to sustain not only economic activity but also — through its induced effects — private investment.

Cyclical policies could probably be made more effective by a better knowledge of the cyclical situation, its foreseeable change, and the impact times of the measures taken. More simply, such an improvement could also be obtained by a more durable and consistent implementation of these policies, with an allowance for the effects of measures enacted earlier. Indeed, the close succession of recovery plans and restrictive plans goes some way to explaining the ineffectiveness of the policies appplied during the first oil crisis.

CHAPTER 5
A joint estimation of demand for investment and labor*
by
Pierre-Alain Muet , Pierre Villa and Michel Boutillier

Introduction

Until the late 1960s, the demand for labor had never been studied jointly with the investment function.[1] Yet the theoretical framework generally used to define the latter combines in a symmetrical manner a demand for capital and a demand for labor that depend on the same parameters. This separation is also found in econometric models, which provide distinct specifications and — usually — estimates for the two functions: the investment resulting from an intertemporal optimization, and the employment resulting from the short-term maximization of corporate profits.

This simplification accurately reflects the differences between the forecasting horizons on which investment and employment decisions are based. However, it has the disadvantage of adopting only one of the two functions — in practice, the investment function — to test certain hypotheses concerning the production function. The simultaneous estimate of demand for investment and labor should therefore allow a better assessment of the validity of a priori hypotheses on the production function than can be obtained from the investment function alone.

However, if the direct estimate of the production function requires only hypotheses relating to that function, the estimate of demand factors introduces four types of hypotheses, respectively concerning:
- the specification of the production function;
- the functioning of markets and the information perceived by firms;
- corporate behavior (generally reduced to profit maximization);
- adjustment lags.

The interpretation of the estimates in terms of production-function

---

* Originally published as "Une estimation conjointe des demandes d'investissement et de travail," *Annales de l'INSEE* 38-39:237-258, 1980.

1. The earliest work on the subject was notably done by Coen and Hickman [1970] and Nadiri and Rosen [1969; 1974].

parameters is therefore contingent on the last three hypotheses.

The present chapter reports the joint estimation of investment-demand and labor-demand functions based on annual and quarterly French national accounts series.The opening section summarizes the theoretical foundations and the specification of the estimated equations.

1. SPECIFICATION OF THE INVESTMENT DEMAND AND LABOR DEMAND

This section recapitulates the discussion of investment demand in Chapter 2 above. We assume that firms determine their demand for investment and labor by maximizing their discounted profit subject to the production-function constraint. We can thus define two major demand functions: *notional demand* , which corresponds to the conventional hypotheses of neoclassical general equilibrium; and *effective demand* , which assumes that firms adjust to a given expected change in demand for their output — this corresponds to the standard Keynesian hypothesis in macroeconomic analysis.

With perfect competition and in the absence of rationing in the different markets, the demands for investment (or capital) and labor that maximize the firm's profits depend solely on expected real costs:

$$
(1) \quad
\begin{cases}
K^d = K^d \left(\dfrac{c^*}{p}, \dfrac{w^*}{p} \right) \\[2em]
N^d = N^d \left(\dfrac{c^*}{p}, \dfrac{w^*}{p} \right)
\end{cases}
$$

c is the user cost of capital, w the wage rate, p the price of value added, N employment, K capital (I will denote investment). The asterisk denotes expected values and the index d the demands (or desired values). The elasticities of factor demands with respect to costs are generally all negative; they become very high when returns to scale tend toward unity. As an example, with the Cobb-Douglas function, we get log-linear functions that yield linear relationships between growth rates through logarithmic differentiation :

$$
(2)\begin{cases}
(\overset{o}{K})^d = \left(\dfrac{I}{K}\right)^d - \delta = -\dfrac{\beta}{1-(\alpha+\beta)}(\overset{o}{w/p})* - \dfrac{1-\beta}{1-(\alpha+\beta)}(\overset{o}{c/p})* + \dfrac{\gamma}{1-(\alpha+\beta)} \\[4mm]
(\overset{o}{N})^d = -\dfrac{1-\alpha}{1-(\alpha+\beta)}(\overset{o}{w/p})* - \dfrac{\alpha}{1-(\alpha+\beta)}(\overset{o}{c/p})* + \dfrac{\gamma}{1-(\alpha+\beta)}
\end{cases}
$$

Clearly, this notional-demand model is highly unrealistic, since firms' investment and employment decisions are generally based on expected changes in demand for their output. Moreover, notional demands are defined only on the restrictive assumption of diminishing returns to scale.

When we assume that firms adjust capital and labor to the expected change in demand Q*, the postulated optimization behavior simply becomes a minimization of total production costs along the isoquant corresponding to output Q*. This yields *effective demands* for investment and labor, determined here by expected demand Q* and — depending on the degree of elasticity of substitution — on the relative capital-labor cost (c/w)*. With a Cobb-Douglas function, for example, we get :

$$
(3)\begin{cases}
K^d = A^{-\frac{1}{\alpha+\beta}}(Q^*)^{\frac{1}{\alpha+\beta}}(c/w)*^{-\frac{\beta}{\alpha+\beta}} e^{-\frac{\gamma}{\alpha+\beta}t} \\[4mm]
N^d = A^{-\frac{1}{\alpha+\beta}}(Q^*)^{\frac{1}{\alpha+\beta}}(c/w)*^{+\frac{\alpha}{\alpha+\beta}} e^{-\frac{\gamma}{\alpha+\beta}t}
\end{cases}
$$

which again leads to a linear relationship between growth rates. When the production function is not of the Cobb-Douglas type, the form of the demand functions becomes more complicated; in particular, it ceases to be log-linear. By differentiating these functions, *we can nevertheless find a general relationship between the growth rates of factor demands and those of output (Q*) and relative cost (c/w)*.*

For if we assume the production function to be homogeneous and of degree v, we obtain the demand functions through differentiation:

$$(4) \quad \begin{cases} \dfrac{dK^d}{K^d} = \dfrac{1}{v}\dfrac{dQ^*}{Q^*} - \beta\,\sigma\,\dfrac{d(c/w)^*}{(c/w)^*} + d_1 \\[3ex] \dfrac{dN^d}{N^d} = \dfrac{1}{v}\dfrac{d\,Q^*}{Q^*} + (1-\beta)\,\sigma\,\dfrac{d\,(c/w)^*}{(c/w)^*} + d_2 \end{cases}$$

v   stands for production-function returns to scale, σ for elasticity of substitution and β for the ratio $w^*N/(w^*N + c^*K)$. This coefficient is constant in the long term if technical progress is Harrod-neutral and if the real wage rate grows at the same pace as technical progress — as was generally the case in the French economy during the estimation period. By contrast, the coefficient varies in the short term with relative cost, but we will show that such changes are negliglible compared to fluctuations in the growth rate of relative cost.

The reader will note that equations (4) are analogous to Slutsky's consumption-function equations. The influence of production — or the isoquant shift — is comparable to the "income effect" and the second term represents the substitution effect. This general formulation allows us to give a simple specification for effective-demand models. These then take the form of linear relationships between the variables' growth rates:

$$(5) \quad \begin{cases} \left(\dfrac{I}{K}\right)^d = \dfrac{1}{v}\overset{o}{Q}{}^* - \beta\,\sigma\,(\overset{o}{c/w})^* + (d_1 + \delta) \\[3ex] (\overset{o}{N})^d = \dfrac{1}{v}\overset{o}{Q}{}^* + (1-\beta)\,\sigma\,(\overset{o}{c/w})^* - d_2 \end{cases}$$

To obtain the model linking actual investment and employment to the observed variables, we must allow for implementation times and the formation of expectations. Investment and employment decisions rest on the anticipated change in explanatory variables. In the absence of direct information on these expectations, it is generally assumed that they are based on changes observed in the past. They are accordingly represented by distributed-lag functions of the explanatory variables. The form and length of the distributed-lag function mainly depend on the forecasting horizon (Muet [1979 b]). Furthermore, in an economy enjoying steady-state long-term growth, expectations ought to rise at the constant growth rate of the economy. This aspect is implicitly taken into account when the model is specified in terms of growth rate. Expected growth is then expressed by a distributed-lag function of the observed growth rate .

The lags for adjustment of actual values to desired values constitute the second factor in the introduction of distributed lags. Conventional formalization (as in Muet [1979b]) leads to geometric lag distributions or, when several factors are involved, to cross geometrical distributions (as in Pouchain [1980]). However, the non-diagonal terms are hard to display econometrically. For the sake of simplicity, we will therefore preserve separate lag distributions for capital and labor.

By combining expectation lags and adjustment lags, we can consequently give a general specification of the effective-demand model in the form:

(6)
$$
\begin{cases}
\dfrac{I}{K} = \dfrac{1}{v}\, \Phi_1\,(L)\,\overset{o}{Q} - \beta\, \sigma\, \Phi_2\,(L)\,(\overset{o}{c/w}) + d_1 \\[2em]
\overset{o}{N} = \dfrac{1}{v}\, \Phi_3\,(L)\,\overset{o}{Q} + (1 - \beta)\, \sigma\, \Phi_4\,(L)\,(\overset{o}{c/w}) + d_2
\end{cases}
$$

where Φ_1, Φ_2, Φ_3 and Φ_4 are standardized lag functions. In practice, we will choose first-order lag distributions for these various functions on annual data and polynomial distributions for estimates on quarterly series.

2. ESTIMATES ON ANNUAL SERIES

The data used for the estimate concern the full range of non-financial enterprises.[2] In addition, only equipment capital has been included. Plant and office structures are not affected by a possible capital-labor substitution. We begin by examining first the independent estimate of the two functions, then their simultaneous estimate. Beforehand, we will mention the estimate of notional demands, but only briefly, since its unrealistic character is amply demonstrated by the adjustments given here.

2.1. Notional demands

The estimates for investment (as in Chapter 2 above) have shown that the only price variable that undisputably influenced investment was the user cost

---

2. All the series except employment are given in Appendix 1 to Chapter 2 above.

of capital. This finding is confirmed by the estimate of labor demand. The estimates below show that wage-rate elasticities do not differ significantly from zero, while those of the user cost of capital are negative on investment and positive on employment (the specification uses first-order lag distributions with the same parameter λ) :

Investment

(7)
$$\left(\frac{I}{K}\right)_{(t)} = 0.89 \left(\frac{I}{K}\right)_{-1} - 0.015 \, (\overset{o}{c}/p) - 0.033 \, (\overset{o}{c}/p)_{-1}$$
$$\phantom{\left(\frac{I}{K}\right)_{(t)} = } {}_{(4.7)} \phantom{\left(\frac{I}{K}\right)_{-1}} {}_{(1.3)} \phantom{- 0.015 \, (\overset{o}{c}/p)} {}_{(2.7)}$$

$$+ 0.09 \, (\overset{o}{w}/p) - 0.04 \, (\overset{o}{w}/p)_{-1} + 0.011$$
$$ {}_{(1.4)} \phantom{\, (\overset{o}{w}/p)} {}_{(0.5)} {}_{(0.5)}$$

$$R^2 = 0.79 \qquad DW = 1.92 \qquad OLS \qquad (1957\text{-}1974)$$

Employment

(8)
$$\overset{o}{N} = -0.14 \, \overset{o}{N}_{-1} + 0.058 \, (\overset{o}{c}/p) - 0.05 \, (\overset{o}{c}/p)_{-1}$$
$$\phantom{\overset{o}{N} = } {}_{(t)} {}_{(0.5)} \phantom{\, \overset{o}{N}_{-1}} {}_{(2.6)} \phantom{+ 0.058 \, (\overset{o}{c}/p)} {}_{(0.2)}$$

$$+ 0.05 \, (\overset{o}{w}/p) + 0.25 \, (\overset{o}{w}/p)_{-1} + 0.002$$
$$ {}_{(0.3)} \phantom{\, (\overset{o}{w}/p)} {}_{(1.2)} {}_{(0.3)}$$

$$R^2 = 0.51 \qquad DW = 2.5 \qquad OLS \qquad (1957\text{-}1974).$$

This user-cost influence with opposite signs is clearly incompatible with the notional-demand model specification, since the model assumes all the elasticities to be negative. On the other hand, this result tallies with the specification of the effective-demand model, in which the user cost comes into play only through substitution and therefore has a positive effect on employment and a negative effect on investment. However, the fact that the cost of labor has no significant impact on either employment or investment suggests that the influence of the user cost of capital does not reflect this substitution effect alone.

2.2. Effective demands: independent estimates

In the first part of this chapter, we have shown that a general formulation of the effective-demand model could be expressed in terms of the production function's returns to scale v, the share of wages in output β, and the elasticity of substitution σ. While coefficient β is generally stable in the long term, it varies in the short term with changes in the relative capital-labor cost

$$\left(\beta = \frac{wN}{cK + wN} \right)$$

It is strictly constant only when the production function is of the Cobb-Douglas type. We must therefore begin by making sure that our approximation is acceptable, that is, that changes in β are negligible compared to changes in the growth rate of the relative capital-labor cost. If we calculate the coefficient of the correlation between $\beta_o(c/\overset{o}{w})$ and $(c/\overset{o}{w})$, we get $R^2 = 0.994$, which shows that the variance of β (c/w) is almost entirely due to that of $c/\overset{o}{w}$. In other words, β can be regarded as constant with respect to $c/\overset{o}{w}$. Finally, before carrying out the estimate, we must specify the distributed-lag form.

On the basis of our results for investment (Chapter 2 above), we have chosen first-order distributions for the different functions, with each model estimated using non-linear least squares (NLLS) applied to the autoregressive forms. With conventional notation for distributed lags, the functions can be expressed as follows:

$$(9) \quad \begin{cases} \dfrac{I}{K} = \dfrac{a_0 + a_1 L}{1 - \lambda_1 L} \overset{o}{Q} + \dfrac{b_0 + b_1 L}{1 - \lambda_2 L} (c/\overset{o}{w}) + d \\[4mm] \overset{o}{N} = \dfrac{a'_0 + a'_1 L}{1 - \lambda'_1 L} \overset{o}{Q} + \dfrac{b'_0 + b'_1 L}{1 - \lambda'_2 L} (c/\overset{o}{w}) + d \end{cases}$$

Table 1 presents the result of these independent estimates, which are largely convergent as regards the values assignable to production-function parameters. The long-term coefficients (LTC) of the output growth rate are identical (0.62) and reflect fairly strongly increasing returns to scale. The coefficient of the relative capital-labor cost is positive for employment and negative for investment — an accurate reflection of the substitution effect described by the effective-demand model. Moreover, in both estimates, the long-term coefficient of relative cost is weak and corresponds to a low value for the elasticity of substitution. This value is theoretically equal to the sum of the absolute values of the the two coefficients, that is, 0.075. It will be noted that all the long-term coefficients differ significantly from zero.

TABLE 1 : **Independent estimates of effective demands**

	Investment (I/K)			Employment (N)		
	Estimated coefficients	Standard deviations	t statistics	Estimated coefficients	Standard deviations	t statistics
Demand (Q) :						
a_0	0.143	(0.049)	2.9	0.306	(0.150)	2.0
a_1	0.163	(0.046)	3.5	0.320	(0.170)	1.9
λ_1	0.503	(0.080)	6.3	- 0.006	(0.329)	0.0
LTC...........	0.620	(0.135)	4.6	0.620	(0.178)	3.5
ML............	1.550	(0.330)	4.6	0.505	(0.297)	1.7
Relative cost (c/w) :						
b_0	- 0.008	(0.005)	1.5	0.049	(0.019)	2.6
b_1	- 0.019	(0.007)	1.5	0.016	(0.029)	0.6
λ_2	- 0.215	(0.220)	1.0	- 0.428	(0.380)	1.1
LTC...........	- 0.022	(0.011)	2.0	0.053	(0.023)	2.3
ML............	0.510	(0.150)	3.5	- 0.086	(0.206)	0.4
d	0.054	(0.014)	3.9	0.026	(0.014)	1.9
Adjustment characteristics NLLS 1957-1974	$R^2 = 0.88$ DW = 2.22 $S = 0.197 . 10^{-2}$			$R^2 = 0.7$ DW = 1.91 $S = 0.50 . 10^{-2}$		

Lastly, the comparison of the distributed lags reveals a remarkable ranking of adjustments: adjustment lags for capital are longer than those for labor, and the response times to production variables are longer than the response times to changes in relative costs, as summed up by the mean-lag

(ML) value. The estimate also shows that one can specify the distributed lags by adopting a first-order distribution for the acceleration effect of investment (a_1 , a_2 , and λ_1 differ significantly from zero) and a finite distribution for the other distributed lags by deleting the parameters that do not differ significantly from zero ($\lambda_1' = \lambda_2' = \lambda_2 = b_1' = 0$).

The following section presents the simultaneous estimate of the model thus defined.

2.3. Effective demands: simultaneous estimates

If we spell out the theoretical values of the long-term coefficients and take into account the observations above, we can write the model as:

$$
(10) \quad
\begin{cases}
\dfrac{I}{K} = \dfrac{1}{v} \ \dfrac{a + (1 - a)\, L}{1 - \lambda_1\, L}\ \overset{o}{Q} - \beta\, \sigma\, [b + (1 - b)\, L]\, \overset{o}{(c/w)} + d \\[4mm]
\overset{o}{N} = \dfrac{1}{v}\, [a' + (1 - a')\, L]\, \overset{o}{Q} + (1 - \beta)\, \sigma\, \overset{o}{(c/w)} + d'
\end{cases}
$$

The results of the estimate based on the maximum-likelihood method are listed in Table 2. These figures are admittedly not very different from the estimates calculated independently, but the coefficients are estimated with greater accuracy, as shown by the Student t values. Returns to scale exhibit a rather strong increase, and we can consider that they differ significantly from unity with a less than 5% probability of error.

The elasticity of substitution is estimated accurately and the result obtained closely matches the estimates for investment (Chapters 2 and 3 above). *Assuming a putty-putty production function corresponding to our specification, the response of investment and employment to the relative capital-labor cost is compatible with a low elasticity of substitution, which we can estimate at between 0.05 and 0.11 with a 5% probability of error.*

To conclude, we shall examine how our results respond to changes in pre-set specifications. As regards error autocorrelation, it ought not to affect our results significantly, since the employment function is not estimated in autoregressive form. As for the investment function, the studies conducted on the same data have shown that this autocorrelation does not affect the estimate (Chapter 2 above).

TABLE 2 : **Simultaneous estimate of effective-demand function parameters**

	Production-function parameters			Distributed-lag parameters			
	v	β	σ	a	λ	a'	b
Estimated coefficients......	1.721	0.397	0.083	0.520	0.507	0.514	0.343
Standard deviations........	0.307	0.095	0.014	0.091	0.067	0.120	0.078
t statistics	5.6	3.6	5.6	5.7	7.5	4.2	4.4

If we constrain coefficient β to the value 0.6, the elasticity of substitution decreases slightly (0.06 with a standard deviation of 0.01), while the other coefficients are virtually unaffected. Lastly, even the elimination of the 1963 point by means of a "dummy" variable introduced for the employment function (the variance observed being due to the inflow of the French-settler population from Algeria following that country's independence) does not affect the results obtained earlier.

Graphs 1 and 2 present the influence of the growth rates for gross domestic product and for the relative capital-labor cost on investment and employment. The simulation shows that if the influence on investment of user-cost changes is weaker than that of growth, it is of roughly equal magnitude on employment. The simulations given here correspond to the model estimated without the year 1963 for the employment function.

GRAPH 1: **Influence of demand and the relative capital-labor cost on effective demand for employment**
(annual data)

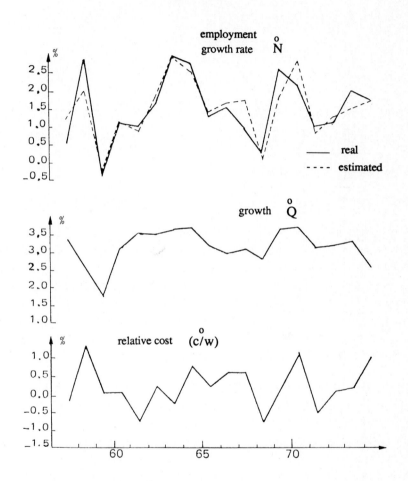

GRAPH 2: **Influence of demand and the relative capital-labor cost on effective demand for investment**
(annual data)

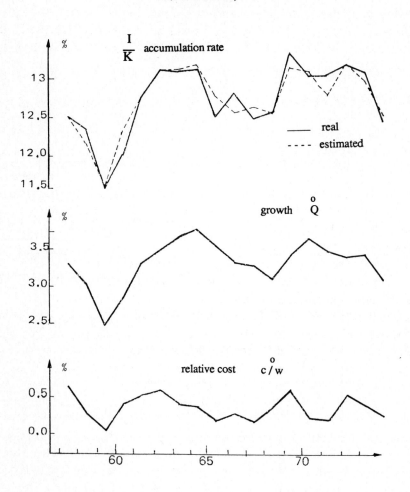

3. ESTIMATES ON QUARTERLY DATA

This section gives the independent and simultaneous estimates on quarterly series using the base-1962 quarterly accounts and the 1946-1959 accounts (Bournay and Laroque [1979]). As the results obtained are significantly affected by the measurement of the user cost of capital, we shall begin by examining the latter.

3.1. Measuring the user cost of capital

Under certain assumptions (identical tax and economic amortization rate, absence of financial constraints), the user cost of capital can be written, using the earlier notations:

$$c = (1 - \theta) \cdot q \cdot (r - \overset{o}{p}{}^* + \delta). \text{ FISC}$$

θ is the rate of corporation tax ($\theta = 0.5$) and δ the tax and economic amortization rate. FISC measures the impact of taxation changes, p^* expected inflation, q the investment price and r the nominal interest rate.

The series compiled by Malinvaud [1971] and used in the annual estimate overlooks economic amortization; it measures expected inflation by the difference between the yield on unindexed bonds and the yield on the Caisse Nationale de l'Energie [state energy-investment fund] indexed bonds. This expression overestimates the effect of the real interest rate and underestimates that of taxation. The breakdown of the growth rate of the user cost of capital thus defined (written c_1) shows that its variability is largely due to the term $(r-p^*)$. To test the stability of the econometric results, we have calculated two other user-cost series (c_2 and c_3) using bond yields as nominal interest rates and two other measures for expected long-term inflation.[3] The discrepancies mainly concern the changes in user cost from 1955 to 1962. The inflation expectations are much higher at the start of the period than in the Malinvaud series. As a result, the user cost rises in 1959 and 1960, and subsequently falls, rather than falling steadily. This difference in the user-cost curve, as we shall see, has a sizable effect on the econometric results.

---

3. These other two measures also use the gap between the Caisse Nationale de l'Energie indexed-bond yield and the non-indexed bond yield. The expected inflation thus obtained is applied directly to the calculation of c_3, whereas it is smoothed in c_2 (see de Ménil , and Porcher [1977]).

3.2. Independent estimates

For the quarterly data, we have chosen finite lag distributions, which we have estimated using the Almon method. The model becomes:

$$
(12) \quad \left\{
\begin{array}{l}
\dfrac{I}{K} = \displaystyle\sum_{i=0}^{n} a_i \overset{o}{Q}_i + \sum_{j-1}^{m} b_j \overset{o}{(c/w)}_{-j} + d \\[3em]
\overset{o}{N} = \displaystyle\sum_{i=0}^{n'} a'_i \overset{o}{Q}_i + \sum_{j=1}^{m'} b'_j \overset{o}{(c/w)}_{-j} + d'
\end{array}
\right.
$$

The estimates cover (a) the entire economy excluding agriculture; (b) manufacturing industries. Table 3 lists the results for the period 1958.I - 1974.IV — for which we have the three measures of user cost — and for the period 1958.I-1977.IV for c_2 and c_3 .

The estimates of investment demands are very stable when we change the definition of the user cost of capital. Returns to scale approximate 1.7 for the whole economy and 1.25 for manufacturing. Nevertheless, they are certainly overestimated, for if the true model is — as we believe — an infinite distribution, the fact of estimating only a finite distribution underestimates the long-term coefficient.

The autocorrelation of errors shown up by the Durbin and Watson coefficient may reflect in particular this incomplete lag specification. The long-term coefficient of relative cost is negative and differs significantly from zero, but it is three times smaller on average than the coefficient estimated on annual data. We find virtually the same mean lags as in the annual estimate: between six and eight quarters for the acceleration effect and approximately two to three quarters for relative cost. The latter coefficient, however, is never estimated accurately — as evidenced by the very large value of its standard deviation. This imprecision is partly due to the choice of formulation, which assumes identical expectations for user cost and wages. Now the user cost already embodies expectations about the cost of capital. It should therefore affect corporate decisions more promptly, as suggested by the immediate impact of tax deductions on investment in 1969 and 1976 in France.[4]

---

4. An estimate that distinguishes between the real cost of capital (c_2) and the wage rate yields a long-term coefficient of -0.004 (0.002) and a mean lag of 0.4 (0.3) for the former and +0.07 (0.02) and 2.8 (2.0) for wage costs.

The long-term elasticity of employment demand with respect to production is also smaller than unity and leads to very high returns to scale (on the order of two). These are presumably overestimated for the reasons already set out regarding investment.

Also, the mean lag — approximately two to three quarters — is comparable to the mean lag in the annual estimate. The effect of the relative capital-labor cost is, on the other hand, highly responsive to the definition of the user cost of capital. The coefficient is positive only for the first quarter. It differs significantly from zero only for the quarterly series corresponding to the Malinvaud series used in the annual estimate (c_1 series).

The nature of the results is not noticeably modified by introducing recent years in the estimation period. In particular, the influence of user cost on employment is not significant except for the estimate covering the whole economy (with the definition c_2). At all events, the coefficient remains very small (0.004). Moreover, the long-term coefficients of demand decrease in all the equations. This change reflects not greater returns to scale, but longer investment decision and implementation times — consecutive to the fall in capacity-utilization rates and the increase in the proportion of replacement investment. For employment, this coefficient decrease reflects the lengthening of the productivity cycle already observed on annual and sectorial data in other studies.

On the whole, the findings match those of the estimates calculated on annual data, except for the influence of the relative capital-labor cost on employment. The significant and sizable effect (if we refer to the simulation presented in Graph 1) shown up by annual data is mainly due to the special measure chosen for expected inflation.

3.3. Simultaneous estimate

The estimation method used here is the maximization of likelihood. The lag pattern is pre-set and derived from unconstrained estimates:

$$(13) \begin{cases} \dfrac{I}{K} = \dfrac{1}{v} \sum_{i=0}^{n} a_i \overset{o}{Q}_{-i} - \beta \sigma \sum_{j=0}^{m} b_j \overset{o}{(c/w)}_{-j} + d_1 \qquad \sum_{i=0}^{n} a_i = \sum_{i=0}^{m} b_j = 1 \\[4ex] \overset{o}{N} = \dfrac{1}{v} \sum_{i=0}^{n'} a'_i \overset{o}{Q}_{-i} + (1 - \beta) \sigma \sum_{j=0}^{m'} b'_j \overset{o}{(c/w)}_{-j} + d_2 \qquad \sum_{i=0}^{n'} a'_i = \sum_{i=0}^{m'} b'_j = 1 \end{cases}$$

TABLE 3: **Independent estimates on quarterly series**

Coefficients	Period : 1958-I		
	Entire economy		
	C_1	C_2	C_3
Investment function			
Long-term coefficient of $\overset{\circ}{Q}$...............	0.64	0.55	0.56
Standard deviation........................	(0.08)	(0.08)	(0.08)
Mean lag (quarter)........................	6.6	6.3	6.3
Standard deviation........................	(0.8)	(0.9)	(0.9)
POLYNOMIAL FORM	3rd degree, unconstrained		
	15 lags		
Long-term coefficient of (c/w)...........	- 0.024	- 0.015	- 0.013
Standard deviation........................	(0.009)	(0.004)	(0.004)
Mean lag (quarter)........................	3.1	3.1	3.1
Standard deviation........................	(16)	(17)	(22)
POLYNOMIAL FORM		2nd degree,	
	7 lags	7 lags	7 lags
R^2	0.56	0.61	0.60
DW	0.80	0.81	0.80
Employment function			
Long-term coefficient of $\overset{\circ}{Q}$...............	0.46	0.49	0.50
Standard deviation........................	(0.06)	(0.06)	(0.06)
Mean lag (quarter)........................	2.6	2.6	2.6
Standard deviation........................	(0.2)	(0.2)	(0.2)
POLYNOMIAL FORM...............		2nd degree,	
(c/w)..	0.015	- 0.001	- 0.001
Standard deviation........................	(0.005)	(0.002)	(0.002)
$(c/w)_1$..	- 0.004	- 0.002	- 0.002
Standard deviation........................	(0.005)	(0.002)	(0.002)
R^2	0.62	0.58	0.58
DW	1.10	0.97	0.96

to 1974-IV			Period 1958-I to 1977-IV			
Manufacturing only			Entire economy		Manufacturing only	
C_1	C_2	C_3	C_2	C_3	C_2	C_3
0.81	0.80	0.80	0.33	0.30	0.65	0.64
(0.08)	(0.09)	(0.08)	(0.04)	(0.05)	(0.05)	(0.05)
7.9	7.8	7.7	5.7	5.7	7.6	7.6
(0.9)	(1.0)	(1.0)	(0.9)	(1.1)	(0.8)	(0.9)
3rd degree, unconstrained			3 rd degree, unconstrained		3 rd degree, unconstrained	
19 lags			15 lags		19 lags	
- 0.020	- 0.006	- 0.007	- 0.016	- 0.011	- 0.003	- 0.002
(0.009)	(0.003)	(0.003)	(0.004)	(0.003)	(0.003)	(0.003)
2.4	1.3	1.2	3.3	3.4	1.1	0.7
(22)	(95)	(65)	(14)	(28)	(285)	(593)
last lag constrained to 0			2nd degree, last lag constrained to 0			
7 lags	5 lags	4 lags	5 lags	4 lags	5 lags	4 lags
0.68	0.67	0.68	0.62	0.58	0.82	0.82
0.53	0.50	0.50	(0.19)	(0.16)	(0.51)	(0.50)
0.51	0.51	0.51	0.38	0.38	0.42	0.41
(0.07)	(0.07)	(0.06)	(0.07)	(0.04)	(0.04)	(0.04)
2.7	2.8	2.8	2.3	2.3	2.5	2.5
(0.2)	(0.2)	(0.2)	(0.1)	(0.1)	(0.1)	(0.1)
last lag constrained to 0			2nd degree, last lag constrained to 0,			
6 lags			6 lags			
0.017	-0.003	0.003	0.004		- 0.002	- 0.002
(0.010)	(0.004)	(0.004)	(0.002)	( )	(0.004)	(0.003)
-0.008	-0.004	-0.006	- 0.002	- 0.002	- 0.004	- 0.005
(0.010)	(0.004)	(0.004)	(0.002)	(0.002)	(0.004)	(0.003)
0.53	0.52	0.53	0.62	0.63	0.53	0.60
0.76	0.73	0.75	1.03	1.02	0.95	0.84

The results in Table 4 confirm the assessments obtained for unconstrained adjustments. While the elasticity of substitution generally differs significantly from zero, the substitution effect is not properly measured except with the c_1 definition of user cost or, for the entire economy, with the c_2 definition.

In the other cases, β is greater than one, producing a negative effect of (c/w) on employment that counteracts the substitution effect. Furthermore, even with c_2 (whole economy), the estimate is already largely meaningless since β does not differ significantly from one. The value for the elasticity of substitution is much smaller than the one yielded by the annual-data estimate. The simulations reported in Graphs 3 and 4 show that the influence of user cost is distinctly weaker than the influence of demand.

The estimate for 1958.I-1977.IV corroborates the previous findings. As in the unconstrained estimates, we observe longer lags and higher returns to scale, which can be interpreted in the same manner.

Conclusion

The joint estimates of factor demands on annual and quarterly data bear out the results obtained for investment:
- returns to scale increase;
- the influence of user cost corresponds to a low elasticity of substitution when the model is putty-putty;
- adjustment lags are shorter for relative factor costs than for demand.
Although they comply with this ranking, the adjustments for employment are consistently shorter than for investment.

The quarterly-data estimates furnish a sizably smaller assessment of the elasticity of substitution than the annual-data estimates. This finding can be easily interpreted if we consider the "true" model to be of the putty-clay type. In this case, the putty-putty specification measures the apparent elasticity that comes into play in the *ex ante* choice of production technique. For a same lifetime and a same long-term elasticity of substitution, this apparent elasticity (equal to the product of the elasticity of substitution by the investment-to-capital ratio) is four times smaller at the quarterly level than at the annual level. Now, with our putty-putty specification, the quarterly data yield an elasticity of substitution equivalent to between a third and a quarter of the elasticity estimated from annual data.

TABLE 4 Simultaneous estimates on quarterly series

$$\left.\begin{aligned}
\frac{I}{K} &= \frac{1}{v}\sum_{i=0}^{n} a_i \overset{\circ}{Q}_{-i} - \beta\sigma\sum_{j=0}^{m} b_j (\overset{\circ}{c/w})_{-j} + d_1 \qquad \sum_{i=0}^{n} a_i = \sum_{j=0}^{m} b_j = 1 \\[2mm]
\overset{\circ}{N} &= \frac{1}{v}\sum_{i=0}^{n'} a'_i \overset{\circ}{Q}_{-i} + (1-\beta)\sigma\sum_{j=0}^{m'} b'_j (\overset{\circ}{c/w})_{-j} + d_2 \qquad \sum_{i=0}^{n'} a'_i = \sum_{j=0}^{m'} b'_j = 1
\end{aligned}\right\} \quad (13)$$

| Coefficients | Period 1958-I to 1974-IV | | | | | | Period 1958-I to 1977-IV | |
| | Entire economy | | | Manufacturing | | | Entire economy | Manufacturing |
	C_1	C_2	C_3	C_1	C_2	C_3	C_2	C_3
v	2.07	2.00	1.97	1.73	1.73	1.68	2.70	1.88
Standard deviation	(0.18)	(0.16)	(0.16)	(0.13)	(0.13)	(0.13)	(0.19)	(0.10)
β	0.57	0.97	1.17	0.64	1.88	4.7	0.95	12.3
Standard deviation	(0.14)	(0.14)	(0.23)	(0.21)	(2.4)	(14)	(0.10)	(123)
σ	0.031	0.015	0.011	0.032	0.028	0.001	0.014	0.016
Standard deviation	(0.009)	(0.004)	(0.004)	(0.012)	(0.004)	(0.004)	(0.004)	(0.4)
n'	15	15	15	19	19	19	15	19
n	6	6	6	6	6	6	6	6
m'	6	6	6	6	4	4	6	4
m	0	0	0	0	0	0	0	0
Investment equation DW	0.80	0.79	0.78	0.67	0.63	0.62	0.19	0.67
Employment equation DW	1.0	0.92	0.68	0.67	0.71	0.68	0.79	0.65
d	0.015	0.015	0.015	0.013	0.014	0.014	0.017	0.015
	(0.000 7)	(0.000 6)	(0.000 6)	(0.000 8)	(0.000 8)	(0.000 8)	(0.000 3)	(0.000 5)
d	-0.003	-0.004	-0.000 4	-0.008	-0.000 8	-0.009	-0.000 3	-0.007
	(0.000 6)	(0.000 6)	(0.000 6)	(0.000 9)	(0.000 9)	(0.000 9)	(0.000 5)	(0.000 6)

GRAPH 3　**Influence of demand and relative cost on investment**

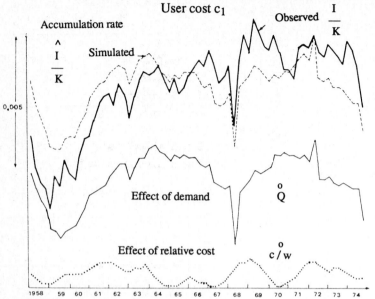

User cost c_1

Accumulation rate

$\overset{\wedge}{\dfrac{I}{K}}$

Simulated →

Observed $\dfrac{I}{K}$

0.005

Effect of demand

$\overset{o}{Q}$

Effect of relative cost

$\overset{o}{c/w}$

1958　59　60　61　62　63　64　65　66　67　68　69　70　71　72　73　74

GRAPH 4: **Influence of demand and relative cost on employment**

User cost c_1

Employment growth rate

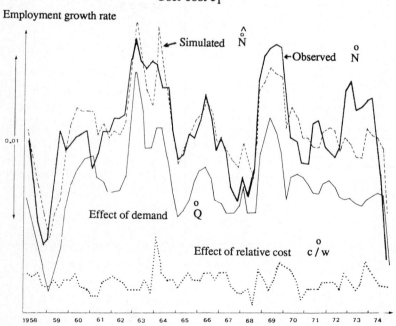

← Simulated　$\overset{\wedge}{\overset{o}{N}}$

←Observed　$\overset{o}{N}$

0.01

Effect of demand　$\overset{o}{Q}$

Effect of relative cost　$\overset{o}{c/w}$

1958　59　60　61　62　63　64　65　66　67　68　69　70　71　72　73　74

Moreover, the simulations reveal that the relative cost has a strong influence on employment in the annual-data estimate. This result is largely due to the user-cost series used. It is all the more fragile as it mainly reflects the impact of the expected real interest rate — and therefore of long-term expectations about inflation — on factor demands. The quarterly-data estimates calculated with the aid of other price-expectation assessments do not conclusively demonstrate that such an influence exists. The substitution effect is therefore uncertain. However, our estimates do not enable us to reject it. Indeed, it is probable that the factor costs are not fully described. A more thorough measure would require a broader definition of labor costs including hiring, dismissal, and personnel management costs. It would also require a greater integration of costs linked to capital use — such as equipment service-life — and of financial constraints, which have been left aside here.

CHAPTER 6
The dynamics of investment and employment with
capital and labor adjustment costs*
by
Patrick Artus and Bernard Migus

Introduction

Many studies describe how capital adjusts to its desired long-term level in the presence of capital adjustment costs (Hayashi [1982]; Abel and Blanchard [1983]; Blanchard and Sachs [1982 a, b]; d'Autume and Michel [1984]).

The present chapter sets out to introduce an adjustment cost for employment as well. This is intended to take into account the rigidity of employment--which is certainly very high, at least in France. We introduce the possibility of the firm's being demand-constrained, without examining the potential shift from a constrained to an unconstrained regime or vice-versa. This type of shift has already been studied by Malgrange and Villa [1984]; an investment model with several regimes has already been developed and estimated by Artus and Muet ([1983], Chapter 8 below) but in the static case, where the firm is unable to anticipate whether it will be constrained or not in the future.

Changes in capital, employment and output are analyzed here in the cases where demand constraints either are never active or permanently limit the firm's potential output. In the latter case, we introduce a dynamic of the adjustment of expected demand to its long-term level. This allows us to incorporate in the model an effect of the short-term economic cycle and to represent the productivity cycle. The description of expected demand is therefore somewhat more sophisticated than in many applied studies, where it is calculated solely by smoothing observed past demand.

We go on to demonstrate the existence of a single, stable, optimal path converging toward the long-term values of the endogenous variables, and we estimate the models that have been developed.

---

* Originally published as "Dynamique de l'investissement et de l'emploi avec coûts d'ajustement sur le capital et le travail," *Annales d'Economie et de Statistique* (formerly *Annales de l'INSEE*) 2:75-100, Apr.-June 1986.

1. MODEL WITH DEMAND CONSTRAINT

1.1. The firms' program

Firms maximize their expected and discounted intertemporal profit under the constraints of demand satisfaction and capital accumulation. At each period (t_0) they calculate this maximization, thereby defining an optimal path over $[t_0,\infty[$. To simplify our notations, we postulate $t_0 = 0$ throughout. Capital and employment are subjected to adjustment costs, calculated so as to cancel each other out on the steady-state-growth path defined later. These costs are incorporated in simple, quadratic form.

The firms' program in $t_0 = 0$ is therefore written:

$$(1) \quad \text{Max} \sum_{j=0}^{\infty} \frac{1}{(1+r)^j} \left[p_j \bar{D}_j - w_j N_j - p_j^I I_j - \frac{\gamma}{2} p_j^I \frac{(I_j - (g+\delta) K_{j-1})^2}{\bar{I}_j} \right. $$
$$\left. - \frac{\mu}{2} w_j \frac{(N_j - (1+n) N_{j-1})^2}{\bar{N}_j} \right]$$

under the constraints

$$(2) \qquad \bar{D}_j = f_j(N_j, K_j) \quad \text{(given demand)}$$

which, inverted, gives :

$$(2') \qquad N_j = e_j (\bar{D}_j , K_j)$$

where the functions f and e are time-dependent (technical progress);

and:

$$(3) \qquad K_{j-1} (1 - \delta) + I_j \quad \text{(capital accumulation)}$$

where:

r: discount rate, assumed constant
p_j :   expected production price for ... + j, exogenous
$\bar{D}_j$:   expected demand in $t_0 + j$
N_j: employment

p_j^I: investment price (expected, exogenous)

I_j: investment

δ : capital depreciation rate (exogenous)

K_j: existing capital during period $t_o + j$, including investment carried out at the start of the period

f_j: production function, linking total demand to capital and employment (putty-putty hypothesis)

γ, μ : adjustment-cost coefficients

I, N : exogenous variables, homogeneous with investment and employment, used for making the profit function homogeneous

w : cost of labor.

In steady-state growth, where volumes grow at rate g (equal to the expected growth rate of D) and employment at rate n (equal to g - Π, where Π is the exogenous growth rate of labor productivity), we get:

$$K_j = (1 + g) K_{j-1}$$

and thus:

$$I_j = K_j - (1 - \delta) K_{j-1}$$

as well as:

$$N_j = (1 + n) N_{j-1}$$

During steady-state growth, the quadratic adjustment costs introduced cancel each other out. Capital and employment levels on the steady-state-growth path therefore do not depend on adjustment costs. In particular, this maximization program defines an optimal path over [o, ∞[for K and N, given the expected values of the exogenous factors (p_j, w_j, D_j, p_j^I) and the initial capital stock (K_{-1}). The program therefore determines the capital at the end of the initial period 0, that is, K_o . Demand in 0, $\overline{D}_o$, is assumed not to be observed at the time of the firms' capital and investment decisions. We shall describe below our hypothesis concerning the manner in which they calculate D_o from observed demand values. If *ex post* actual demand D_o differs from expected demand $\overline{D}_o$, we suppose that only employment can be adjusted to satisfy (2), whereas the capital remains identical to the one chosen at the beginning of the period, K_o . Therefore, the employment adjustment cost produces an effect only at the moment when factor levels are chosen in response to expected demand, and not *ex post* after the demand has been observed.

Despite the apparent symmetry of adjustment costs, an asymmetry therefore exists between the treatment of capital and that of employment. If the firm's demand forecast proves inaccurate *ex post*, the firm cannot modify the capital stock but will be able to adapt employment. We therefore use a solution fairly similar to the one found in the literature on labor contracts: employees and firms agree on wages and employment in advance and, *ex post*, the employees must provide all the labor demanded by the firms at the agreed wage. The consequences of this hypothesis must be clearly set out.

Let us place ourselves *ex ante* on a steady-state-growth path where there are no adjustment costs. If observed demand exceeds expected demand, our hypothesis implies that the quantity of labor effectively provided will increase with respect to the predicted optimal quantity. This change is no doubt achieved mainly through overtime (conversely, low demand would be met by layoffs). The profit equation shows that the firm, in this case, incurs a wage cost and an adjustment cost. The simplification consists of making this adjustment cost identical to the cost incurred when employment varies: no distinction is made between employment and working time in the supply of work hours.

-If observed demand exceeds expected demand, the quantity of labor increases. This raises the reference base for calculating the adjustment costs in the optimal path of the following period. As a result, the quantity of labor will be greater on that path in the short term. We therefore assume the firm will not seek a rapid return of the employment utilization rate to its normal value. The inertia induced by adjustment costs is identical here for working time and employment.

- If observed demand greatly exceeds expected demand, it may be in the firm's interest not to satisfy the demand in full, since the marginal productivity of labor diminishes with the additional utilization of labor. There is a demand threshold beyond which demand is rationed (a shift into excess demand occurs in the goods market). We have assumed that this threshold was never met and, in this section, have deliberately envisaged an excess supply of goods.

We have sought to keep the specifications in this chapter fairly simple. The objective of firms could be made more complex by introducing an extra factor (the working time) and costs induced by changes in factor utilization from normal levels (see an example for capital in Artus, Laroque and Michel [1984]). To permit a rigorous analysis of the maximization problem, we have purposely included only two production factors. We have refused to incorporate *ex post* into the model an employment-adjustment mechanism that did not proceed from the firm's optimization behavior.

Lastly, we were unable to introduce disequilibrium estimates in the estimation of the dynamic model--a sufficiently complex process in itself. As a result, we have ruled out a priori the possibility of excess demand for goods in the model constrained *ex ante*.

1.2. Optimality conditions

We use (2') to identify N_j in (1) and to treat a problem involving capital alone; similarly, we replace I_j by its expression in (3). The expression to be maximized is therefore:

$$
(1') \quad \sum_{j=0}^{\infty} \frac{1}{(1+r)^j} \left[p_j \bar{D}_j - w_j e_j(\bar{D}_j, K_j) - p_j^1 (K_j - (1-\delta) K_{j-1}) \right.
$$
$$
- \frac{\gamma}{2} p_j^1 \frac{(K_j - (1+g) K_{j-1})^2}{\bar{I}_j}
$$
$$
\left. - \frac{\mu}{2} w_j \frac{(e_j(\bar{D}_j, K_j) - (1+n) e_j(\bar{D}_{j-1}, K_{j-1}))^2}{\bar{N}_j} \right]
$$

which, when derived with respect to K_j , yields:

$$
(4) \quad -w_j e_K'(\bar{D}_j, K_j) - p_j^1 + p_{j+1}^1 \frac{1-\delta}{1+r} \frac{\gamma p_j^1}{\bar{I}_j} (K_j - (1+g) K_{j-1})
$$
$$
+ \frac{(1+g)}{1+r} \frac{\gamma p_{j+1}^1}{\bar{I}_{j+1}} (K_{j+1} - (1+g) K_j) - \frac{\mu w_j}{\bar{N}_j} (e(\bar{D}_j, K_j)
$$

$$-(1+n)\,e\,(\bar{D}_{j-1},\,K_{j-1}))\,e'_K\,(\bar{D}_j,\,K_j)+\frac{\mu\,w_{j+1}}{\bar{N}_{j+1}}\,\frac{(1+n)}{(1+r)}\,(e\,(\bar{D}_{j+1},\,K_{j+1})$$

$$-(1+n)\,e\,(\bar{D}_j,\,K_j))\,e'_K\,(\bar{D}_j,\,K_j)=0$$

where, for simplicity, we have omitted the time index of the employment function e.

Equation (4) expresses the zero value of the discounted profit connected with the operation that consists of increasing the capital by dK in j, then selling that extra investment (of which $dK(1-\delta)$ remains) in $j + 1$. This operation:
- makes it possible to reduce employment in j (gain: $we'_K\,e'_K > 0$);
- costs the capital purchase price minus its resale value:

$$\left(-p'_j+\frac{1-\delta}{1+r}p'_{j+1}\right)$$

- increases the adjustment cost of capital in $+ j$ if the capital was increasing in the reference situation (otherwise, the cost is reduced)

(term $-\dfrac{\gamma p'_j}{\bar{I}_j}(K_j-(1+g)\,K_{j-1})$);

- reduces the adjustment cost of capital correlatively in $j + 1$;
- reduces the adjustment cost of labor in j   since the surplus capital allows the firm to use less labor   and increases it in $j+ 1$.

It will be shown in Appendix 1 that the Hessian in (1') is indeed such as to produce a maximum.

1.3.   Steady-state growth

On a steady-state-growth path, we have:

$$K_j = K_0\,(1 + g)^j\;;\;\bar{D}_j = \bar{D}_0\,(1 + g)^j\;;\;N_j = N_0\,(1 + n)^j$$

The inverted production function is such that:

(5) $e_j\,(\bar{D}_0(1 + g)^j,\,K_0\,(1 + g)^j = N_0\,(1 + n)^j\;;\;e_j$ grows at the rate $1 + n$.

(4) is then very simply written:

(6) $\quad -e'_{jK}(\bar{D}_0(1+g)^j, K_0(1+g)^j) = \dfrac{p^l_j}{w_j} - \dfrac{1-\delta}{1+r}\dfrac{p^l_{j+1}}{w_{j+1}}$

e'_{jK} , on account of (5), grows at the rate $(1+n)/(1+g)$; it follows that (p/w) must grow at that same rate. Let ρ stand for the growth rate of prices (p and p^l). We get:

$$\frac{p^l_j}{w_j} = \left(\frac{1+n}{1+g}\right)^j \frac{p^l_0}{w_0}$$

This yields the optimality condition for steady-state growth:

(7) $\quad e'_{jK}(\bar{D}_0, K_0) = \dfrac{p^l_0}{w_0}\left(1 - \dfrac{1-\delta}{1+r}(1+\rho)\right),$

that is, the entirely standard expression in the static case, with user cost of capital defined as :

$$p^l_0\left(1 - \frac{1-\delta}{1+r}(1+\rho)\right) \approx p^l_0(r-\rho+\delta)$$

We shall subsequently assume that expected prices and wages grow at constant rates starting from the observed price, and that for all paths we therefore have:

$$p_j = p_0(1+\rho)^j, \qquad p^l_j = p^l_0(1+\rho)^j, \qquad w_j = w_0\frac{(1+\rho)^j(1+g)^j}{(1+n)^j}$$

Expected demand is more complex to handle, as we shall see below.

1.4. Expected demand

We have tried in this chapter to offer a more refined presentation of changes in expected demand than is customary. Firms invest at the start of the period, since the capital obtained after investment is used for production during the period. We therefore assume that firms must determine expected demand values over [0, ∞[from the observation of its past values over]- ∞, -1] . We distinguish the medium-term trend of demand, derived from a fairly long lag on observed values:

$$\bar{D}_{-1} = \frac{1}{M} \sum_{i=1}^{M} D_{-i}(1+\bar{g})^{i-1}; \qquad \bar{D}_{+j} = \bar{D}_{-1}(1+g)^{j+1}$$

where $\bar{g}$ is the average growth rate of demand over the last M periods. From date -1 on, this medium-term demand increases at the expected growth rate of demand, namely, g. In the short term, observed demand may diverge from this trend. We assume that firms expect demand to fall back in line with the trend gradually as follows:

(8) $\bar{D}_j = \theta\bar{D}_{j-1}(1 + g) + (1 - \theta)\bar{\bar{D}}_j$

Hereafter, to simplify our equations, the variables used are transformed variables obtained by dividing the initial variables by their steady-state-growth value, using the variables' expected growth rates over the period [0, ∞[that is:

$$\bar{D}'_j = \frac{\bar{D}_j}{(1+g)^j} \quad ; N'_j = \frac{N_j}{(1+n)^j} \quad ; K'_j = \frac{K_j}{(1+g)^j} \quad ;$$

$$p'_j = \frac{p_j}{(1+\varrho)^j} \quad ; p_j'^{\mathrm{I}} = \frac{p_j^{\mathrm{I}}}{(1+\varrho)^j} \quad ; w'_j = \frac{w_j(1+n)^j}{(1+\varrho)^j(1+g)^j}$$

$$\bar{I}'_j = \frac{\bar{I}_j}{(1+g)^j} \quad ; \bar{N}'_j = \frac{\bar{N}'_j}{(1+n)^j} .$$

This gives: $w'_j = w_0$, $p'^{\mathrm{I}}_j = p_0$, $p'_j = p_0$, $N'_j = N_0$, $I'_j = I_0$.

Accordingly, (8) can be written, by iteration and by substituting transformed variables:

(9) $\bar{D}'_j - \bar{\bar{D}}'_j = \theta^{j+1}(\bar{D}'_{-1} = \bar{\bar{D}}'_{-1})$

As demand in -1 is observed, $\bar{D}'_{-1} = D'_{-1}$ (D: observed demand). We can also note that, by definition, $\bar{\bar{D}}'_j = \bar{D}'_{-1}$, since the demand trend grows at rate g.

Thus, through (9), the short-term curve of demand — which will be very important for determining the investment level — depends on its medium-term trend and on the speed at which firms (parametered by θ) expect demand to revert to its trend after short-term deviations.

There is obviously a strong dissymmetry between the sophisticated handling of demand expectations and the very simple handling of price and wage expectations (expected prices and wages grow at a constant rate). Again, we could imagine a more general model (with complex dynamics) in which all expectations had a long-term and a short-term component.

1.5. Solution

The solution consists in integrating (4), an equation that exhibits second-order differences in K and includes $\bar{D}$ which, as we have just seen, diverges from the long-term demand trend $\bar{\bar{D}}$. We linearize (4) around the optimal path for steady-state growth defined by (7) calculated for the demand trend $\bar{D}'_{-1}$.
K' stands for capital (constant when transformed variables are used) on this path. Using transformed variables, (4) becomes:

$$
\begin{aligned}
&- w_0\, e'_K (\bar{D}'_j, K'_j) - p_0 \\
(4')\quad &-p_0(1+\rho)\frac{1-\delta}{1+r} - \frac{\gamma p'_0}{\bar{I}_0}(K'_j - K'_{j-1}) + \frac{\gamma p'_0}{\bar{I}_0}\frac{(1+\rho)(1+g)}{1+r}(K'_{j+1} - K'_j) \\
&- \frac{\mu\, w_0}{\bar{N}_0}(e(\bar{D}_j, K'_j) - e(\bar{D}'_{j-1}, K'_{j-1}))\, e'_K(\bar{D}'_j, K'_j) \\
&+ \frac{\mu\, w_0}{\bar{N}_0}\frac{(1+\rho)(1+g)}{1+r}(e(\bar{D}'_{j+1}, K'_{j+1}) - e(\bar{D}'_j, K'_j))\, e'_K(\bar{D}'_j, K'_j) = 0
\end{aligned}
$$

Hence, after linearization:

$$
\begin{aligned}
&(K'_{j+1} - K')\left(\frac{\mu\, w_0}{\bar{N}_0(1+\eta)}\, e'^2_K + \frac{\gamma p'_0}{\bar{I}_0(1+\eta)} \right) \\
&+ (K'_j - K')\left(-w_0\, e''_{K^2} - \frac{\gamma P'_0}{\bar{I}_0}\left(1 + \frac{1}{(1+\eta)}\right) - \frac{\mu\, w_0}{\bar{N}_0}\, e'^2_K\left(1 + \frac{1}{1+\eta}\right) \right)
\end{aligned}
$$

$$(10) \quad + (K'_{j-1} - K') \left(\frac{\gamma p'_0}{I_0} + \frac{\mu w_0}{N_0} e'^2_K \right)$$

$$= (\bar{D}'_{j+1} - \bar{D}'_{j-1}) \frac{\mu w_0}{N_0 (1+\eta)} e'_D e'_K$$

$$+ (\bar{D}'_j - \bar{D}^1_{-1}) \left(-w_0 e''_{KD} - \frac{\mu w_0}{N_0} e'_D e'_K \left(1 + \frac{1}{1+\eta} \right) \right)$$

$$+ (\bar{D}'_{j-1} - \bar{D}'_{-1}) \frac{\mu w_0}{N_0} e'_D e'_K$$

where $1 + \eta = \quad 1 + \eta = \dfrac{1+r}{(1+\rho)(1+g)}$

and all the derivatives are taken at the point $(\bar{\bar{D}}'_{-1}, K')$.
The resolution of (10) is given in Appendix 2.

We get:

$$(11) \quad K'_j - K' = (K'_{-1} - K') \lambda_1^{j+1} + (\bar{D}'_{-1} - \bar{\bar{D}}'_{-1}) \frac{A \theta^2 + B \theta + C}{E \theta^2 + F \theta + G} (\theta^{j+1} - \lambda_1^{j+1})$$

λ_1 is the only stable solution (meeting the transversality condition) of the characteristic polynomial of the left-hand member of (10), θ is the demand adjustment coefficient seen in (9). For the reasons given in Appendix 2, we make the rather logical assumption that $\theta < \lambda_1$, in other words, that the expected speed of return of demand to its long-term trend level is greater than the speed of adjustment of capital to its long-term objective.

We then obtain $\quad \dfrac{A \theta^2 + B \theta + C}{E \theta^2 + F \theta + G} > 0$

where A, B and C are the coefficients of the right-hand member of (10), E, F and G those of the left-hand member. Since $\theta < \lambda_1$, we can see that if demand is depressed in the short term $(\bar{D}'_{-1} - \bar{\bar{D}}'_{-1} < 0)$, capital is augmented compared to a path where $\bar{D}'_{-1} = \bar{\bar{D}}'_{-1}$. The reason is the following: As θ is small, demand rapidly catches up with its long-term level. Initial employment $(e(D_{-1}, K_{-1}))$ is below the level needed to satisfy long-term demand $(e(\bar{\bar{D}}, K_{-1}))$.

As θ is small, employment will have to expand quickly from $(e(D_{-1},K_{-1}))$ to $e(\bar{\bar{D}}, K_{-1})$. This will entail a high adjustment cost that firms can reduce by increasing their capital at the outset with respect to the optimal reference path. Only capital K'_0 is derived from (1), since in $t = 1$ firms calculate a new optimal path on $[1, \infty[$. For the estimate, we shall therefore use (11) with j=0. We can, however, observe that $\theta^{j+1} - \lambda_1^{j+1}$ (the correction term) is equal, of course, to 0 for $j = 1$, then decreases, and finally increases toward 0. The divergence from the reference path therefore increases before gradually disappearing. It is interesting to study the effect of the introduction of this demand-expectation flexibility on the short-term changes in labor productivity.

If demand expectations are fulfilled $(D'_0 = \bar{D}'_0)$:

$$N'_0 = e\,(\bar{D}'_0, K'_0) \qquad\qquad (e'_D > o, e'_k < o)$$

We assume that stationary equilibrium $(\bar{D}'_{-1} = \bar{\bar{D}}'_{-2})$ prevailed in - 1.

In 0, expected wages and prices do not change, but long-term demand grows from $\bar{\bar{D}}'_{-2}$ to $\bar{\bar{D}}'_{-1} = \phi\,\bar{\bar{D}}'_{-2}, \phi > 1$. We then get:

$$\bar{D}'_0 = \theta\,\bar{D}'_{-2} + (1-\theta)\,\bar{D}'_{-1} = \frac{\theta + (1-\theta)\,\varphi}{\varphi}\,\bar{D}'_{-1}$$

$$(\bar{D}'_{-1} < \bar{D}'_0 < \bar{D}'_{-2})$$

(11) implies that:

$$\frac{K'_0}{\bar{D}'_0} = (1 - \lambda_1)\left(\frac{\bar{K}'}{\bar{\bar{D}}'_{-1}}\right)\frac{\bar{\bar{D}}'_{-1}}{\bar{D}'_0} + \lambda_1\left(\frac{\bar{K}'}{\bar{\bar{D}}'_{-1}}\right)\frac{\bar{\bar{D}}'_{-2}}{\bar{D}'_0}$$

$$+ \frac{A\theta^2 + B\theta + C}{E\theta^2 + F\theta + G}\,(\theta - \lambda_1)\,\frac{1-\theta}{\theta + (1-\theta)\phi}$$

where $(K'/\bar{\bar{D}}'_{-1})$ is the inverse of capital productivity in stationary equilibrium. This yields:

(12) $\quad \dfrac{K_0'}{\bar{D}_0'} = \dfrac{(1-\lambda_1)\,\varphi + \lambda_1}{(1-\theta)\,\varphi + \theta}\left(\dfrac{\bar{K}'}{\bar{D}_{-1}'}\right) + \dfrac{A\,\theta^2 + B\,\theta + C}{E\,\theta^2 + F\,\theta + G}(\theta - \lambda_1)\dfrac{1-\varphi}{\theta + (1-\theta)\,\varphi}$

If expected demand were assumed to remain at the level of long-term demand, we would have $\bar{D}_j' = \bar{D}_{-1}'$ for all $j(\theta = 0)$, and :

(13) $\quad \dfrac{K_0'}{\bar{D}_0'} = \left(\dfrac{\bar{K}'}{\bar{D}_{-1}'}\right)\left(\dfrac{(1-\lambda_1)\,\varphi + \lambda_1}{\varphi}\right) - \dfrac{C}{G}\lambda_1\dfrac{1-\varphi}{\varphi}$ $\qquad$ ($G < 0$)

The term $\quad -\dfrac{C}{G}\lambda_1\dfrac{1-\varphi}{\varphi}\quad$ is positive, $\dfrac{(1-\lambda_1)\,\varphi + \lambda_1}{\varphi} < 1$: we can

therefore have $\dfrac{K_0'}{\bar{D}_0'} > \dfrac{\bar{K}'}{\bar{D}_{-1}'}\quad$ if the term $\dfrac{-C}{G}\lambda_1\dfrac{1-\varphi}{\varphi}$ is large enough.

At the very opposite end, for the maximum permitted value of $\theta(\theta = \lambda_1)$,

$\dfrac{K_0'}{\bar{D}_0'} = \left(\dfrac{\bar{K}'}{\bar{D}_{-1}'}\right).$

When demand expectations are very rigid ($\theta = \lambda_1$) and are slow to adjust to long-term demand, capital productivity does not fluctuate. When demand adjusts rapidly to long-term demand (small θ), if

$$-e_D'\,e_K'/[(\bar{N}_0\,\gamma\,p_0/\mu\,w_0\,\bar{I}_0) + e_K'^2]$$

is large (high employment adjustment cost (μ/N_0), capital productivity falls when demand rises. If the production function f is homogeneous of degree 1, capital and labor productivities vary inversely.[1] By introducing the pattern of

---

1. Since $\bar{D}'_0 = f(N'_0, K'_0)$, in other words, with homogeneity of degree one: $1 = f\left(\dfrac{N'_0}{\bar{D}'_0}, \dfrac{K'_0}{\bar{D}'_0}\right).$

adjustment to long-term demand, we can therefore generate a productivity cycle (increase in labor productivity when demand rises) if the employment adjustment cost is high enough.

It is important to note that the productivity cycle defined here differs from the one generally introduced in macroeconomic models. *Ex post*, here, employment adjusts freely in order to satisfy actual demand; *ex ante*, a productivity cycle appears when we calculate productivity from expected short-term demand (we therefore have a productivity cycle with perfect expectations). The particular productivity cycle is not due simply to employment inertia (the presence of the adjustment-cost term parametered by μ) but to the combination of employment inertia (if $\mu = 0$, $\lambda_1 = 0$ and there is no productivity cycle) and the allowance made in the expectations for the short-term cyclical situation (D' $\neq$ D').

Appendix 2 also shows that capital inertia (λ_1) rises with adjustment costs for both factors (γ and μ) and with expected long-term demand D' .

2. MODEL WITH NO DEMAND CONSTRAINT

2.1. The firms' program

Firms proceed with their "notional" investment here, since the quantity of goods sold equals the supply of goods. Capital and employment are subjected to the same adjustment costs as before. The notations are identical. The firms' program at date 0 is written:

$$
(14) \quad \text{Max} \sum_{j=0}^{\infty} \frac{1}{(1+r)_j} \left[p_j f_j(N_j, K_j) - w_j N_j - p_j^I I_j - \frac{\gamma}{2} p_j^I \frac{(I_j - (g+\delta) K_{j-1})^2}{\bar{I}_j} \right.
$$

$$
\left. - \frac{\mu}{2} w_j \frac{(N_j - (1+n) N_{j-1})^2}{\bar{N}_j} \right]
$$

subject to the constraint

$$
(3) \quad K_j = K_{j-1}(1-\delta) + I_j
$$

2.2. Optimality conditions

Substituting (3) for I_j in (14) and deriving with respect to K_j and N_j , we get the optimality conditions:

(15) $\qquad f_K'(N_j', K_j') = \dfrac{p_0^I}{p_0}\left(1 - \dfrac{1-\delta}{1+r}(1+\rho) + \dfrac{\gamma}{I_0}(K_j' - K_{j-1}')\right.$

$$- \dfrac{\gamma}{I_0}\dfrac{1+q}{1+r}(1+\rho)\,(K_{j+1}' - K_j')\bigg)$$

(16) $\qquad f_N'(N_j', K_j') = \dfrac{w_0}{p_0}\left(1 + \dfrac{\mu}{\bar{N}_0}(N_j' - N_{j-1}')\right.$

$$- \dfrac{\mu}{\bar{N}_0}\dfrac{(1+g)(1+\rho)}{(1+r)}(N_{j+1}' - N_j')\bigg)$$

Equation (15) reflects the fact that the use of one additional unit of capital in the period j produces zero profit—if we take into account the purchase cost, the resale value, the additional adjustment cost in j and the latter's reduction in j +1. Equation (16) indicates that the use of one additional unit of labor in j produces zero profit.

In steady-state growth, we find the usual conditions again:

$$f_K' = \frac{p^I}{p}\left(1 - \frac{1-\delta}{1+r}(1+\rho)\right), \qquad f_N' = \frac{w}{p}$$

The Hamiltonian's concavity at optimum with respect to K and N follows from the same reasoning as given in Appendix 1.

2.3. Solution

As before, (15) and (16) must be linearized around the stationary solution (using transformed variables) and integrated. The values for employment and capital in the stationary solution will be written N' and K'. As previously:

$$1 + \eta = \frac{1+r}{(1+g)(1+\rho)}$$

We obtain:

$$(17) \qquad f''_{KN}(N', K')\,(N'_j - N') + (K'_{j+1} - K')\frac{p^I_0}{p_0}\frac{\gamma}{\bar{I}_0}\frac{1}{1+\eta}$$

$$+ (K'_j - K')\left[f''_{K^2}(N', K') - \frac{p^I_0}{p_0}\frac{\gamma}{\bar{I}_0} - \frac{p^I_0}{p_0}\frac{\gamma}{\bar{I}_0}\frac{1}{1+\eta} \right]$$

$$+ (K'_{j-1} - K')\left(\frac{p^I_0}{p_0}\frac{\gamma}{\bar{I}_0} \right) = 0$$

$$(18) \qquad f''_{KN}(N', K')\,(K'_j - K')(N'_{j+1} - N')\left(\frac{w_0}{p_0}\frac{\mu}{\bar{N}_0}\frac{1}{(1+\eta)} \right)$$

$$+ (N'_j - N')\left(f''_{N^2}(N', K') - \frac{w_0}{p_0}\frac{\mu}{\bar{N}_0} - \frac{w_0}{p_0}\frac{\mu}{\bar{N}_0}\frac{1}{(1+\eta)} \right)$$

$$+ (N'_{j-1} - N')\left(\frac{w_0}{p_0}\frac{\mu}{\bar{N}_0} \right) = 0$$

This can be written:

$$(19) \qquad \begin{pmatrix} N'_{j+1} - N' \\ N'_j - N' \\ K'_{j+1} - K' \\ K'_j - K' \end{pmatrix} = A \begin{pmatrix} N'_j - N' \\ N'_{j-1} - N' \\ K'_j - K' \\ K'_{j-1} - K' \end{pmatrix}$$

with:

$$
A = \begin{pmatrix}
-f''_{N^2}\dfrac{p_0}{w_0}\dfrac{\bar N_0}{\bar\mu}(1+\eta) & \vdots & -(1+\eta) & \vdots & -f''_{KN}\dfrac{p_0}{w_0}\dfrac{\bar N_0}{\bar\mu}(1+\eta) & \vdots & 0 \\[2pt]
+(1+\eta)+1 & \vdots & & \vdots & & \vdots & \\[2pt]
1 & \vdots & 0 & \vdots & 0 & \vdots & 0 \\[2pt]
-f''_{KN}\dfrac{p_0}{p'_0}\dfrac{\bar I_0}{\gamma}(1+\eta) & \vdots & 0 & \vdots & -f''_{K^2}\dfrac{p_0}{p'_0}\dfrac{\bar I_0}{\gamma}(1+\eta) & \vdots & -(1+\eta) \\[2pt]
& \vdots & & \vdots & +(1+\eta)+1 & \vdots & \\[2pt]
0 & \vdots & 0 & \vdots & 1 & \vdots & 0
\end{pmatrix}
$$

The characteristic polynomial $D(\lambda)$, where λ stands for the eigen values of the dynamic system (1), is written:

$$
(20) \qquad D(\lambda) = -\lambda^2 (f''_{KN})^2 \frac{p_0}{p'_0}\frac{p_0}{w_0}\frac{\bar I_0}{\gamma}\frac{\bar N_0}{\mu}(1+\eta)^2
$$

$$
+\left(\lambda^2+\lambda\left(f''_{N^2}\frac{p_0}{w_0}\frac{\bar N_0}{\mu}(1+\eta)-(1+\eta)-1\right)+1+\eta\right)
$$

$$
\times\left(\lambda^2+\lambda\left(f''_{K^2}\frac{p_0}{p'_0}\frac{\bar I_0}{\gamma}(1+\eta)-(1+\eta)-1\right)+(1+\eta)\right)
$$

We show in Appendix 3 that $D(\lambda)$ has two zeros between 0 and 1 and that the two other roots correspond to divergent dynamics.

Let B be the matrix of the coordinates of A's eigen vectors in the base $(N'_{j+1} - N', N'_j - N', K'_{j+1} - K', K'_j - K')$. B is such that the first two eigen vectors correspond to the divergent eigen values.

We therefore have:

$$
(21) \qquad B\begin{pmatrix} N'_{j+1}-N' \\ N'_j-N' \\ K'_{j+1}-K' \\ K'_j-K' \end{pmatrix} = \begin{pmatrix} 0 \\ 0 \\ c_3\,\lambda_3^{j+1} \\ c_4\,\lambda_4^{j+1} \end{pmatrix}
$$

where λ_3 and λ_4 are the stable eigen values.

The four-equation system of (21), with the equations taken at the point j=-1, enables us to calculate the integration constants c_3 and c_4. N'_{-1} - N', K'_{-1} and K' are known at the time of the firms' decision.

As we have determined c_3 and c_4, as well as λ_3 and λ_4 (through the calculation of the D (λ) zeros), (21) allows us to calculate K'_0 - K' and N'_0 - N' in terms of $c_3 \lambda_3$ and $c_4 \lambda_4$. K'_1 - K' and N'_{-1}- N' are eliminated, for they will be determined on an optimal path over [1, ∞ [and not on the [0, ∞ [path examined here.

3. ESTIMATE

3.1. Specification

To estimate the models, we must specify the production function f. We have chosen a Cobb-Douglas type function, which, as it must meet the steady-state growth conditions (5), is written:

$$(22) \qquad \bar{D}_j = Q_0 \, N_j^\alpha \, K_j^\beta (1+g)^{(1-\beta)j} (1+n)^{-\alpha j}$$

Hence

$$(23) \qquad N_j = \left(\frac{\bar{D}_j}{Q_0} \right)^{1/\alpha} K_j^{-\beta/\alpha} (1+g)^{-[(1-\beta)/\alpha]j} (1+n)^j$$

for the function e.

This allows us to identify all the expressions that appear in the preceding developments when shifting to transformed variables. For the constrained regime (section 1 above), optimal capital in a steady-state-growth situation (defined by (7)) is written:

$$(24) \qquad K' = \bar{D}'^{1/(\alpha+\beta)} \left(\frac{\beta}{\alpha} \right)^{\alpha/(\alpha+\beta)} \left[\frac{w_0}{p_0^1 (1-[(1-\delta)/(1+r)](1+\rho))} \right]^{\alpha/(\alpha+\beta)} Q_0^{-1/(\alpha+\beta)}$$

For the regime with no constraint (section 2 above), optimal capital and employment in a steady-state-growth situation are given by:

(25)

$$K' = \alpha^{\alpha/1 - (\alpha + \beta)} \, \beta^{(1 - \alpha)/(1 - (\alpha + \beta))} \left(\frac{w_0}{p_0}\right)^{-\alpha/(1 - (\alpha + \beta))} \left(\frac{c_0}{p_0}\right)^{-(1 - \alpha)/(1 - (\alpha + \beta))}$$

$$N' = \alpha^{(1 - \beta)/(1 - (\alpha + \beta))} \, \beta^{\beta/(1 - (\alpha + \beta))} \left(\frac{w_0}{p_0}\right)^{-(1 - \beta)/(1 - (\alpha + \beta))} \left(\frac{c_0}{p_0}\right)^{-\beta/(1 - (\alpha + \beta))}$$

where $\quad c_0 = p_0^I \left(1 - \dfrac{1 - \delta}{1 + r}(1 + \rho)\right) \quad$ is the user cost of capital.

3.2.   Series

We have estimated the models using French quarterly series for the period 1963-1982. The series used cover all non-financial firms. They consist of:

D and Q: value added of non-financial firms
p: price of this value added
w: wage cost per capita (including firms' social-security contributions)
N: employment in non-financial firms
K: net capital of non-financial firms
p^I :   investment price
r: interest rate on private bonds

The conversion to transformed variables requires a knowledge of the variables' expected growth rates.

The expected growth rates of volumes (g) and employment (n) have been calculated on a moving average from the observed growth rates of value added and of the workforce. The length of the moving average was subjected to an iterative procedure during the estimation, eventually leading us to choose moving averages over the last six quarters.

The expected growth rate of prices could not be taken as equal to a moving average of observed growth rates of prices, for in that case we would not always have had $1 + r > (1+ \rho)(1+g)$.

In keeping with METRIC (INSEE [1981], p. 288), we chose for long-term price-rise expectations a variable calculated by taking 90% of the past price rise (again measured on a six-quarter average), from which we subtracted 1.5 points a year.

This new variable, consistently smaller than actual inflation, effectively leads to $1 + r > (1+\rho)(1+g)$ in all points, a prerequisite for the stability of the optimal paths.

3.3. Model with demand constraint

As the firm is assumed to adujst its optimal path in every period, the equation to estimate for capital is (11), where we posit $j = 0$, which determines the capital at the end of the decision period. Adding a random factor ε_k, assumed to be normal, zero-mean, and with a standard deviation σ_k, we get:

$$(26) \quad K'_0 = K' + (K'_{0-1} - K') \lambda_1 + (\bar{D}'_{-1} - \bar{\bar{D}}'_{-1}) \frac{A\,\theta^2 + B\,\theta + C}{E\,\theta^2 + F\,\theta + G} (\theta - \lambda_1) + \varepsilon_K$$

where λ_1 is the root included between 0 and 1 of the left-hand member of (10), and K' is the long-term level of capital (see (24)). $\bar{D}$ and $\bar{\bar{D}}$ are defined in 1.4; A, B, C, E, F and G in 1.5.

The parameters to be estimated are:
- α and β, the capital and labor coefficients in the Cobb-Douglas production function;
- Q_0, the production-function constant;
- M, the maximum lag used to compose the long-term demand series; after an iterative procedure, M was set at nine quarters;
- θ, the speed of adjustment of demand to its long-term level (see (8));
- $\mu/\bar{N}_0$ and $\gamma/\bar{I}_0$, the coefficients of user cost of capital and employment.

The estimation procedure is as follows. For given parameter values:
- we calculate the coefficients, then the roots of the characteristic polynomial of (10);
- we choose the root that is smaller than 1 (λ_1);
- we calculate the coefficients of the second member of (10);

- we can then calculate the likelihood of the system to be estimated: for capital, it is equation (26); for employment — which, in the short term, adjusts so as to meet real (not expected) demand — it is the equation equivalent to (23) in which transformed variables are used and a random term ($\varepsilon_N \sim (0, \sigma_N)$) has been added, yielding:

$$(27) \qquad N'_0 = Q_0^{-1/\alpha} \, D_0'^{1/\alpha} \, K_0'^{-\beta/\alpha} + \varepsilon_N$$

The likelihood of (26)-(27) is maximized using an iterative procedure. The results are given in the first column of Table 1.

The coefficients of the production function exhibit slightly diminishing returns to scale ($\alpha + \beta = 0,85$).

The estimated coefficients of the adjustment costs are such that a 1% rise in employment in one quarter would increase the wage cost by 0.74%, while a 1% rise in capital in one quarter would reduce profit by the equivalent of 3.14% of the capital's value, or, to put it differently, by 12.52% of the output value or 27.89% of the wage cost. The adjustment cost of capital therefore seems to be much greater than the adjustment cost of employment, and explains the strong inertia obtained in capital adjustment.

The eigen value λ_1 averages 0.970, indicating a mean lag for capital of eight years. The extreme values obtained for λ_1 over the period are 0.962 and 0.987. The other eigen value, corresponding to an unstable dynamic, varies from 1.030 to 1.043.

λ_1 displays particularly high values in the low-growth years 1975 and 1980-1981-1982, suggesting a very slow capital adjustment then; λ_1 falls to its lowest values between 1966 and 1972.

θ is found to equal 0.26, pointing to a rapid adjustment of expected short-term demand to its long-term level.

The term $\qquad \dfrac{A\,\theta^2 + B\,\theta + C}{E\,\theta^2 + F\,\theta + G}(\theta - \lambda_1) \qquad$, which multiplies $\bar{D}'_{-1} - \bar{\bar{D}}'_{-1}$

(see (26)), averages -0.196. The denominator's smaller-than-unity eigen value $E\theta^2 + F\theta + G$ varies between 0.87 and 0.92; θ is always smaller than that value, and $\qquad \dfrac{A\,\theta^2 + B\,\theta + C}{E\,\theta^2 + F\,\theta + G}$

is always positive (see Appendix 2).

3.4. Model without demand constraint

The equations to be estimated for capital and employment are taken from system (21), as explained in 2.3. This leads, for each period, to system (28):

$$
\begin{aligned}
K_0' - K' &= k_0 (K_{-1}' - K') + k_1 (N_{-1}' - N') \\
N_0' - N' &= n_0 (K_{-1}' - K') + n_1 (N_{-1}' - N')
\end{aligned}
\tag{28}
$$

where K' and N', the optimal long-term levels of capital and employment, are given by (25).

As we have seen in 2.3, k_0, k_1, n_0 and n_1 are not constants but must be calculated for each period from the coordinates of the eigen vectors of (19) in the system $(N'_0, N'_{-1}, K'_0, K'_{-1})$ and from the non-divergent eigen values of (19), written λ_3 and λ_4 in (21). These coordinates and eigen values are determined by the totality of the model's parameters and exogenous variables. As expected demand is not included, there are fewer parameters to be estimated here. They are α, β, Q_0 (Cobb-Douglas function coefficient) and the adjustment costs μ/N_0 and γ/I_0.

The estimate of the unconstrained model for the entire period yields results that can undoubtedly be described as scarcely credible. The accuracy of the equations is good (see the second column of Table 1) but the mean coefficient of K'_{-1} - K' in the equation for K'_0 - K' (see (28)) is 0.995, while the mean coefficient of N'_{-1} - N' in the equation for N'_0 - N' is 0.998 (the mean value of k_1 is 0.0024, that of n_1 is 0.0004).

System (28) is almost reduced to $K'_0 = K'_{-1}$, $N'_0 = N'_{-1}$, implying that the long-term values K' and N' furnished by (25) are clearly not the objectives of capital and employment.

This inertia obtained in the estimate is reflected by the rise in the coefficients of adjustment costs $\mu/\overline{N}_0$ and $\gamma/\overline{I}_0$ (see Table 1).

TABLE 1

	Model with demand constraint	Model without constraint
Production-function coefficients :		
α	0.42 (12.1)	0.52 (14.7)
β	0.43 (11.4)	0.33 (8.8)
Q_0	4.51 (155.6)	5.36 (163.8)
Adjustment costs :		
μ/N_0	0.0010 (3.2)	0.0027 (3.8)
γ/I_0	0.00048 (1.7)	0.00092 (2.7)
Demand adjustment :		
θ	0.26 (1.9)	
Equation for K' :		
Standard deviation (mean % of K').......	0.24 %	0.35 %
DW	1.33	0.71
Equation for N' :		
Standard deviation (mean % of N').......	0.63 %	0.32 %
DW	1.30	0.46

in parentheses under the coefficients : t statistics

Once again, we encounter the familiar phenomenon that the capital and employment equations of the "true neoclassical model" (Chapter 2 above) — where expected output does not appear — give very poor empirical results. Here, the poor results are of a different nature. They do not consist of abnormal values for the parameters of relative factor prices or parameters of the production function (these are, in fact, reasonable here). Rather, they consist of extremely long adjustment lags for production factors.

Of course, we could argue that, in the unconstrained regime, relative-price changes are very slow to be incorporated into firms' decisions. But the slowness is so great here — mean adjustment times of 50 years for capital and 125 years for employment ! — that it must certainly reflect the inappropriateness of the unconstrained model for the overall period mean.

Conclusion

In this chapter, we have been able to derive the optimal paths of employment and capital explicitly in the cases where the firm is demand-constrained or not. Our findings indicate that the adjustment costs of capital are much greater than those of employment, and that the model without demand constraints yields poor results. We could generalize the model by introducing a more sophisticated expectation pattern — not only for demand, but also for factor costs — than is used in the standard investment models. However, this would obviously complicate the model's specification. We could also refine the production function by distinguishing between employment and working times both in their contribution to output and in the adjustment costs that they generate for firms when they vary.

APPENDIX 1

Calculation of the Hessian of (1')

The derivative of (1') with respect to K_j is:

$$-\frac{w_j}{(1+r)^j}e''_{K^2} - \frac{\mu\,w_j}{\bar{N}_j}(N_j-(1+n)\,N_{j-1})\,e''_{K^2} + \frac{\mu\,w_{j+1}}{\bar{N}_{j+1}}(N_{j+1}-(1+n)\,N_j)\,e''_K$$

$$(e'_{K^2} > 0)$$

Its negativity is assured if:

$$\frac{w_j}{(1+r)^j}e''_{K^2}\left[\frac{\mu\,(N_j-(1+n)\,N_{j-1})}{\bar{N}_j} - \frac{w_{j+1}}{w_j}\,\frac{\mu}{1+r}\cdot\frac{(N_{j+1}-(1+n)\,N_j)}{\bar{N}_{j+1}} + 1\right] > 0.$$

At the optimum, this is verified as follows. If we differentiated (1) directly with respect to N_j, we would have:

$$-\frac{w_j}{(1+r)^j} - \mu\frac{w_j}{\bar{N}_j}\,\frac{1}{(1+r)^j}(N_j-(1+n)\,N_{j-1})$$

$$+ \frac{\mu\,w_{j+1}}{\bar{N}_{j+1}}\,\frac{(1+n)}{(1+r)^{j+1}}\cdot(N_{j+1}-(1+n)\,N_j)+\eta_j=0,$$

where $n_j \geq 0$ is the multiplier associated with (2') (where $N_j \geq e(\bar{D}_j, K_j)$).
Hence the positivity at the optimum of the bracketed term and the negativity of the second derivative.

APPENDIX 2

Resolution of the differential equation (10)

Let us first consider the general solution of the equation without the second member. We see that the characteristic polynomial is such that:

$$P(0) = \frac{\gamma p_0^l}{\bar{I}_0} + \frac{\mu w_0}{\bar{N}_0} e_K'^2 > 0$$

$$P(1) = -w_0 e_K''^2 < 0.$$

Therefore, at least one root lies between 0 and 1. The root product equals

$$\frac{1+r}{(1+\rho)(1+g)}.$$

If $1 + r \geq (1 + \rho)(1 + g)$ (the nominal interest rate is greater than or equal to the growth rate of nominal output), which we will posit subsequently, then the product of the roots is greater than 1. As a result, one of the roots must necessarily lie between 0 and 1, and another root be greater than 1. The transversality condition (non-divergence of long-term capital) restricts us to the root with a value between 0 and 1, written λ_1 . The reason for this is that since the product of the roots is equal to

$$\frac{1+r}{(1+\rho)(1+g)}$$

the root greater than 1 is greater than

$$\frac{1+r}{(1+\rho)(1+g)}.$$

Using transformed variables, program (1) is written:

$$\text{Max} \sum_{j=0}^{\infty} \frac{1}{(1+\eta)^j} \left[p_0 \bar{D}_j' - w_0 - p_0^l I_j' \right.$$

$$\left. + \frac{\gamma}{2} p_0^l \frac{1}{\bar{I}_0} (K_j' - K_{-1}')^2 - \frac{\mu}{2} \frac{w_0}{\bar{N}_0} (N_j' - N_{-1}')^2 \right].$$

The usual transversality condition is written:

$$\lim_{j \to \infty} \frac{1}{(1+\eta)^j} K_j' = 0,$$

which effectively requires us to omit the root greater than

$$1 + \eta = \frac{1 + r}{(1 + \rho)(1 + g)}.$$

The general solution of the equation without the second member is therefore written:

$$K'_j - K' = \widetilde{A}\,\overline{\lambda}_1{}^{j+1}$$

Using (9), we can write the second member:

$$\theta^{j+2}(\bar{D}'_{-1} - \bar{\bar{D}}'_{-1})\frac{\mu\,w_0}{N_0(1+\eta)}\,e'_D\,e'_K + \theta^{j+1}(\bar{D}'_{-1} - \bar{\bar{D}}'_{-1})$$

$$\times\left(-w_0\,e''_{KD} - \frac{\mu\,w_0}{\bar{N}_0}\,e'_D\,e'_K\left(1 + \frac{1}{1+\eta}\right)\right)$$

$$+ \theta^j(\bar{D}'_{-1} - \bar{\bar{D}}'_{-1})\frac{\mu\,w_0}{\bar{N}_0}\,e'_D\,e'_K,$$

which will be noted as $\theta^j\,(\bar{D}'_{-1} - \bar{\bar{D}}'_{-1})\,(A\theta^2 + B\theta + C)$.
A special solution of (10) whose first member will be written:

$$E\,(K'_{j+1} - K') + F\,(K'_j - K') + G\,(K'_{-1} - K')$$

can be found in the form:

$$K_j{}' - K' = x\,\theta^{j+1}$$

if θ differs from λ_1, which is the root with a value between 0 and 1 of the characteristic polynomial of (10). We then have:

$$E\times\theta^2 + F\times\theta + G\,x = (\bar{D}'_{-1} - \bar{\bar{D}}'_{-1})\,(A\,\theta^2 + B\,\theta + C)$$

Hence

$$x = (\bar{D}'_{-1} - \bar{D}'_{-1}) \frac{A\,\theta^2 + B\,\theta + C}{E\,\theta^2 + F\,\theta + G}.$$

For the sign of x to be non-ambiguous, we subsequently assume that $\theta < \lambda_1$ (therefore, that $E\theta^2 + F\theta + G > 0$) and that $\theta < \bar{\lambda}_1$, root with a value between 0 and 1 of $A\theta^2 + B\theta + C$ (there is only one $\bar{\lambda}_1$ root, for $C > 0$ and $A+B+C<0$).
Hence $\dfrac{A\,\theta^2 + B\,\theta + C}{E\,\theta^2 + F\,\theta + G} > 0.$

λ_1 and $\bar{\lambda}_1$ cannot be classified.

The condition $\theta < \lambda_1$ and $\theta < \bar{\lambda}_1$ means that the expected speed of the return of demand to its long-term level is high. In particular, it exceeds the speed of adjustment of capital to its long-term target, which seems logical enough.

In these conditions,

$$\frac{A\,\theta^2 + B\,\theta + C}{E\,\theta^2 + F\,\theta + G} > 0.$$

The general solution of the equation with the second member is written :

$$K'_j - K' = \tilde{A}\,\lambda_1^{j+1} + (\bar{D}'_{-1} - \bar{D}'_{-1}) \frac{A\,\theta^2 + B\,\theta + C}{E\,\theta^2 + F\,\theta + G}\,\theta^{j+1}$$

The value of $\tilde{A}$ will be set allowing for the initial value of K'. We should therefore have:

$$K'_{-1} - K' = \tilde{A} + (\bar{D}'_{-1} - \bar{D}'_{-1}) \frac{A\,\theta^2 + B\,\theta + C}{E\,\theta^2 + F\,\theta + G}$$

Hence the final general solution:

$$K'_{-1} - K' = \left(K'_{-1} - K' - (\bar{D}'_{-1} - \bar{D}'_{-1}) \frac{A\theta^2 + B\theta + C}{E\theta^2 + F\theta + G} \right) \lambda_1^{j+1}$$

$$+ (\bar{D}'_{-1} - \bar{D}'_{-1}) \frac{A\theta^2 + B\theta + C}{E\theta^2 + F\theta + G} \theta^{j+1}$$

$$= (K'_{-1} - K') \lambda_1^{j+1} + (\bar{D}'_{-1} - \bar{D}'_{-1}) \frac{A\theta^2 + B\theta + C}{E\theta^2 + F\theta + G} (\theta^{j+1} - \lambda_1^{j+1})$$

We can analyze the variance of the eigen value λ_1, which stands for the inertia of capital.

The characteristic polynomial of the left-hand member of (10) is written:

$$\frac{\lambda^2}{1+\eta} - \left(1 + \frac{1}{1+\eta} + \frac{w_0 \, e_K''^2}{(\mu w_0/\bar{N}_0) \, e_K'^2 + \gamma \, (p_0^I/\bar{I}_0)} \right) \lambda + 1 = 0.$$

The solution smaller than 1 (λ_1) grows with the adjustment-cost parameters (γ and μ). The bigger these are, the more inert the capital. e'_K is given by (7)

$$\left(-e'_K = \frac{p_0^I}{w_0} \left(1 - \frac{1-\delta}{1+r}(1+\rho) \right) \right)$$

Normally, if demand D grows, e'_K decreases and λ_1 increases.

APPENDIX 3

Analysis of the dynamics of (19)

The product of the roots of D (λ) is $(1 + \eta)^2 > 1$ if we make the same assumption as before, that is, $1 + r > (1 + \rho)(1 + g)$.

The root sum is the opposite of the coefficient of λ_3, namely:

$$2+2\frac{1+r}{(1+g)(1+\rho)} -f''_{N^2}\frac{p_0}{w_0}\frac{\bar{N}_0}{\mu}\frac{(1+r)}{(1+g)(1+\rho)} -f''_{K^2}\frac{p_0}{p'_0}\frac{\bar{I}_0}{\gamma}\frac{1+r}{(1+g)(1+\rho)} > 4.$$

We observe that:

$$D(0) = \frac{(1+r)}{(1+g)(1+\rho)} \cdot \frac{1+r}{(1+g)(1+\rho)} > 1 \qquad \text{(the root product)}$$

$$D(1) = (f''_{N^2} f''_{K^2} - (f''_{KN})^2) \left(\frac{p_0}{p'_0}\frac{p_0}{w_0}\frac{\bar{I}_0}{\gamma}\frac{\bar{N}_0}{\mu}\frac{(1+r)^2}{(1+g)^2(1+\rho)^2} \right) > 0$$

if the production function f meets the standard conditions — which is especially the case with the Cobb-Douglas function chosen here.
Let us consider the element of D(λ) :

$$\lambda^2 + \lambda \left(f''_{K^2}\frac{p_0}{p'_0}\frac{\bar{I}_0}{\gamma}\frac{1+r}{(1+g)(1+\rho)} - \frac{1+r}{(1+g)(1+\rho)} - 1 \right) + \left(\frac{1+r}{(1+g)(1+\rho)} \right)$$

written Q (λ) .

$$Q(0) = \frac{1+r}{(1+g)(1+\rho)} > 0;$$

$$Q(1) = f''_{K^2} \frac{p_0}{p_0^1} \frac{\bar{I}_0}{\gamma} \frac{1+r}{(1+g)(1+\rho)} < 0.$$

The product of the roots $Q(o)$ being greater than 1, $Q(\lambda)$ has a single root between 0 and 1, written λ_q.

$$D(\bar{\lambda}_Q) = -\bar{\lambda}_Q^2 (f''_{KN})^2 \frac{p_0}{p_0^1} \frac{p_0}{w_0} \frac{\bar{I}_0}{\gamma} \frac{\bar{N}_0}{\mu} \frac{(1+r)^2}{(1+g)^2(1+\rho)^2} < 0.$$

D therefore has at least two zeros between 0 and 1. As the sum of D's roots is greater than

$$2 + 2 \frac{1+r}{(1+g)(1+\rho)}$$

D has only two zeros between 0 and 1. The two other roots correspond to divergent dynamics, and the corresponding integration constants will therefore equal zero.

CHAPTER 7
Production functions with the energy factor :
estimations for the major OECD countries*
by
Patrick Artus and Claude Peyroux

Introduction

The main purpose of this chapter is to present estimates of production functions comprising three factors (capital, labor and energy) for five leading industrial   countries: the United States, West Germany, France, Japan and Britain. These estimates make it possible to measure the degree and speed of response to relative price changes in investment, employment and demand for energy in each country. As a result, they contribute to an understanding of the economic adjustment mechanisms consecutive to oil-price rises. The final estimates given concern production-factor demand equations (for investment, energy and employment) in a putty-clay context-in other words, assuming that substitution between these factors can only take place at the time the equipment is purchased. The final estimates yield the parameters of the production function itself, as well as the year-by-year values of the price elasticities relating to factor demands. They therefore enable us to take a stand in the debate on the impact of oil-price rises on labor productivity, notably in the United States. Berndt [1980] argues for a very weak impact on the basis of a mainly statistical analysis that is open to question. The reader will see that we reach an entirely different conclusion.

The model used here is not a short-term one, since capital is not regarded as fixed but as gradually adjusting itself like the variable factors to the optimal levels simultaneously resulting from relative prices. This constitutes an improvement not only, of course, on simple, isolated energy-demand functions (ex. Hogan [1980]) but also on many energy-specific models (ex. Nordhaus [1980]) and on production functions that specify an a priori ranking of factor

* Originally published as "Fonctions de production avec facteur energie: estimations pour les grands pays de l'OCDE," Annales de l'INSEE 44:3-39, 1981.

demands (Helliwell and MacRae [1980]).

Naturally, our estimates afford only a very partial insight into the effects of rises in energy prices or the real wage rate. At the end of the chapter, we can merely simulate, using other relative-price hypotheses, how firms would have behaved assuming they had minimized their costs and, by meeting demand, had no influence on volume traded. This approach is totally different from those elaborated in the sizable literature that has blossomed in recent years on the subject of overall economic reactions to oil-price rises (ex. Bruno and Sachs [1979a, 1979b] ; Bruno [1978]). Such work generally presents short-term, fixed-capital models organized around a goods-supply function (which therefore supposes profit maximization) and an overall demand function, together with a labor-market equilibrium and a hypothesis on the formation of the real wage rate. What happens, then, in these models if the price of imported intermediate goods rises ? Output falls, and so must the demand for labor, putting a downward pressure on the wage rate. The slower the fall in wages, the larger the drop in supply in the short term. The short-term model is often accompanied by a money-market equilibrium, as in Bruno and Sachs [1979a] or Findlay and Rodriguez [1977]. This equilibrium determines the consumption price and — since the price of domestic output derives from the goods-market equilibrium — the exchange rate as well.

The literature also contains occasionally surprising findings on the long-term effects of price rises in imported intermediate goods. For example, Obstfeld [1980] shows that, in the long run, the return to the economy's equilibrium utility (and therefore to a certain level of expenditure) and to an equilibrium in the goods market definitely implies an improvement in the terms of trade and, in some cases, generates current-account surpluses. To induce constant utility and balance the goods market, a larger share of demand needs to be channeled toward imported goods, since profitable supply diminishes. This shift is ensured by the improvement in the terms of trade.

This chapter is divided into three parts. Part 1 provides a summary of recent work and empirical findings regarding the introduction of energy in production functions. Part 2 reports on two types of econometric results: an estimate of translog cost-function parameters, so as to allow comparisons with existing results which often use this approach and to permit the testing of certain hypotheses on the weak separability of production factors ; and an estimate of the putty-clay production functions, which constitute the core of the chapter.[1] Part 3 applies the results of these estimates to simulate the effects of historical changes in factor relative prices. As explained above, these effects are limited to the demanded quantities of capital, labor and energy.

1. SUMMARY OF RECENT WORK

Recent years have seen considerable advances in the study of possibilities for substitution between the energy factor and non-energy inputs, labor and capital as a function of their prices at a given output level. These developments are due to the theoretical investigations into new multi-factor production functions that impose no restrictions on elasticities of substitution, unlike the classic Cobb-Douglas and CES functions.

The earliest empirical research in the mid-1970s involved an estimate for the United States of a production function with three or four factors : capital (K), labor (L), energy (E) and non-energy raw materials (M). Subsequently, international comparisons between the major developed countries were effected using time series and country cross-section series. This work raised the complex issue of defining the links between capital and energy. For some authors these two factors are substitutable ; for others, complementary. The first attempt to reconcile these two viewpoints was to regard capital and energy as complementary in the short run and substitutable in the long run. Berndt and Wood [1978] offer another interpretation of this difference by distinguishing between two ways in which energy-price changes influence capital demand. By considering K and E bundled together as S, the authors identify a direct substitution effect inside S between K and E, and an effect due to the substitution between S and the other production factors at a given level of total output. For Berndt and Wood, the substitution or complementarity of K and E therefore depends on the relative size of the direct effect compared with the indirect effect.

We begin with a brief survey of the findings of certain investigations carried out in recent years. Space precludes a discussion of all the studies on the subject. Those described here provide a good illustration of the issue and

---

1. Most of the estimates given in this chapter were calculated as part of the medium-term forecast modeling program of the OECD Economics and Statistics Department.

yield interesting results. The most noteworthy in our view are the following :

- Berndt and Wood [1975] offered what is regarded as the protoype of the KLEM models, as the authors were the first to use a four-factor translog cost function.
- Griffin and Gregory [1976] analyze the effects of substitution between K and E using intercountry cross-section data and not single-country time series as in the preceding paper. Here again a translog cost function is used, but with only three factors (K, L, E). The reason given by the authors is that the estimate of a cost function based on single-country time series can serve only to determine the short-term effects where E and L are substitutable and E and K complementary−whereas in the long term E and K are expected to be substitutable.

- Pindyck [1979] explores the links between K and E by decomposing energy into four components − coal, oil, gas and electricity− using international time series. Pindyck initially uses a homogeneous translog cost function for the prices of the four types of energy (see Appendix to this chapter) ; he assumes the total cost function to be once again translog, but not homogeneous.

- Berndt and Wood [1978] analyze the reasons for the discrepancies among econometric findings on the capital-energy connection. The authors focus on the following explanation : the usual omission of non-energy raw materials (M) biases the estimated elasticities of substitution. For let us suppose that the f(K, L, E, M) function offers weak separability into a bundle V = g (K, L, E) and M (see Appendix). We then have :

$$Q = f (K, L, E, M) = h \{g (K, L, E), M) = t (V, M).$$

In these conditions, Berndt and Wood show that the price elasticities E_{ke} and E_{ek} (with Q constant) are provided by :

$$E_{ke} = E_{ke}^* + N_E \, E_{vv}$$
$$E_{ek} = E_{ek}^* + N_k \, E_{vv}$$

where :

E_{ke}^* and E_{ek}^* are the cross price elasticities of K and E with respect to the constant bundle V;

N_E and N_K are the optimal shares (see Appendix) of factors E and K in the total production cost of V (cost function linked to g(K, L, E)) ;
E_{vv} is V's own-price elasticity, with Q constant.

Thus, in a three factor function we measure E_{ke} or E_{ek} , whereas in a four-factor function we measure E_{ke} or E_{ek} . Now if E_{ke} or E_{ek} is positive, $N_E E_{VV}$ or $N_k E_{vv}$ is always negative for E_{vv} is negative. Therefore the sign of E_{ke} will depend on the size of the two opposite effects E_{ke} and $N_k E_{vv}$.

The various studies performed lead to highly varying estimates of inter-factor elasticities of substitution. This may be due to the biases indicated by Griffin and Gregory [1976] and Berndt and Wood [1978]. To illustrate the discrepancy, we list in Table 1 the mean estimates obtained for these elasticities in six different studies on US manufacturing. In addition to the four summarized above, we have included the study by Ozatalay (similar to Pindyck [1979] as to the type of data but using four production factors instead of three) and the study by Hudson and Jorgenson [1974], which resembles Berndt and Wood's first paper [1975].

While there is a convergence on the seeming substitutability of capital and labor on the one hand, and labor and energy on the other, a great uncertainty appears to prevail as to the interaction — complementarity or substitutability — between capital and energy.

If we turn to the findings by Pindyck [1979] and Griffin and Gregory [1976] for the countries for which additional estimates are provided in the present chapter, we obtain Table 2.

For all countries, we find clearcut substitutabilities between all factors. It should be pointed out that none of these studies covers the period after the first oil crisis and that this can cause our results to differ significantly.

Investment and Factor Demand

TABLE 1.   **Elasticity of substitution for the United States**

Authors - estimate period	Capital/Labor A KL	Capital/ Energy A KE	Labor/Energy A LE
GRIFFIN and GREGORY 1955-1969..............................	0.06	1.07	0.87
HUDSON and JORGENSON 1947-1971..............................	1.08	- 1.39	2.16
BERNDT and WOOD 1947-1971..............................	1.01	- 3.53	0.68
PINDYCK 1959-1973..............................	1.41	1.77	0.05
OZATALAY 1963-1974..............................	1.08	1.22	1.03
BERNDT and WOOD 1947-1971..............................	-	- 6.84	-

TABLE 2.   **Elasticity of substitution for other countries**

Authors - estimate period	Capital/Labor A KL	Capital/ Energy A KE	Labor/Energy A LE
WEST GERMANY			
Pindyck..	0.71	0.66	1.23
Griffin-Gregory............................	0.50	1.03	0.78
FRANCE			
Pindyck..	0.72	0.56	1.17
Griffin-Gregory............................	0.41	1.05	0.78
BRITAIN			
Pindyck..	0.64	0.36	1.10
Griffin-Gregory	0.39	1.04	0.87
JAPAN			
Pindyck	0.70	0.74	1.15

2. ECONOMETRIC STUDY

The econometric study is arranged in two parts. In the first, we reestimate the conventional three-factor translog function (that is, in the putty-putty case) for four major countries.[2] This estimate allows us to test various hypotheses of weak separability (see Appendix) between labor (L) and the capital-energy bundle (K,E), as well as between energy and value added (K,L). In the second part, we estimate a putty-clay production function of the mixed CES/Cobb-Douglas type and of the two-level CES type (see Appendix). The estimates were calculated on annual series for 1963 to 1978 (or 1979) and concern all private-sector branches. The sources are national accounts, wholesale price indexes and International Energy Agency statistics.

2.1. Translog cost function

This estimate only requires a simultaneous estimate (here, using Zellner's minimum-distance method) of the equations for the optimal share of two of the three factors in total cost. We chose labor and energy (see Appendix). We tried, however, to accommodate cyclical swings by adding to these basic equations either the capacity utilization rate (calculated a priori from the survey variables) or its changes. We assumed here that factors are not at their optimal level when the capacity-utilization level is abnormal, or that the factors adjust to capacity utilization and that when the latter's level varies, the factor shares deviate from the optimum. The translog cost function does not lend itself well to the direct introduction of adjustment speeds. We are therefore led to the somewhat ad hoc addition of the utilization rate.

The results of these estimates are reported in Table 3.

In every case, a substitutability appears between labor and capital, and between labor and energy. The substitutability is particularly strong between capital and labor in West Germany, the United States and France; between labor and energy in the United States and West Germany. By contrast, the situations vary as regards the capital-energy relation. We find a limited substitutability in Britain and complementarity in all other countries. It remains to be determined whether this discrepancy is due to inter-country differences or to econometric difficulties (which we noted previously in the studies on the United States). Subsequent estimates will help to shed light on this question. The very low capital-energy substitutability for Britain occurs

---

2. We have not calculated this estimate for Japan, owing to the oddity — not to say implausibility — of the available series for that country's real energy consumption. We have also excluded Canada because of the difficulty of isolating its energy-sector investment, which has expanded considerably in recent years.

TABLE 3.   **Putty-putty translog function**

	Capacity utilisation rate				a_L	KL	LE	a_E
	Level		Variation					
	Labor	Energy	Labor	Energy				
Britain					0.14 (3.1)	- 0.13 (8.3)	- 0.01 (6.0)	0.026 (12.2)
	0.68 (3.5)	- 0.003 (0.3)			- 0.62 (2.8)	- 0.19 (9.5)	- 0.01 (4.1)	0.029 (2.3)
			- 0.06 (0.3)	0.01 (1.3)	0.14 (3.0)	- 0.13 (8.3)	- 0.01 (6.5)	0.027 (12.7)
France					0.33 (6.8)	- 0.06 (4.1)	- 0.028 (5.5)	0.009 (0.9)
	- 0.06 (0.2)	0.20 (3.5)			0.40 (1.3)	- 0.056 (3.0)	- 0.032 (8.0)	- 0.196 (3.3)
			- 0.03 (0.1)	0.03 (0.6)	0.33 (6.7)	- 0.059 (4.0)	- 0.028 (5.6)	0.009 (0.8)
West Germany					0.38 (4.1)	- 0.026 (1.3)	- 0.004 (1.1)	0.03 (2.8)
	0.26 (1.6)	0.02 (0.9)			0.07 (0.3)	- 0.038 (1.9)	- 0.008 (2.7)	0.013 (0.6)
			-0.24 (1.5)	0.04 (4.2)	0.40 (4.7)	- 0.021 (1.1)	- 0.003 (1.3)	0.021 (3.5)
United States					0.41 (4.0)	- 0.045 (1.5)	0.011 (2.3)	- 0.027 (1.9)
	0.04 (0.3)	- 0.01 (0.8)			0.31 (1.1)	- 0.060 (1.3)	0.006 (0.8)	- 0.026 (0.8)
			- 0.21 (2.4)	0.007 (0.8)	0.45 (4.9)	- 0.031 (1.2)	0.012 (2.2)	- 0.027 (1.8)

1. Coefficients of price logarithms in the cost function
2. Coefficients of price-logarithm products

KE	Labor share			Energy share			Partial elasticities of substitution in 1978		
	R	DW	SEE	R	DW	SEE	Capital-labor	Capital-energy	Labor-energy
- 0.019 (33.9)	0.82	0.92	0.025	0.99	1.82	0.0009	0.43	0.13	0.66
- 0.019 (20.2)	0.90	1.42	0.019	0.99	1.88	0.0009	0.14	0.14	0.66
- 0.019 (35.0)	0.82	0.94	0.025	0.99	1.85	0.0008	0.42	0.13	0.66
- 0.072 (21.7)	0.62	1.57	0.017	0.97	1.57	0.003	0.65	- 0.95	0.61
- 0.085 (19.8)	0.62	1.50	0.017	0.98	2.08	0.003	0.67	- 1.30	0.57
- 0.072 (21.3)	0.62	1.56	0.017	0.97	1.39	0.003	0.66	- 0.95	0.61
- 0.032 (10.2)	0.11	1.11	0.022	0.83	1.90	0.002	0.93	- 0.07	0.87
- 0.038 (12.7)	0.24	1.56	0.020	0.80	1.99	0.002	0.82	- 0.23	0.78
- 0.033 (15.6)	0.23	0.94	0.021	0.92	2.08	0.001	0.90	- 0.08	0.92
- 0.040 (12.1)	0.17	0.73	0.013	0.98	1.86	0.001	0.79	- 0.70	1.36
- 0.037 (0.3)	0.19	0.71	0.013	0.98	1.73	0.001	0.73	- 0.61	1.21
- 0.041 (11.7)	0.41	1.19	0.011	0.98	2.01	0.001	0.86	- 0.78	1.43

neither in Pindyck [1979] nor in Griffin and Gregory [1976].

The cyclical situation represented by the capacity-utilization rate is important, but to a degree and in a manner that vary with each country. The utilization-rate level significantly influences the make-up of total cost in Britain and France ; its variations are significant in West Germany and the United States. In theory, because of their high rigidity, we could have expected labor and capital to occupy larger shares of total cost in depression phases and smaller shares during an expansionary phase or a strong upswing. By contrast, energy consumption ought to respond closely to output changes, and its share of total cost should vary with the utilization rate. These effects are not observed consistently. A counter-example is provided by the positivity of the capacity-utilization rate in the equation for the labor-linked share of total cost in Britain.

2.2.   Separability tests

The test for weak separability is equivalent to a standard test for constraints on the coefficients of the two equations used (shares of labor and energy in total cost : see Appendix). Table 4 lists the values of the weighted sums of residual squares and Fischer's F statistics for the unconstrained estimates, the estimate with a weak-separability hypothesis for labor (where $\dfrac{\gamma_{KL}}{\gamma_{LE}} = \dfrac{a_K}{a_E}$), and the estimate with a weak-separability hypothesis for energy (where $\dfrac{\gamma_{KE}}{\gamma_{LE}} = \dfrac{a_K}{a_L}$).

These two types of separability are the most naturally plausible : machines representing a mix of capital and energy combined with labor ; or the standard national-accounting distinction between intermediate consumption of energy and value added.

Table 4 shows that no weak-separability hypothesis is rejected at the 5% level. The test therefore does not seem to be very powerful. Later in this chapter, we report on production functions with a weak-separability hypothesis for labor, which yielded better results on estimates of two-level CES type functions. Clearly it would have been better to be able to reject certain types of separability as early as this stage.

TABLE 4.   Tests for low separatibility

	S Unconstrained	S S separate	S E separate	F L separate	F E separate
United-States.............................	0.002 490 8	0.002 555 3	0.002 516 0	0.647	0.253
West Germany..........................	0.007 406 7	0.007 413 8	0.007 638 5	0.024	0.782
France..	0.004 508 5	0.005 260 9	0.004 523 0	4.172	0.080
Britain..	0.007 826 9	0.009 052 3	0.009 093 3	3.914	4.045

2.3. Putty-clay model

For this second group of estimates, we abandon the putty-putty model — on which the translog cost function is based — in order to test a putty-clay model, which seems to correspond more closely to reality (see Chapter 3 above for a definition of a test and its application to France). This switch is justified on the grounds that production technology is visibly hard to modify on the existing capital.

The production function used will be either of the mixed CES/Cobb-Douglas or two-level CES type. We shall use the first type when the elasticity of substitution between labor and the capital-energy bundle seems to approximate unity, as the equations to be estimated are much simpler. Also included here is the just-tested hypothesis of weak separability for labor.

The minimization of discounted expected production cost under a demand constraint determines the optimal factor quantities. These are also marginal, since we use a putty-clay model where the substitution applies only to the vintage of equipment to be installed. Firm behavior is assumed to be :

$$\text{Min } u_t\, I_t + w_t\, L_t + e_t\, E_t$$
$$H\,(I_t, L_t, E_t)$$

and the expression of factor demands, in the two-level CES function :

$$\left(\frac{I}{Q}\right)^*_t = Q_0^{-1} e^{-rT} \cdot \left[\left(a_K{}^\sigma + a_E{}^\sigma \left(\frac{e}{u}\right)_t^{1-\sigma}\right)^{\frac{\sigma_1-1}{\sigma-1}} + a_L\,\tau_1\left(\frac{w}{u}\right)_t^{1-\sigma_1}\right]^{\frac{\sigma_1}{1-\sigma_1}} \cdot$$

$$a_K{}^\sigma \cdot \left[a_K{}^\sigma + a_E{}^\sigma \left(\frac{e}{u}\right)_t^{1-\sigma}\right]^{\frac{\sigma_1-\sigma}{\sigma-1}}$$

$$\left(\frac{E}{\bar{\bar{Q}}}\right)_t^* = Q_0{}^{-1}e^{-rT}\cdot\left[\left(a_K{}^\sigma\left(\frac{u}{e}\right)_t^{1-\sigma} + a_E{}^\sigma\right)^{\frac{\sigma_1-1}{\sigma-1}} + a_L{}^{\sigma_1}\left(\frac{w}{e}\right)_t^{1-\sigma_1}\right]^{\frac{\sigma_1}{1-\sigma_1}}\cdot$$

$$a_E{}^\sigma\cdot\left[a_K{}^\sigma\left(\frac{u}{e}\right)_t^{1-\sigma} + a_E{}^\sigma\right]^{\frac{\sigma_1-\sigma}{\sigma-1}}$$

$$\left(\frac{L}{\bar{\bar{Q}}}\right)_t^* = Q_0{}^{-1}e^{-rT}a_L{}^{\sigma_1}\cdot\left[\left(a_K{}^\sigma u_t^{1-\sigma} + a_E{}^\sigma e_t^{1-\sigma}\right)^{\frac{\sigma_1-1}{\sigma_1}} + a_L{}^{\sigma_1} w_t^{1-\sigma}\right]^{\frac{\sigma_1}{1-\sigma_1}}\cdot w^{-\sigma_1}$$

where :

I: investment;

Q: desired production-capacity variation;

r: autonomous rate of technical progress;

e: energy price;

w: wage cost;

u: user cost of capital;

σ_1: elasticity of substitution between labor and the capital-energy bundle;

σ: elasticity of substitution between capital and energy;

E: optimal quantity of energy allocated to the new vintage;

L: optimal quantity of labor allocated to the new vintage;

H: represents the production function;

Q_0, a_k, a_L, a_E, are constants.

Like Ando, Modigliani, Rasche and Turnovsky [1974], followed by de Menil and Yohn [1977], we define the user cost of capital in a manner consistent with this intertemporal minimization as :

$$u = \frac{F}{1-v}\cdot P_I\cdot\frac{i-\overset{\circ}{w}}{1-[1-1/(1+i-\overset{\circ}{w})]^T}$$

which allows a return to a static minimization.

F : variable representing investment-specific taxation (tax deductions of 1967, 1968, 1969, 1975, 1976) ;

P_I : capital-goods purchase price ;

v : apparent rate of direct corporation tax, calculated as a moving average over a long period, since it is an expected rate ;

i : nominal long-term interest rate ;

ω : expected growth rate of wage cost (represented by a four-year lag ; no specific measure is available here).

T : equipment lifetime, assumed fixed.

As we use three production factors, we must also, in principle, define a user cost of energy u_e equal to :

$$u_e = e_t \frac{i - \overset{\circ}{w}}{i - \overset{\circ}{e}} \frac{1 - \left(\dfrac{1}{1 + i - \overset{\circ}{e}}\right)^T}{1 - \left(\dfrac{1}{1 + i - \overset{\circ}{w}}\right)^T}$$

The user cost is equal to the current energy price only if e = w , that is, if firms expect unit labor and energy costs to grow at the same pace. In the empirical study that follows, we have made such an assumption so as to avoid complications and arbitrary definitions. The issue unquestionably calls for further study. To simplify the notations, we shall designate as e what should be called u_e .

In the CES and Cobb-Douglas functions, the factor-demand expressions become :

$$\left(\frac{I}{Q}\right)_t^* = Q_o^{-1} e^{-rT} \left(\frac{a}{1-a}\right)^{1-a} a_K{}^\sigma \left(\frac{w}{u}\right)_t^{1-a} \left[a_K{}^\sigma + a_E{}^\sigma \left(\frac{e}{u}\right)_t^{1-\sigma}\right]^{\frac{a}{1-\sigma} - 1}$$

$$\left(\frac{E}{Q}\right)_t^* = Q_o^{-1} e^{-rT} \left(\frac{a}{1-a}\right)^{1-a} a_E{}^\sigma \left(\frac{w}{e}\right)_t^{1-a} \left[a_K{}^\sigma \left(\frac{u}{e}\right)_t^{1-\sigma} + a_E{}^\sigma\right]^{\frac{a}{1-\sigma} - 1}$$

$$\left(\frac{L}{Q}\right)_t^* = Q_o^{-1} e^{-rT} \left(\frac{1-a}{a}\right)^a \left(\frac{u}{w}\right)_t^a \left[a_K{}^\sigma + a_E{}^\sigma \left(\frac{e}{u}\right)_t^{1-\sigma}\right]^{\frac{a}{1-\sigma}}$$

where a is the capital-energy bundle's share of total cost. The desired production-capacity variation will, as in Bischoff [1971], be written simply as :

$$\overline{Q} = \sum_i a_i \left(X_{-i} - (1 - \delta) X_{-i-1}\right)$$

where :

    X : output (calculated, in this three-factor function, as value added + intermediate consumption of energy) ;

    δ : capital depreciation rate, assumed constant and applied equally to all vintages. For the estimate we carry Q into the right-hand member and include the a_i coefficients among the parameters to be estimated

2.4. Putty-clay model estimate

This estimate was calculated in two different ways : by estimating the investment equation alone ; by estimating all three factor-demand equations using the maximum-likelihood method (the three equations have some of the parameters in common.[3]). For the other two cases, we have had to construct series for the factor quantities allocated to the new equipment vintage on the basis of total quantities used. We have decided to confine ourselves initially to the investment equation, as it is the only one for which statistical observations of the explained variable are available. Furthermore, as the variables explained in the equations given above originate in the production function, they correspond to a full utilization of production capacity.

If EF is total employment, we can define EF*, the employment occurring at full capacity utilization, as :

$$EF^* = EF. \frac{\overline{Tu}}{Tu}$$

where T_u is the capacity utilization rate and T_u its mean. We can then measure L, marginal employment, by :

$$L = EF^* - (1 - \delta) EF^*_{-1} = \frac{\overline{Tu}}{Tu} EF - (1 - \delta) \frac{\overline{Tu}}{Tu_{-1}} EF_{-1}$$

that is, the difference between present optimal employment and the preceding optimal employment that persists on unscrapped equipment. The same calculation can be made for energy consumption.

a. Investment equation alone

The findings are reported   in Tables 5 and 6. For Britain, West Germany and Japan, we had to use a two-level CES production function, as the elasticity of substitution with labor was visibly smaller than unity. In this case, the equation to be estimated became highly non-linear and very difficult, obliging

---

3. As mentioned in the tables of results, we have had to posit a priori certain lag coefficients on production as equal to the values obtained in the estimate of the investment equation alone; certain elasticities of substitution have had to be subjected to iterative procedures. This was due to the estimation difficulties we encountered.

TABLE 5. Three-factor investment function estimates

CES + Cobb-Douglas function

	Constant	Labor coefficient in Cobb-Douglas	Capital/Energy elasticity of substitution	Energy-price expectation lag	Accelerator lag				Autonomous technical progress	R	DW	See
					a	a	a	a				
West Germany	- 1.6 (1.9)	0.25 (1.8)	0.60 (2.6)	1 year	0.31 (14.1)	0.30	0.25 (22.7)	0.14 (7.8)	- 0.006 (0.7)	0.99	2.01	0.026
	- 2.7 (1.8)	0.50	0.78 (3.1)		0.32 (16.0)	0.30	0.24 (21.8)	0.14 (12.7)	- 0.019 (6.9)	0.98	1.99	0.028
France	- 1.7 (3.1)	0.63 (2.7)	0.37 (1.6)	3 years	0.40 (4.9)	0.37 (4.4)	0.23		- 0.029 (1.7)	0.97	1.04	0.052
United States	- 2.9 (3.6)	0.92 (3.3)	0.26 (1.4)	2 years	0.24 (10.0)	0.30	0.28 (23.3)	0.18 (15.0)	0.005 (0.9)	0.96	2.19	0.033
	- 2.1 (63.0)	0.65	0.14 (1.0)		0.24 (10.0)	0.30	0.28 (25.4)	0.18 (16.4)	0.009 (2.6)	0.96	1.98	0.033
Japan	0.09 (1.6)	0.36 (2.4)	0.30 (2.3)	2 years	0.19 (4.7)	0.30	0.31 (15.5)	0.20 (10.0)	- 0.022 (1.3)	0.98	1.98	0.037
	0.09 (1.6)	0.52	0.40 (5.7)		0.18 (4.5)	0.30	0.31 (15.5)	0.21 (10.5)	- 0.039 (6.3)	0.98	2.10	0.037

1. Set a priori as equal to the share of labor in total cost.

TABLE 6.   **Three-factor investment function estimates**

Two-level CES function

	Constant	Labor/(Capital and Energy) elasticity of substitution	Capital/Energy elasticity of substitution	Energy-price expectation lag	Accelerator lag				Autonomous technical progress	R	DW	See
					a	a	a	a				
Britain	- 0.52 (4.9)	0.20	0.41 (1.2)	1 year	0.16 (4.4)	0.30	0.32 (17.8)	0.22 (12.2)	0.004 (1.5)	0.94	1.58	0.033
West Germany	- 2.29 (5.2)	0.50	0.60 (3.6)	1 year	0.33 (16.5)	0.30	0.23 (22.9)	0.14 (14.0)	- 0.011 (5.8)	0.98	2.28	0.028
Japan	- 0.94 (18.7)	0.50	0.28 (4.5)	2 years	0.18 (5.0)	0.30	0.31 (17.2)	0.21 (11.7)	- 0.020 (3.4)	0.98	1.94	0.035

1. Coefficient obtained by iterative procedure

us to use an iterative procedure on one of the elasticities of substitution instead of estimating it directly. Where we kept a mixed CES/Cobb-Douglas function,[4] we constrained the labor coefficient in the Cobb-Douglas function to be equal to labor's share of total cost when the coefficient spontaneously diverged from that share too sharply.

We find considerable differences among the capital-energy elasticities of substitution estimated for each country : virtually no substitution in the United States ($\sigma = 0.14$), moderate substitution in France, Japan and Britain (σ between 0.30 and 0.40) and very high substitution in West Germany (σ in the 0.60 range). This may seem surprising, as one assumes industrial structures to be fairly similar in all these countries.

The elasticity of substitution between labor and the capital-energy bundle was constrained to 1 for France and the United States [5] ; we find 0.50 for West Germany and Japan, and a remarkably low 0.20 for Britain.

We can also use these estimates to calculate the elasticity of demand for energy relative to its price. This is, of course, the elasticity characteristic of the new vintage, which applies to total energy consumption only in the long run, after all the capital stock has been replaced.[6] The means obtained are :

United States	0.28
West Germany	0.64
France	0.49
Britain	0.35
Japan	0.48

---

4. We also report our findings for West Germany and Japan in this case. For Britain, the elasticity of substitution with labor is too low to enable us to do so.

5. After being found very close to one. In an initial study with a two-level CES function, the optimal values obtained in this first stage (after an iterative procedure in steps of 0.05 on σ) were 1.00 for France and 1.10 for the United States.

6. This price elasticity is given in the CES + Cobb-Douglas case by :

$$ -\sigma + (a - 1 + \sigma) \cdot a_E{}^\sigma \cdot \left(a_k{}^\sigma \left(\frac{u}{\rho} \right)^{1-\sigma} + a_E{}^\sigma \right)^{-1} $$

and by :

$$ -\sigma + \frac{(\sigma - \sigma_1)\, a_E{}^\sigma}{a_k{}^\sigma \left(\dfrac{u}{e} \right)^{1-\sigma} + a_E{}^\sigma} + \sigma_1\, a_E{}^\sigma \frac{p^{\sigma - \sigma_1}}{p^{1-\sigma_1} + a_L{}^{\sigma_1} \left(\dfrac{u}{e} \right)^{1-\sigma_1}} $$

where

$$ P = \left[a_k{}^\sigma \left(\frac{u}{e} \right)^{1-\sigma} + a_E{}^\sigma \right]^{\frac{1}{1-\sigma}} $$

in the double CES case.

TABLE 7.   **Simultaneous estimate of investment, energy and labor :**

CES + Cobb-Douglas function

	Lagged labor	Investment constant	Labor constant	Energy constant	Capital/Energy elasticity of substitution	Accelerator			
						a	a	a	a
West Germany	0.13 (6.5)	- 1.77 (7.2)	793 (2.9)	1956 (1.7)	0.45 (2.2)	0.32 (6.4)	0.30	0.24 (10.0)	0.14 (5.8)
United-States	0.22 (3.9)	- 2.09 (99.8)	- 3.55 (6.8)	- 4.86 (39.4)	0.10 (1.2)	0.28 (28.9)	0.30	0.26 (28.9)	0.16 (17.8)

	Autonomous technical progress	Investment			Labor			Energy		
		R	DW	See	R	DW	See	R	DW	See
West Germany	- 0.016 (2.7)	0.97	1.64	0.028	0.88	2.19	0.049	0.31	2.36	0.182
United States	0.007 (3.1)	0.94	1.59	0.032	0.25	0.17	0.146	0.24	1.52	0.256
France	0.018 (3.6)	0.78	1.89	0.11	0.55	1.84	0.061	0.72	2.47	0.152

1. Coefficients set a priori.

TABLE 8.   **Simultaneous estimate of investment, energy and labor :**

Two-level CES function

	Investment constant	Labor constant	Energie constant	Lagged labor	Elasticity of substitution L, (K-E)	Elasticity of substitution K, E	Accelerator			
							a	a	a	a
Britain	- 0.51 (115)	- 5.53 (12.9)	- 2.82 (13.8)	0.52 (9.0)	0.20	0.35 (2.5)	0.16 (5.7)	0.30	0.32 (22.9)	0.22 (15.7)
Japan	- 0.86 (24.9)	- 8.30 (13.9)	- 3.68 (19.5)		0.50	0.19 (4.9)	0.18	0.30	0.31	0.21

	technical progress	Investment			Labor			Energy		
		R	DW	See	R	DW	See	R	DW	See
Britain	0.004 (2.2)	0.94	1.59	0.029	0.84	2.19	0.112	0.10	1.71	0.208
Japan	- 0.016 (3.4)	0.97	1.17	0.035	0.87	1.32	0.192	0.24	1.52	0.56

1. Coefficients set a priori.
2. Coefficients obtained by iterative procedure.

Two countries stand out as atypical : the United States, where energy consumption is virtually unresponsive to price ; and West Germany, where it is extremely so.

b. Simultaneous estimate of demand for the three factors

The results are listed in Tables 7 and 8. By adding lagged labor to the equation, we introduced the possibility that the labor allocated to the new vintage could adjust slowly to its optimal level. The elasticities of substitution obtained are close to those found with the investment equation alone, although generally somewhat lower between capital and energy. The same country ranking appears. We can observe that the response of factor demands to output changes also exhibits a wide diversity. The response is very prompt in France, prompt in West Germany and the United States, and highly spread out over time in Britain and Japan, where the accelerator is no doubt also responsible for smaller swings.

It is also interesting to determine whether energy price rises stimulate investment or not. Of course, that depends on the relative intensity of substitution between capital and energy, and between labor and the capital-energy bundle. The form chosen for the production function naturally forces a capital-energy substitution in the inner CES, but not overall.

Finally, more expensive energy leads to investment growth :

- in the CES + Cobb-Douglas case, if $1 - a < \sigma$ (a : labor coefficient) ;
- in the double CES case, if σ (capital/energy) $> \sigma_1$ (labor/capital/ energy) ; this condition, however, is necessary but not sufficient.[7]

In the CES + Cobb-Douglas case, the first condition is met only for West Germany when the investment equation alone is estimated ; it never occurs when the three factor-demand equations are estimated simultaneously. In the two-level CES, the second condition is always met only for Britain. Therefore, we observe that in most cases (France, Japan, the United States, possibly West Germany) energy savings are achieved through capital savings and an increased use of labor. Macroeconomically speaking, investments linked to energy savings do not stimulate the economy.

---

7. In this case, the derivative of I* with respect to $\underline{e}$ is complicated, and there is no variable-independent analytical condition that allows it to be positive.

These findings can be compared with the ones obtained using the translog cost function applied to a putty-putty model. The latter analysis reveals that in two countries   West Germany and Britain there is an overall presumption of substitutability between capital and energy. For these countries, the translog cost function estimate yielded a positive or very slightly negative partial elasticity of substitution (Britain and West Germany respectively). Conversely, both approaches confirmed that higher energy prices reduced investment in the United States and France. The two sets of findings are thus wholly consistent.

3.   INTERPRETATION : EFFECTS OF RELATIVE-PRICE SHIFTS BY COUNTRY

3.1.   Relative prices

The estimate of putty-clay production functions for the major OECD countries provides estimates of the elasticities of substitution between capital, labor and energy and enables us to interpret observed changes in production-factor productivity. The estimates reported in this section are derived from the investment equation alone, owing to the statistical uncertainty affecting the series on employment and energy allocated to the new vintage.

Labor and energy variations are linked to the full-capacity optimal employment and energy coefficients, which can be measured by means of the equation investment's estimated parameters (such as elasticity of substitution and rate of technical progress) and the capacity utilization rate. For labor, we get :

$$L^{**} = l^* \cdot \bar{Q}$$

where :

L** : marginal demand for labor, optimal, at full capacity ;
l*   : optimal (marginal) labor coefficient, measured by means of the investment equation parameters ;
$\bar{Q}$: gross desired change in capacity, defined earlier ;

and :

$$EF^{**} = EF^{**}_{-1} (1 - \delta) + L^{**}$$

where :

EF** : optimal total employment at full capacity ;
   σ : capital depreciation rate ;

and lastly :

$$EF^* = EF^{**} \frac{Tu}{\overline{Tu}}$$

where:

EF* : effective optimal total employment ;
Tu: capacity utilization rate (with a mean of $\overline{Tu}$).

Finally, we estimate an equation for the adjustment of observed employment to optimal employment :

$EF = \lambda EF_{-1} + (1 - \lambda) EF^*$, used to effect the simulations reported below. The same treatment is applied to intermediate energy consumption. We shall now analyze the impact on investment, employment and energy consumption of changes in relative factor prices in the United States, France, Britain and West Germany in the light of these estimates, assuming constant demand and output.

The changes in the relative price of energy were fairly similar in all countries (Table 9) : it fell in the second half of the 1960s, especially in Britain, regained its 1964 level in 1971 or thereabouts, then rose sharply in 1974. The series used for West Germany, however, shows that the energy price was lower there than in the other countries at the end of the period.

The long-term change in the relative price of labor and capital (which can be interpreted as a real wage rate) varies widely from one country to another : between 1964 and 1978, the increase was 20-30 % in the United States, approximately 200 % in West Germany and Britain, and 240 % in France, which recorded the heaviest such distortion in prices. These long-term differences are largely due to those relative to the change in the real wage rate. From 1964 to 1978, per capital wage costs rose by 24 % in the United States, 54 % in Britain, 82 % in West Germany and 89 % in France. In the short run, the fluctuations generally stemmed from changes in the expected real interest rate and in investment incentives. The patterns for each country can be summarized as follows :

- *United States*: : The widest swings occurred in 1975-1976, when the real interest rate was nearly equal to zero, causing the relative cost of labor to grow, and in 1977-1978, when the opposite trend prevailed.

- *France* : The swings in the relative capital-labor cost were very abrupt. In 1968-1969, we observe the effects of wage rises (27 % in two years) and investment incentives, followed in 1972-1973 by the effects of low interest rates. In 1975 and 1976, all factors combined to drive up the relative cost of labor : low interest rates, heavy wage increases (the average real wage rate rose 7.3 % in two years) and tax incentives to investment. Finally, in 1979, the expected rise in inflation reduced the user cost of capital.

- *Britain*: In 1970, strong inflation drove down the real interest rate, while wage costs soared (+13 %), causing a sharp rise in the relative price of labor. The user cost of capital was high in 1973 and 1974, owing to real interest rate levels (4 % and 7.8 % respectively). By contrast, from 1976 on, real interest rates remained negative, the user cost stayed low and the relative cost of labor stayed high.

- *West Germany* : The most notable changes were: a rise in the relative cost of labor in 1970-1971 (due to very steep increases in the wage rate : 16.5 % in 1970 and 11.1 % in 1971), followed by a drop in 1973-1974 (due to the levels reached by the real interest rate : 3.7 % in 1973 and 5.2 % in 1974), and a recovery in 1975, coinciding with the renewed fall in interest rates and tax relief on investment.

3.2. Effect of relative prices

We now turn to a country-by-country analysis of the impact of relative-price changes. The method used is the following: taking the estimates of optimal capital, labor and energy coefficients for each vintage of equipment, we calculate what the investment, employment and energy consumption would have been :

i. if the relative price of energy and capital had stayed at its 1964 level ;
ii. if all the relative prices had stayed at their 1964 level.
We further assume that *demand, and therefore output and installed capacity,*

kept their historical values, as did prices. Of course, this is a purely notional hypothesis, for the variance on investment and employment would have entailed changes in output, wages and prices. The hypothesis is particularly unrealistic for France and West Germany, where autonomous technical progress is strong, leading to a sharp fall in the demand for labor even if its relative price does not rise. We shall now examine the four countries in succession.

TABLE 9.   **Relative factor prices**

1964 = 100

	United-States		France		Britain		West Germany	
	I	II	I	II	I	II	I	II
1964	100	100	100	100	100	100	100	100
1965	105.2	99.5	104.6	95.8	102.0	98.9	100.9	92.7
1966	105.0	97.7	110.2	95.0	108.7	98.8	102.9	88.1
1967	108.1	98.5	110.2	89.5	114.8	100.8	108.4	94.4
1968	111.6	94.3	133.7	99.9	113.3	95.7	115.6	99.9
1969	112.3	90.4	154.2	103.7	107.2	86.0	118.2	91.5
1970	110.4	91.9	144.7	93.6	124.1	88.6	128.6	88.9
1971	115.7	101.3	159.4	105.2	139.4	98.4	152.3	101.0
1972	117.6	99.1	177.3	105.9	155.1	100.3	169.6	105.0
1973	119.2	102.6	201.8	111.4	141.2	84.0	150.6	92.3
1974	120.2	144.7	202.4	175.1	120.3	96.5	162.5	110.2
1975	127.8	166.7	237.2	182.2	173.3	134.9	192.6	134.4
1976	137.1	167.6	243.9	181.2	222.3	178.3	183.0	124.6
1977	129.3	162.4	229.1	167.6	230.2	197.5	206.3	131.1
1978	120.9	147.4	240.8	158.0	193.5	154.3	206.2	124.9
1979			277.3	191.8				

I   Labor price
      Capital price

II   Energy price
      Capital price

- *United States* (Table 10)

As the elasticity of substitution between capital and energy was weak, the 1974 rise in the energy price induced a substitution of labor for the energy-capital bundle. This rise caused investment to shrink by about 7 % from 1975 to 1978, and energy consumption by 4.3 % by the end of the period. Employment, on the other hand, expanded, and the estimated equations indicate that between 1974 and 1978 the energy-price rise trimmed annual labor productivity gains by about 0.5 %.

The relative price of labor had a strong and contrary effect. Its increase steadily boosted investment (by an average 7.8 % in this second scenario), thereby also expanding energy consumption (by nearly 6 % in 1978) and slowing employment. If the relative prices of all factors had remained constant, employment, according to the estimates, would have been 3.1 % higher by the end of 1978. This figure is, however, much lower than the one obtained for France and West Germany as shown below.

- *France* (Table 10)

As with the United States, the elasticities of substitution in France were such that the 1974 energy-price rise cut both investment and energy consumption (by 7.2 % and 10.5 % respectively by the end of the period). It naturally increased employment and, according to these estimates, caused labor productivity gains to fall by an annual 0.7 % from 1975 to 1979.

It is a totally academic hypothesis to assume that real wage costs could have remained constant from 1964 on. The exercise nevertheless shows that in France — owing to the sizable increase in the relative cost of labor, and because of the unitary elasticity of substitution between labor and the capital-energy bundle — substantial changes appeared in the production-factor levels, especially after 1968 and in 1975-1976: investment and energy consumption were sharply stimulated, and employment sharply curtailed (by 15.8 % in the simulation for 1979 !).

- *Great Britain* (Table 10)

Unlike the two preceding countries, the elasticity of substitution between capital and energy estimated for Britain is greater than that between labor and the capital-energy bundle (0.41 versus 0.2). The 1974 energy-price rise therefore caused investment to expand — by more than 2 % on average between 1975 and 1978. Given the very low elasticity for labor, energy-price changes had little effect on employment and virtually no observable impact on labor-productivity growth in recent years. The fall in the relative price of energy and capital at the end of the 1960s had led to an energy overconsumption of about 2 %, which appears with a lag linked to the relative-cost expectation lag. The distortion in the relative price of labor observed for the past fifteen years had the usual effects (more investment, less employment, more consumption), but was also diminished by the lower value of the elasticity of substitution. Overall, changes in factor costs have certainly had less impact in Britain than in the other countries.

- West Germany (Table 10)

As in Britain, the 1974 energy-price rise boosted investment, according to our estimates based on the investment equation alone. Between 1975 and 1978, the investment level was on average 3.2 % higher than if the relative price of energy had remained constant. The induced fall in energy consumption reached 4 % by the end of 1978, and additional employment 1 %. These figures are considerably lower than in France and the United States, for the corresponding elasticity of substitution is only 0.5 in West Germany. A heavy overconsumption of energy is observed until 1974, owing to its low relative price (94.8 with respect to capital from 1965 to 1973, with 1964 = 100). The sharp rise in the relative cost of labor unquestionably caused significant changes in production-factor demand. Under the (extreme) hypothesis that all relative prices remained at their 1964 levels, employment in 1978, according to this calculation, would have been 22.2 % higher than its observed level ! We must repeat that this is a purely academic assumption, but it nevertheless suggests the magnitude of the phenomena at work. The substitution of capital for labor accelerated after the large wage increases of 1970-1971 and the investment incentives of 1975.

The distortion in relative prices varied from country to country, affecting them in different ways. The variance is due either to the distortion intensity (for example, the small rise in the relative cost of labor in the United States) or to the characteristics of factor substitution in each country. Our main findings are the following: (1) in two countries, France and the United States, the 1974 energy-price rise was a major factor in slowing labor productivity; (2) in two countries too, France and West Germany, the increase in the

TABLE 10.   Deviations induced by stability of relative prices[1] (%)

	Investment		Total employment		Energy consumed	
	I	II	I	II	I	II
United-States						
1964.........................	0	0	0	0	0	0
1970.........................	- 1.2	- 7.3	0.7	2.2	- 0.1	- 3.0
1974.........................	2.8	- 8.8	0.2	3.3	- 0.6	- 6.3
1975.........................	6.5	- 9.2	- 0.2	3.3	0.4	- 6.1
1976.........................	7.7	- 12.2	- 0.7	3.5	2.0	-5.7
1977.........................	7.5	- 9.0	- 1.3	3.6	3.5	- 5.8
1978.........................	6.4	- 6.0	- 2.2	3.1	4.3	- 5.9
France						
1964.........................	0	0	0	0	0	0
1970.........................	- 0.6	- 23.3	0.6	4.6	- 1.6	- 9.5
1974.........................	4.1	- 35.0	0.2	10.9	- 0.8	- 19.6
1975.........................	6.3	- 40.0 ·	- 0.5	12.0	2.0	- 19.9
1976.........................	7.5	- 40.3	- 1.3	13.0	4.6	- 20.7
1977.........................	7.0	- 38.2	- 2.4	13.5	6.6	- 21.8
1978.........................	6.2	- 40.5	- 3.4	14.0	8.1	- 22.7
Britain						
1964.........................	0	0	0	0	0	0
1970.........................	0.5	- 3.1	- 0.2	- 0.1	- 1.2	- 1.9
1974.........................	0.1	- 2.9	0.1	0	- 1.7	- 4.4
1975.........................	- 1.4	- 10.2	- 0.1	0.4	- 1.8	- 4.6
1976.........................	- 2.8	- 15.3	0	0.6	- 0.3	- 3.9
1977.........................	- 3.3	- 16.3	0.1	0.8	2.1	- 2.7
1978.........................	- 2.0	- 12.5	- 0.3	0.6	4.1	1.8
West Germany						
1964.........................	0	0	0	0	0	0
1970.........................	1.5	- 7.2	0.8	3.7	- 2.6	- 4.4
1974.........................	- 1.2	- 17.2	0.8	13.8	- 2.5	- 10.1
1975.........................	- 3.7	- 24.3	1.1	16.4	- 0.9	- 9.7
1976.........................	- 2.8	- 22.1	0.3	18.1	0.9	- 9.6
1977.........................	- 3.4	- 26.0	- 0.6	19.6	2.0	- 9.7
1978.........................	- 2.7	- 25.5	- 1.0	22.2	4.0	- 9.6

1. Variance between the levels of investment, etc., calculated assuming a constant price and the levels
obtained with observed relative prices, using the estimated equations, on a year-by-year basis.
I = Constant relative price of energy ; II = All relative prices constant.

relative cost of labor greatly distorted the production technique; (3) in Britain, relative prices had only a moderate effect on the economy.

Conclusion

Until now, energy was generally omitted from the production functions used in macroeconomic models. The oil-price rises of 1974 and 1979 require that gap to be filled, for the estimates calculated show that firms' energy consumption behavior is not passive. On the contrary, they make decisions on energy at the same time as on employment and investment. Moreover, the major industrial countries appear to be very dissimilar in this respect throughout our study. The underlying differences in productivity gains and unemployment among these countries can be explained if we include that third production factor.

The investigations reported on here must, of course, be supplemented by further work, as they employ many simplifying hypotheses. Ideally, one should be able to endogenize not only the input substitution but also scrappings, without imposing a given behavior a priori as is customary in capital-vintage functions. The analysis should include price formation, which is the key element of supply behavior. These various issues are already being examined. However, we have preferred to assume a fixed scrapping rate here, as no statistics on the volume of discarded equipment are available for any country. Although one can endogenize the scrapping rate by using the factor-demand equations, such a procedure is questionable owing to its indirect nature and the confusion it creates between scrapping and replacement investment. Nevertheless, it is very likely that sale prices are insufficiently flexible to preserve the return on total capital stock when wages or intermediate-consumption prices undergo violent swings. Our simulations, which are linked to the impact of energy-price rises, therefore undoubtedly overestimate the production capacity and consequently the employment subsequent to these rises. On the other hand, they underestimate the latter's effect on investment, since a part of the scrapped equipment must be replaced.

Appendix

The following is a brief but, in our view, necessary summary of the few basic characteristics of the three-factor functions used in this chapter. Fuss and MacFadden [1979] give a full analysis of production functions, cost functions, their close interrelation (production-duality theory) and their properties. The authors notably furnish full demonstrations of the results we shall use.

A. Translog cost function

Introduced by Christensen, Jorgenson and Lau [1973], the transcendental logarithmic (translog) cost function approximates to the second order by a power of Log P any function that can be differentiated continuously twice. The translog function is written :

$$\text{Log } G = \text{Log } a_0 + \sum_i a_i \text{ Log } P_i + \frac{1}{2} \sum \sum \gamma_{ij} \text{ Log } P_i \text{ Log } P_j$$

with :

i, j = K, L, E (as in all that follows) ;

$a_0 > 0$

P_i = price of production factor i.

A.1. *All cost functions are homogeneous of degree one in price*

They therefore exhibit a constant return to scale :

$$\mu = \left(\sum_i P_i \frac{\partial G}{\partial P_i} \right) / G$$

equal to unity. This property entails the conditions :

$$\sum_i a_i = 1 \quad \forall i \qquad \text{and} \qquad \sum_j \gamma_{ij} = 0 \quad \forall j$$

The equality of the second partial derivatives of Log G imposes the equalities :

$$\forall ij \quad \gamma_{ij} = \gamma_{ji}$$

as well as :

$$\sum_i \gamma_{ij} = 0 \qquad \forall i$$

A.2. *Optimal share of factors in total cost : M_i*

$$M_i = \frac{X_i^* P_i}{\sum_i X_i^* P_i}$$

with X_i^* = demand for factor i at the optimum.

The simple expression of M_i results from the following important property, called Shephard's lemma : at the optimum, we have $X_i^* = \frac{\partial G}{\partial P_i}$,

which allows a straightforward deduction of factor-demand functions from the cost function. We get :

$$M_i = \frac{P_i}{G} \cdot \frac{\partial G}{\partial P_i} = \frac{\partial \, \text{Log} \, G}{\partial \, \text{Log} \, P_i} = a_i + \sum_j \gamma_{ij} \, \text{Log} \, P_j$$

Thus the translog cost function has the crucial property that *the share of factors in total cost M_i are a linear function of the parameters to be estimated.* This explains the function's frequent use.

A.3. *Elasticity of substitution : A_{ij}*

In the case of a three-factor function, there are several definitions of the elasticity of substitution that generalize the two-factor case. We shall use only one of these definitions in this chapter: Allen's partial elasticity of substitution A_{ij} (Allen [1938]). Uzawa's theorem [1962] allows a simple expression of A_{ij} , for we obtain :

$$\forall i \neq j \quad A_{ij} = \frac{G \cdot \frac{\partial^2 G}{\partial P_i \, \partial P_j}}{\left(\frac{\partial G}{\partial P_i}\right)\left(\frac{\partial G}{\partial P_j}\right)} \quad ; \quad A_{ii} = \frac{G \cdot \frac{\partial^2 G}{\partial P_i^2}}{\left(\frac{\partial G}{\partial P_i}\right)^2}$$

where $\forall i, j \; A_{ij} = A_{ji}$. Diewert [1974] showed that the existence of a cost function implies that the A_{ii} own elasticities *are negative.*

The calculation and use of the A_{ij} elasticities of substitution are justified by their connections with the E_{ij} price elasticities. For we have the equations :

$$E_{ij} = \frac{\partial \, \text{Log} \, X_i}{\partial \, \text{Log} \, P_i} = M_j A_{ij}$$

As :

$$\forall i \quad \sum_i E_{ij} = 0,$$

it follows that :

$$\forall i \quad \sum_j M_j A_{ij} = 0$$

Given that :

$$\forall_i A_{ii} < 0$$

we get :

$$\forall i \quad \sum_{j \neq i} M_j A_{ij} > 0$$

Thus, in a three-factor function, the elasticities of substitution are all positive, or one of them is negative and the other two positive. If $A_{ij} > 0$, then $E_{ij} > 0$ and the two factors i and j are substitutable. If $A_{ij} < 0$, then $E_{ij} < 0$ and the two factors i and j are complementary. As a result, in the three-factor case : either all the factors are substitutable ; or two factors are complementary and the third is substitutable for the first two.

A.4. Separability

The separability of a production function $f(X_1, X_2, X_3, ..., X_n)$ is characterized by the independence of the marginal substitution rate :

$$R_{ij} = \frac{\partial f}{\partial X_i} / \frac{\partial f}{\partial X_j}$$

between two factors with respect to a change in another factor X_k . In the general case, the separability can be either strong or weak. Let S be a partition of N, the set of n production factors, such that :

$$N = N_1 \cup N_2 ... \cup N_s \text{ and } N_r \cap N_t = O \quad \forall_r \neq t$$

Strong separability :

$$\frac{\partial R_{x_i\ x_j}}{\partial X_k} = 0 \qquad \forall i \in N_i, \forall j \in N_j \text{ et } R \notin N_i \cup N_j$$

Weak separability :

$$\frac{\partial R_{x_i\ x_j}}{\partial X_k} = 0 \qquad \forall i, j \in N_e \text{ et } R \notin N_e$$

These two definitions are valid for a particular combination of factors or for any combination. In the second case, the function is said to have strong or weak overall separability. An even more restrictive form of this property is additivity. A production function is additive if it takes the form :

$$f(X) = \sum_{i=1}^{s} f^i(X_i)$$

where the f_i functions have the same form as f.

Berndt and Christensen [1973b] have shown that $\underline{f}$ is homogeneous and strongly separable if $A_{ik} = A_{jk}$ for all $i \in N_i, j \in N_j$ and $k \notin N_i \cup N_j$. Similarly, $f(X)$ is homogeneous and has weak separability if $A_{ik} = A_{jk}$ for all i, j $\in N_t$ and K $\notin N_t$. If $n = S$, than all A_{ij} are equal (i≠j). Finally, as a result of the duality between production function and cost function, all cost functions possess dual separability along a price partition if and only if the matching production function is homogeneous and possesses dual separability along the same partition. The same applies to additivity.

Separability is fairly easy to characterize with the translog cost function. If, for example, we test the separability of the three factors into two elements $Z = (K, E)$ and L, the condition is written : $A_{KL} = A_{EL}.$

This leads to one of the following (M_E and M_K being positive) :

- Either

$$\gamma_{kl} = \gamma_{ke} = 0$$

in which case $A_{KL} = A_{EL} = 1$; the translog function becomes a Cobb-Douglas function in V and L ;

- or

$$\frac{\gamma_{KL}}{\gamma_{KE}} = \frac{M_K}{M_E}$$

in which case we can demonstrate the relations :

$$\frac{M_K}{M_E} = \frac{a_K}{a_E} = \frac{\gamma_{KL}}{\gamma_{KE}} = \frac{\gamma_{KK}}{\gamma_{KE}} = \frac{\gamma_{KE}}{\gamma_{EE}}$$

The ratio of capital and energy shares in total cost is constant.

A.5. *Estimate of the translog cost function*

It is sufficient to make a simultaneous estimate (using Zellner's method here) of the optimal share-of-total-cost equations for two of the three factors. We chose labor and energy. Given the homogeneity and equality of second derivatives, we get :

$$M_L = a_L - (\gamma_{LE} + \gamma_{kl}) \, Log \, P_L + \gamma_{LE} \, Log \, P_E + \gamma_{KL} \, Log \, P_k$$
$$M_E = a_E - (\gamma_{LE} + \gamma_{KE}) \, Log \, P_E + \gamma_{LE} \, Log \, P_L + \gamma_{kE} \, Log \, P_k$$

which enable us to determine the five parameters a_L, a_E, $\lambda_{kE}, \lambda_{LE}$.

Statistical test of the factors' separability into two elements,
Z = (K, E) and L.

We have seen that in this case $\quad \dfrac{\gamma_{KL}}{\gamma_{LE}} = \dfrac{a_K}{a_L} \quad$ leaving one less parameter

to estimate. Let N be the number of observations and S^2 a quadratic form of the residuals weighted by the estimated variance-covariance matrix of the two equations' residuals. Without restrictions on γ_{ij}, *we obtain* $\quad S^2 = S_1^2$; with restrictions, $S^2 = S_2^2$. We test the separability, knowing that if it is verified, the variable :

$$\frac{S_2^2 - S}{S_1^2 / (2N - 5)}$$

obeys the Fisher-Snedecor probability distribution with 1 and 2N-5 degrees of freedom.

B.   Mixed CES/Cobb-Douglas or two-level CES production functions

We assume the capital-energy bundle Z is obtained with the aid of a classic CES (Constant Elasticity of Substitution) production function between K and E of the form :

$$Z = \left[a_k \, K^{\frac{\sigma-1}{\sigma}} + a_E \, E^{\frac{\sigma-1}{\sigma}} \right]^{\frac{\sigma}{\sigma-1}}$$

with $0 < \sigma < \infty$.

This function has constant returns to scale , it is additive , and the elasticity of substitution between K and E is constant and equal to σ .

Hanoch [1975a,b] has shown that CES production functions are only a special type of what he calls CRES (Constant Ratio Elasticity of Substitution) functions, with a ratio of $r_{ij}^k = \dfrac{A_{ik}}{A_{jk}}$. Hanoch has also shown that CES functions are "auto-dual" in Houthakker's sense : the cost function and the production function have the same form.

We further assume that the production factors Z and L are linked :

- either by a new CES function, in which case the overall production function, called two-level CES,[8] is written :

$$Q = Q_0 \left[Z^{\frac{\sigma_1-1}{\sigma_1}} + a_L \, L^{\frac{\sigma_1-1}{\sigma_1}} \right]^{\frac{\sigma_1}{\sigma_1-1}}$$

with : $0 < \sigma_1 < + \infty$ $Q_0 > 0$

---

8. Introduced by K. Sato [1967].

- or, when σ_1 is close to unity, by a Cobb-Douglas function, which gives :

$$Q = Q_0 \, Z^a \, L^{1-a}$$

with : $0 < a < 1$.

This makes it more complex to calculate factor demands or optimal shares, notably their non-linearity with respect to the parameters. However, the complexity of the calculations is largely offset by their greatly enhanced flexibility.

CHAPTER 8
Investment with demand, labor
and financial constraints :
the estimation of a multi-regime model*
by
Patrick Artus and Pierre-Alain Muet

Introduction

The conventional approaches to the investment decision of the firm consider either that the firm is always demand-constrained or that it never faces any constraint at all. This chapter is an attempt to enlarge that traditional framework in two directions. First, by combining the two previous approaches and by considering that the firm is sometimes constrained on its output (effective demand) and sometimes not constrained at all (notional demand); next, by including other kinds of constraints as well, like a credit or a labor constraint. The outcome is a distinction between five possible "regimes", each corresponding to a different explanation of observed investment.

Although conventional econometric studies tend to reject the notional-demand model in favor of the effective-demand model with demand constraint (Chapters 2 and 5 above) they conclude, nevertheless, that there is a combined influence of demand and profits. These are said to affect the level of desired investment (Fouquet et al [1978]; Le Marois [1979]; Chapter 2 above), or the speed of its realization (Artus, Muet, Palinkas and Pauly [1981]; Coen [1971]; Eisner [1978 a]; Gardner and Sheldon [1975]; Sarantis [1979]). These models, which can be justified, for example by the aggregation of firms faced with different situations, do not, however, make it possible to distinguish the influence of the various constraints at different periods.

Nor do they provide a very adequate description of these. As regards

* Originally published as "Investment, output and labor constraints and financial constraints : the estimation of a model with several regimes", <u>Recherches Economiques de Louvain</u> 50, no. 1-2, 1984.

available cash-flow, for example, its influence on investment will only appear in situations in which the cash-flow realized and the possibilities of other financing are slight with respect to the desired investment (reflected in the other expressions of effective demand). The only model capable of embodying this constraint is the general expression of effective investment demand as the minimum of the different potential demands. The object of this chapter is precisely to apply the techniques for estimating models with rationing (Fair and Jaffee [1972]; Laffont and Monfort [1976]; Ginsburgh, Tishler and Zang [1980]) to the general expression of investment demand.

These techniques make it possible to determine the parameters of the models adopted, while also showing, in an endogenous manner, the periods in which the various constraints were active or, at least, most probably active. We begin with the specification of the model; we go on to report the estimate of the multi-regime model first omitting, then partially including, a possible constraint on employment.

1. THE SPECIFICATION OF THE MODEL

1.1. Theoretical foundations

We have adopted a putty-clay production function and we suppose that firms determine their investment by maximizing the flow, discounted at the period t, of the profits they expect to make during the new equipment's lifetime, that is :

$$(1) \quad \text{Max} \sum_{i=1}^{T} \frac{p_i \, \Delta Q_i}{(1+r)^i} - p_I \, I - \sum_{i=1}^{T} \frac{w_i \, \Delta L_i}{(1+r)^i}$$

where p_i : production price at date $t + i$;

ΔQ_i : additional production made possible by the investment at date $t + i$;

p : price of the investment at date t;

I : investment at date t;

w_i : wage cost per capita at date $t + i$;

ΔL_i : labor allotted to the date t of investment at date $t + i$;

r : discount rate;

T : expected lifetime of equipment, assumed to be exogenous and fixed (this is only an approximation: see Ando, Modigliani, Rasche and Turnovsky [1974]).

We suppose that technical progress is entirely embodied in the equipment and that physical depreciation is negligible during the equipment lifetime. The production capacity (ΔQ_i) and the labor (ΔL_i) allotted to the investment (I) are thus constant. Let p and α be the expected long-term rate of inflation and that of the increase in real wages respectively. We can rewrite (1) in the following form:

$$(2) \quad \underset{Q, I}{\text{Max}} \quad \sum_{i=1}^{T} \frac{p (1 + \dot{p})^i \Delta Q}{(1 + r)^i} - p_I I - \sum_{i=1}^{T} \frac{w (1 + \dot{p} + \alpha)^i \Delta L}{(1 + r)^i}$$

or

$$(3) \quad \underset{\Delta Q, I, \Delta L}{\text{Max}} \quad \{p' \Delta Q - cI - wL\}$$

in which :

$$(4) \quad p' = p \, \frac{1 + \dot{p}}{1 + \dot{p} + \alpha} \, \frac{r - \dot{p} - \alpha}{r - \dot{p}} \, \frac{1 - \left(\dfrac{1 + \dot{p}}{1 + r}\right)^T}{1 - \left(\dfrac{1 + \dot{p} + \alpha}{1 + r}\right)^T}$$

$$(5) \quad c = \frac{p_I \, (r - p - \alpha)}{(1 + \dot{p} + \alpha) \left[1 - \left(\dfrac{1 + \dot{p} + \alpha}{1 + r}\right)^T \right]}$$

From this point on, we shall call p' "production price" and c "user cost of capital." The latter is corrected by a variable representing investment – specific tax measures. Numerically, p is estimated by comparing the interest rates of indexed and non-indexed bonds (see de Ménil and Porcher [1977]); α is estimated on the basis of the long-term average of increases in real wage costs ; T is set at 14 years.

Thus , the investment decision of firms depends on expected costs, but also on the constraints observed or expected on the various markets. The desired production capacity can be constrained by the expected trend of demand, the manpower allotted to investment by the labor available, and investment itself by the credit available. This is because we consider the credit market to be in a state of disequilibrium, as interest rates are exogenous, being determined essentially by the public authorities. If the firms' demand for credit (investment + change in inventories + miscellaneous - profits) is lower than the banks' credit supply, the investment is not subjected to a financial constraint. In particular, the investment is independent of profits. If, however, demand exceeds the supply of available credit, investment will be rationed.

At this point, we have to make several simplifying assumptions in order to remain in the static framework of equation (3). Investment is of course an intertemporal decision, and in the most complete model all future expected constraints would influence the current investment level. Such a model, however, would be very complicated to estimate, as the constrained or unconstrained paths of output would need to be explicitly determined. We have therefore chosen to add a static output constraint :

$$(6) \qquad \Delta Q \le \overline{\Delta Q}.$$

$\overline{\Delta Q}$ is the capacity change needed to satisfy expected demand, and has to be understood as being a *medium-term expected constraint and not only a current constraint*. A temporarily depressed demand would not, of course prevent firms from investing in order to satisfy future demand. A similar problem arises with the credit supply constraint. We may assume that credit rationing is not expected, but, to keep to a static constraint, we must also assume that after a period when credit has been rationed no compensating rise in investment occurs.

Thus, investment is determined by the following system :

$$(7) \quad \begin{cases} \text{Max } [\, p'\, \Delta Q - c \ I - w \ \Delta L \,] \\ \Delta Q = F\,(I, \Delta L) \\ \Delta Q \le \overline{\Delta Q} \\ \Delta L \le \overline{\Delta L} \\ I \le \overline{I} \end{cases}$$

where F : marginal production function
               $\overline{\Delta Q}$: capacity change needed to satisfy expected demand
               $\overline{\Delta L}$: labor available
               $\overline{I}$: maximum investment corresponding to the available credit

supply.

1.2. The different regimes and the analytical form of functions

The solution of system (7) yields eight possible regimes. However, if we limit ourselves to the determination of investment, the number of regimes is reduced to five. In the absence of a financial constraint ($I < \bar{I}$), four regimes can be envisaged :

a) *Notional demand* $\Delta L < \overline{\Delta L}, \Delta Q < \overline{\Delta Q}$

(8) $\quad F_I' = \dfrac{c}{p'} \quad , \quad F_L' = \dfrac{w}{p'} \quad , \quad \Delta Q = F(I, \Delta L)$

b) *Effective demand (given demand)* $\Delta L < \overline{\Delta L}, \Delta Q = \overline{\Delta Q}$

(9) $\quad \dfrac{F_I'}{F_L'} = \dfrac{c}{w} \quad , \quad \overline{\Delta Q} = F(I, \Delta L)$

c) *Constraint on the labor market* $\Delta L = \overline{\Delta L}, \Delta Q < \overline{\Delta Q}$

(10) $\quad F_I' = \dfrac{c}{p'} \quad , \quad F(I, \overline{\Delta L}) = \Delta Q$

d) *Demand and labor constraint* $\Delta L = \overline{\Delta L}, \Delta Q = \overline{\Delta Q}$

(11) $\quad F(I, \overline{\Delta L}) = \overline{\Delta Q}$

The fifth regime corresponds to a financially constrained investment :

e) *Financial constraint* $I = \bar{I}.$

Finally, the hypothesis that the three constraints will coincide ($\overline{\Delta Q} = F(\bar{I}, \overline{\Delta L})$) has a probability of zero. Rather than adopting a particular form of the *ex ante* production function F, we have preferred to calculate first-order approximations of the exact expressions for the different forms of the investment demand as in Chapter 5 above, by supposing :

- that the production function has returns to scale of order v ;

- that it has an elasticity of substitution σ.

The calculations are laborious, requiring differentiation, Euler's Law, and the definition of the elasticity of substitution. They yield : [1]

- for notional demand :

$$(12) \quad \text{Log } I = - (\beta\sigma + \frac{1 - \beta}{1 - v}) \text{ Log } (\frac{c}{p'}) - \beta (\frac{1}{1 - v} - \sigma) \text{ Log } (\frac{w}{p'})$$

$$< 0 \qquad\qquad\qquad < 0$$

- for effective demand :

$$(13) \quad \text{Log } I = \frac{1}{v} \text{ Log } \Delta\bar{Q} + \sigma\beta \text{ Log } (\frac{w}{c})$$

- for demand with labor constraints :

$$(14) \quad \text{Log } I = - \frac{v}{\left(1 - \frac{1}{v}\right)\eta - \frac{v - \eta}{\sigma}} \text{ Log } \left(\frac{c}{p'}\right) + \left[\frac{1 - \frac{v}{\eta}}{1 - \frac{v}{\eta (1 + \sigma - \frac{\sigma}{v})}}\right] \text{ Log } \Delta\bar{L}$$

$$< 0 \qquad\qquad\qquad > 0$$

- for demand with labor and demand constraints :

$$(15) \quad \text{Log } I = \frac{1}{v (1 - \beta)} \text{ Log } \Delta\bar{Q} - \frac{\beta}{1 - \beta} \text{ Log } \Delta\bar{L}$$

$$\text{where} \quad \beta = \frac{w \Delta L}{w \Delta L + c I} \quad \text{and} \quad \eta = \frac{c I}{p' Q}$$

---

[1] The signs under the coefficents are, in principle, ambiguous ; those given here are, however, by far the most probable.

All these expressions are, of course, first-order approximations, supposing that β and η (the respective cost shares) fluctuate little — which is in fact the case. They have the advantage of being considerably easier to estimate than expressions taken, for example, from a CES function.

The four preceding expressions have been given for the case in which there is no embodied technical progress. If we suppose that there is autonomous technical progress (Hicks neutral), Q (and correlatively p') must be corrected by $e^{\gamma t}$; if the progress concerns labor (Harrod neutral), L and w' must be corrected by $e^{\gamma t}$; if it concerns capital (Solow neutral), I and c' must be corrected by $e^{\gamma t}$. Thus, general formulae can be obtained in all the cases examined.

In order to estimate model (7) completely, we must still define $\overline{\Delta Q}$, $\overline{I}$, and $\overline{\Delta L}$.

1.3. Expected increase in demand

If the time required for realizing investment is θ periods, investment decided upon at each period *t* depends on the gap between the demand expected for period t + θ and the total capacity left after scrapping in this same period, that is :

$$\overline{\Delta Q} = D^a_{t+\theta} - (1 - \delta)\, CAP_{t+\theta-1}$$

$D^a_{t+\theta}$: expected demand for period t + θ
$CAP_{t+\theta-1}$: capacity installed at date t + θ - 1
δ : scrapping rate, assumed to be, in an initial approximation, exogenous and fixed (it depends on T, and is constant only in a situation of steady growth).

We suppose, furthermore, that this growth ΔQ is always positive, which excludes disinvestment in the case of a sharp downturn in demand, and we have chosen adaptive expectations. If, as in Bischoff [1971], we neglect the discrepancy between the installed capacity in t + θ - 1 and the expected demand for this period:

$$(16) \quad \Delta\overline{Q} = \sum_{i=1}^{M} (Q_{-i} - (1-\delta)\, Q_{i-1})$$

We have also adopted an expression correcting this value by the production-capacity utilization rate (see Fouquet and al. [1978]), but this correction does not significantly modify the results obtained in estimating the given-demand model. Thus, we shall limit ourselves below to specification (16).

1.4. Credit supply

We have adopted a highly traditional credit model (see Melitz [1976]; Sterdyniak and Villa [1977]). The cost of distribution by banks is:

$$CD = r_m \cdot RE + C_g \cdot CR$$

where r_m : money-market interest rates;
            RE : refinancing by banks;
            C_g : cost of of credit management;
            CR : distributed credit.

From the equilibrium of the banks' account:

$$RE = CR - DE + RO$$

where

     DE : deposits collected;
     RO : required reserves $(RO = \tau \cdot DE)$;
     τ : rate of required reserves.

we deduce:

$$CD = r_m \ CR \left(1 - \frac{DE}{CR} + \pi\, \frac{DE}{CR}\right) + C_g \ CR$$

The equality of money supply and its counterparts yields :

$$M = CR + S + \text{other}$$

M : money supply
S : gold and foreign currency reserves and accumulated monetary financing by the Treasury.

From which :

$$(17) \quad CD = r_m \ CR \left[1 - \frac{\dfrac{DE}{M}(1-\tau)}{1 - \dfrac{S}{M} - \dfrac{\text{others}}{M}} \right] + C_g \ CR.$$

We suppose that banks maximize their profits. r_b represents the interest rate on credits. The risk of insolvency of firms is taken into account in the form of a marginal cost that grows with their indebtedness. (CR / p_IK) and decreases with their rate of return (π_{-1}). By equalizing the banks' marginal income and marginal cost, we obtain :

$$r_b = r_m \left[1 - \frac{\dfrac{DE}{M}(1-\tau)}{1 - \dfrac{S}{M} - \dfrac{\text{others}}{M}} \right] + C_g + C_0 \ \pi_{-1} + C_1 \ \frac{CR}{p_I \ K}$$

This gives us the linearized equation adopted for credit supply, which also incorporates credit rationing : [2]

$$(18) \quad \frac{CR}{p_I K} = \lambda_0 + \lambda_1 \ r_b - \lambda_2 \ r_m - \lambda_3 \ \frac{DE}{M} \ r_m - \lambda_4 \ r_m \ \tau + \lambda_5 \ \frac{S}{M} \ r_m + \lambda_6 \pi_{-1} + \lambda_7 \ T + \lambda_8 \ FAC$$

---

[2] FAC = Ease of credit avaibility as measured in the French business surveys.

We have also used an autoregressive formulation representing the inertia of credit distribution or the fact that the supply decision does not concern total credits, but only new loans and those that are up for renewal :

$$(19) \quad \frac{CR}{p_I K} = \lambda_0 + \lambda_1 \, r_b - \lambda_2 \, r_m + \lambda_3 \, \frac{DE}{M} \, r_m - \lambda_4 \, r_m \tau + \lambda_5 \, \frac{S}{M} \, r_m + \lambda_6 \, \pi_{-1}$$

$$+ \lambda_7 \left(\frac{CR_{-1}}{p_I K} \right) + \lambda_8 \, T + \lambda_9 \, FAC$$

We suppose that the credit market can be in disequilibrium, as is the case if the rate of interest on debts r_b does not adjust supply to demand. If the credit demand corresponding to the desired investment exceeds the credit supply, the investment is rationed and is determined by:

$$(20) \quad \overline{I} = \Pi \, p_I \, K + CR - CR_{-1} + \text{exogenous} = p_I \, K \left(\Pi + \frac{CR}{p_I K} - \frac{CR_{-1}}{p_I K} + \frac{\text{exogenous}}{p_I K} \right)$$

in which the exogenous variables are the non-bank credits, firms' non-investment costs, leased equipment, and so on. This brings us closer to the disequilibrium hypothesis tested by Laffont and Garcia [1977] than to the credit-market equilibrium hypothesis implicit in several French models. We have carried out Sim's test between the rate of indebtedness of firms ($CR / p_I K$) and the rate of growth of credits provided to firms on the one hand, and the rate of interest on debt r_b on the other. Both tests led to the conclusion that the rate r_b is exogenous (the corresponding Fischer tests are $F_{7,32} = 1.08$ and $F_{7,32} = 1.54$).

1.5. Marginal available labor

This labor force is equal to the sum of non-frictional unemployment and the jobs eliminated by equipment scrapping :

(21) $\overline{\Delta L} = U_{-1} - U_{-1}^F + \delta_1 EF_{-1}$

where

> U : unemployment;
> U^F : frictional unemployment;
> EF : total employment;
> δ_1 : scrapping rate adapted to employment, (differs from the rate for capital because of technical progress).

If, as in Artus, Laroque and Michel [1984], frictional unemployment is represented by :

$U^F = \mu_0 + \mu_1 (EF_{-1} + U_{-1})$,

we get :

(22) $\overline{\Delta L} = \mu_0 + (1 - \mu_1) U_{-1} + (\delta_1 - \mu_1) EF_{-1}$

which will be used from here on.

The estimation of the complete model has been broken down into two stages. In the first stage, we shall suppose that the constraint of the availability of labor is not active, and the complete model can be estimated by using the techniques described previously. In the second stage, we shall reintroduce the possibility that this constraint will apply, and the estimation will be more problematic.

2. ESTIMATES THAT OMIT THE LABOR CONSTRAINT

Thus, model (7) is reduced to cases a, b, and e, with three possible expressions for investment : [3]

---

[3] We omit from (12), (13), and (23) the time trend resulting from technical progress with the neutrality chosen here.

-notional demand

$$(12)\quad \text{Log } I = -\left(\beta\sigma + \frac{1-\beta}{1-v}\right)\text{Log}\left(\frac{c}{p^{\cdot}}\right) - \beta\left(\frac{1}{1-v} - \sigma\right)\text{Log}\left(\frac{w}{p^{\cdot}}\right) + \varepsilon_N = \text{NOT} + \varepsilon_N$$

- effective demand

$$(13)\quad \text{Log } I = \frac{1}{v}\text{Log } \overline{\Delta Q} + \sigma\beta \text{ Log}\left(\frac{w}{c^{\cdot}}\right) + \varepsilon_E = \text{EFF} + \varepsilon_E$$

- investment constrained by the credit supply

$$(23)\quad \text{Log } I = \text{Log } p_I K + \text{Log}\left(\Pi - \frac{CR_{-1}}{p_I K} + \frac{\text{exogenous}}{p_I K} + \lambda_0 + \lambda_1 r_b - \lambda_2 r_m + \lambda_3 \right.$$

$$\left. \frac{DE}{M} r_m - \lambda_4 r_m \tau + \lambda_5 \frac{S}{M} r_m + \lambda_6 \Pi_{-1} + \lambda_7 \frac{CR_{-1}}{p_I K} + \lambda_8 T + \lambda_9 \text{ FAC} \right) + \varepsilon_c = \text{CF} + \varepsilon_c$$

As a constraint on demand or on the credit supply reduces the optimum investment, the general expression of investment demand is : [4]

$$(24)\quad \text{Log } I = \text{Min } (\text{NOT} + \varepsilon_N , \text{EFF} + \varepsilon_E , \text{CF} + \varepsilon_c)$$

The likehood function of the model is derived (see Laffont and Monfort [1976] for the calculation principles) and maximised using the VA13AD routine of the Harwell library. The estimation has been done on **quarterly data**, the sample period being 1968.I to 1981.IV. The long lags in (12) ($M = 16$ quarters) imply that the sample period could not start before 1968.

---

4. The stochastic specification of the model could have been made considerably more sophisticated by supposing, as in Artus, Laroque and Michel [1984], that the random terms were errors stemming from certain exogenous variables of the model. For the sake of simplicity, we have not done so.

The series used are :

I : business fixed investment;
c : user cost of capital, calculated from the interest rate on private bonds (r)
and the long-term expected inflation estimated by comparing the interest rates
on indexed and non-indexed bonds;
p' : deflator for the value added in the business sector, corrected as in section
1.1 above;
w : total wage cost per head in the business sector, including employers' social-
security contributions;
p_I : price of investment goods;
Π : profit rate (gross profits / value of capital) in the business sector;
CR : credit to the business sector (obtained by adding quarterly credit flows to
a benchmark level given by the wealth accounts as recorded in the national
accounts);
r_b : average interest rate on bank credit;
r_m : money-market interest rates;
DE : bank deposits;
M : money supply (M2);
S : official reserves and accumulated monetary financing of the budget deficit;
τ : rate of required reserves (divided by deposits).

2.1. Initial estimates

To get initial values for the parameters, equation-by-equation estimates
are made before the general estimate of (24).

Lags in changes in capacity ΔQ or relative prices are introduced into (12),
(13), and (23). These lags represent: (a) the fact that firms expect these
variables (we suppose these are adaptive expectations); (b) the fact that firms
allow for the investment-completion time in their decision. The investment of
each period is thus determined by:

$$(25) \quad \text{Log } I_t = \sum_{i=0}^{M} \mu_i \text{ Log } I_{t-i}^d , \quad \sum \mu_i = 1$$

where I_{t-i} is the investment decided on in t-i for the period $\{t-i, t-i+M\}$. As $\Sigma\mu_i = 1$, (25) preserves the meaning of the long-term coefficients of the variables in (12), (13), and (23).

We obtain :

$$(12\ b) \quad \mathrm{Log}\ I = \eta_0 + \sum_i \eta_1^i\ \mathrm{Log}\left(\frac{c}{p'}\right)_{-i} + \sum_j \eta_2^j\ \mathrm{Log}\left(\frac{w}{p'}\right)_{-j} + \eta_3\ T + \varepsilon_N \quad = NOT + \varepsilon_N$$

$$(13\ b) \quad \mathrm{Log}\ I = \eta_4 + \sum_i \eta_5^i\ \mathrm{Log}\ (\Delta Q)_{-i} + \sum_j \eta_6^j\ \mathrm{Log}\left(\frac{w}{c}\right)_{-j} + \eta_7\ T + \varepsilon_E \quad = EFF + \varepsilon_E$$

It proved impossible to make simultaneous estimates of the three equations appearing in (24) while complying with the cross-equation constraints stemming from the use of a single production function. If the constraints are imposed, the notional- demand system is eliminated and does not appear at any period. Two hypotheses can be adopted : either this system does not, in fact, appear — that is, firms are always demand-constrained; or the constraints between coefficients cannot be verified — for example, because of adjustment costs.

If, for instance, we include an adjustment cost directly on production, (7) becomes:

(7 a) Max $\{ p'\ \Delta Q - \alpha\ p'\ \Delta Q^2 - w\ \Delta L - c\ I \}$

The effective-demand system is not modified; however, in the notional-demand system, the following must be solved:

$$(26)\quad 1 - \alpha\ \Delta Q - \frac{L_0}{v}\ \Delta Q^{\left(\frac{1}{v} - 1\right)}\left(\frac{w}{p'}\right)^{1 - \sigma(1-\beta)}\left(\frac{c'}{p'}\right)^{(1-\beta)\sigma} - I_0^{\frac{1}{\sigma}}\ \Delta Q^{\left(\frac{1}{\sigma} - 1\right)}\left(\frac{w}{p'}\right)^{\sigma\beta}\left(\frac{c}{p'}\right)^{1-\sigma\beta} = 0$$

2.2. Estimates of a three-regime model: notional demand, effective demand, and credit supply

As stated earlier, notional demand either will be excluded, or will be included without constraint on the coefficients. Table 1 presents the results obtained in both cases.

The econometric results are satisfying with regard to effective demand and differ only slightly from those obtained in the independent estimate. With respect to notional demand, the disappearance of the significance of the real uses cost of capital (c/p') is observed; only the coefficient of real wages (w/p) remains significant. In the estimate over the period as a whole, the influence of the cost of capital probably reflected the substitution effect of the effective-demand model. The estimate of the credit supply function is inaccurate, perhaps because of the small number of periods in which this system is dominant. The accuracy of the investment equation is quite good (standard errors of 1.38 %): this is significantly better than the usual specification, which leads, on French quarterly data, to standard errors ranging between 2.5 and 3.5 %. Only the money-market interest-rate coefficient and the lagged variable are significant. The quarterly probabilities for each regime are reported in Graph 1 and, as annual averages in Table 2.

GRAPH 1. Probabilities of the different regimes

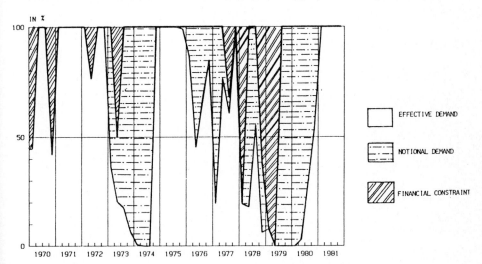

TABLE 1.   **Estimation of a multi-regime model**

	coeffficient	exogenous variable	Without Notional demand	With Notional demand
N	η_0			- 3.24 (0.9)
O	$\Sigma \eta_1^i$	c/p'		0.06 (0.3)
T				
I	$\Sigma \eta_2^i$	w/p'		- 0.81 (3.3)
O				
N	η_3	T		0.022 (3.7)
A				
L				
(NOT)		σ_N		0.028 (3.0)
E	η_4		3.78 (7.0)	2.98 (3.9)
F				
F	$\Sigma \eta_5^i$	ΔQ	0.85 (18.6)	0.96 (12.5)
E				
C	$\Sigma \eta_6^i$	w/c'	0.16 (2.7)	0.20 (3.1)
T				
I	η_7	T	0.001 (1.5)	0.0009 (1.0)
V				
E				
(EFF)		σ_E	0.018 (6.4)	0.017 (6.3)
F C	λ_0		0.11 (0.8)	0.12 (0.2)
I O				
N N	λ_1	r_b	0.13 (1.2)	0.60 (1.0)
A S				
N T	λ_2	r_m	- 0.56 (2.0)	- 1.78 (2.2)
C R				
I A	λ_3	DE/(M r_m)	0.87 (0.4)	3.13 (0.5)
A I				
L N				
** T**	λ_8	T	- 0.0009 (1.0)	- 0.0009 (0.5)
	λ_9	FAC	0 (ε)	0.40 (0.8)
(CF)		σ_c	0.065	0.066
	R^2 DW Standard deviation		0.968 1.129 2.21 %	0.989 1.499 1.38 %

TABLE 2. **Probabilities of the different regimes**

	Without Notional Demand			With Notional Demand		
	NOT	EFF	CF	NOT	EFF	CF
1968		97	3	0	100	0
1969		94	6	0	88	12
1970		95	5	0	72	28
1971		99	1	0	100	0
1972		96	4	0	94	6
1973		92	8	68	20	12
1974		64	36	75	25	0
1975		99	1	0	100	0
1976		100	0	29	71	0
1977		100	0	28	64	8
1978		100	0	41	24	35
1979		42	58	50	2	48
1980		71	29	78	22	0
1981		89	11	0	100	0

The results of the two estimates are not significantly different. The availability of financing limits the investment relatively slightly in 1969-1970 and 1973-1974, and considerably in 1979. According to one estimate, it will also have an effect in 1980, while according to the other it will be in 1978. Demand constraints are predominant throughout, except in 1979 and, in the notional-demand estimate, in 1973-1974, 1978 and 1980, when this regime appears. Thus, the decline in costs or the rise in prices might no doubt have increased the investment before the first oil crisis (1973-1974) and after the second (1979-1980) ; the increase in profits, loosening the financial constraint, would have been truly effective only in 1978-1980.

The estimate of a three-regime model also makes it possible to calculate an indicator of the disequilibrium on the credit market for firms. This indicator (IND) is more precisely the mathematical expectation — conditional on the parameters and the observations of the endogenous variables — of the difference between the potentially feasible investment when the financial constraint is absent and the investment allowed by the credit supply, that is :

$$IND = E (I_1 - CF - \varepsilon_c)$$

where I_1 is the investment that firms would make in the absence of a credit-linked constraint.

To simplify our calculations, and since notional demand could be introduced only by eliminating the constraints on the coefficients, we have restricted ourselves in calculating IND to a model with two modes of determining investment : effective demand and rationing through credit, that is :

$$IND = E (EFF + \varepsilon_E - CF - \varepsilon_c).$$

Thus, IND measures any possible excess (due to available credit) of the investment desired by firms over actual investment and, conversely, the excess of available credit over actual investment allowing for demand constraints and relative prices.[5]

TABLE 3.   **Credit disequilibrium indicator**

1968	- 34.5 %	1973	-13.1 %	1978	-10.2 %
1969	- 27.3 %	1974	-4.2 %	1979	+ 2.1 %
1970	- 16.1 %	1975	- 29.0 %	1980	- 1.0 %
1971	- 22.0 %	1976	- 25.0 %	1981	- 14.7 %
1972	- 12.9 %	1977	- 15.0 %		

The only year in which investment was rationed financially, on an annual average, was 1979, although there are other quarters in which this

---

5 IND is calculated as the mathematical expectation — conditional on each regime and weighted by the regime probability — of the difference between observed investment and the investment corresponding to the other regime.

situation prevails : 74.II (3.6 %) ; 74.III (7.0 %), 80.I (4 %), 80.II (1.1 %). For all other years, on average, the firms' demand for credit is lower than the supply of credit that banks would have wanted to distribute.

Now we shall attempt to reintroduce potential constraints on labor.

3. INTRODUCING THE LABOR CONSTRAINT

In taking into account the possibility of a labor constraint we return to the eight possible regimes—in reality, five regimes for investment. The difficulty here is that observed investment is no longer the minimum of the different possible investment specifications. The solution to (7) is now written :

If $\Delta L < \overline{\Delta L}$, I = Min (notional investment (12), effective (13), $\overline{I}$);
If $\Delta L = \overline{\Delta L}$, I = Min (investment with labor constraint (14), investment with labor and demand constraints (15), $\overline{I}$).

We see, for example, that when the demand constraint is binding, investment is increased by the possible saturation of the labor constraint. We did not wish to carry out far more complicated estimates dealing with both investment and the labor market. This would also have required estimating the equations corresponding to (12) – (15) concerning labor. This operation is made all the more difficult by the fact that we are using a putty-clay model, in which marginal labor ΔL is not an observed variable (the only marginal variable observed is investment). In order to assess the probability of coming up against the constraint $\Delta L = \overline{\Delta L}$, we have estimated (7) in the simplified case where the demand constraint, that is $\Delta Q = \overline{\Delta Q}$, prevails (in view of the preceding results, this case is not unrealistic).

Thus, the possible specifications for investment are (13) (effective demand), (15) (labor and output constraints), and (20) (I = $\overline{I}$). Model (7) is then reduced to :

(27) I= Min {Ī, Max [effective demand (13), labor and demand constraints (15)]}

a model we are able to estimate on the basis of investment alone.

As earlier, we need an initial estimate for investment demand with labor and demand constraints (15). Allowing for these, we obtain the following estimated parameters :

Investment demand

- effective demand :

$$\text{constant} = 2.95 \quad v = 0.89 \quad \gamma = 0.0026 \quad \sigma_E = 0.025$$
$$\quad (0.4) \quad\quad\quad (2.1) \quad\quad (0.8) \quad\quad\quad (1.7)$$

- demand with constraint on ΔL *:*

$$\text{constant} = 2.28 \quad \mu_0 = 62325 \quad \mu_1 = 0.49 \quad \sigma_L = 0.044$$
$$\quad (0.5) \quad\quad\quad (1.3) \quad\quad\quad (1.9) \quad\quad\quad (1.0)$$

- financially constrained investment :

$$\lambda_0 = 0.18 \quad\quad\quad\quad \lambda_1 = 0.06 \quad\quad\quad\quad\quad \lambda_2 = -2.45$$
$$\quad (0.7) \quad\quad\quad\quad\quad\quad (0.1) \quad\quad\quad\quad\quad\quad\quad (2.5)$$

$$\lambda_3 = 4.21 \quad\quad\quad\quad \lambda_7 = 0.84 \quad\quad\quad\quad\quad \lambda_8 = -0.0015$$
$$\quad (3.1) \quad\quad\quad\quad\quad\quad (3.1) \quad\quad\quad\quad\quad\quad\quad (0.2)$$

$$\lambda_9 = 0 \quad\quad\quad\quad\quad \sigma_c = 0.052$$
$$\quad\quad\quad\quad\quad\quad\quad (1.3)$$

Overall : $\quad R^2 = 0.973$

$$\quad\quad\quad DW = 1.17$$

$$\quad\quad\quad \text{standard deviation : 2.15 \%.}$$

As earlier, many parameters of the credit supply equation are not significant ; imposing constraints between the parameters of the two investment functions does not seem to have too adverse an effect on the estimate. The average annual probabilities obtained for each regime are reported in Table 4 and in Graph 2 of Chapter 1 above.

TABLE 4. **Probablilities of the different regimes**

	Effective demand	Demand with $\Delta Q = \overline{\Delta Q}$, L=$\overline{L}$	Financial Constraint
1968	43	56	1
1969	71	28	1
1970	60	12	28
1971	95	5	0
1972	92	2	6
1973	86	1	13
1974	62	0	38
1975	87	12	1
1976	85	3	12
1977	96	4	0
1978	96	4	0
1979	49	1	50
1980	30	20	50
1981	88	12	0

Conclusion

The estimation of a multi-regime model allows a more accurate analysis of the factors that explain investment, by isolating their respective influences during successive periods. Our estimates show that the influence of expected demand is predominant in determining investment, although financial conditions are not negligible.

A growth in expected demand would have increased investment in all years, except perhaps in 1974, 1979 and 1980. On the other hand, a growth in profits, or a drop in production costs, or even a greater distribution of credit, would have had no direct effect on investment in 1968-1969, 1971-1972, 1975 through 1978, and 1981—and, thus, on average, would have been less effective.

The results obtained show, however, that the estimation of credit-market disequilibrium based on investment alone remains relatively fragile, even though the periods in which investment was financially constrained coincide fairly closely with tight credit rationing.

APPENDIX 1

Likelihood and mathematical expectation of the endogenous variable for the two-regime model

We therefore consider the model :

$$Y = \text{Min} \ (a'_1 \ x_1 + \varepsilon_1, \ a'_2 \ x_2 + e_2)$$

$$(\varepsilon_1, \varepsilon_2) \sim N \ (0, \Sigma)$$

$$\Sigma \ = \ \begin{pmatrix} \sigma_1^2 & \sigma_{12} \\ \sigma_{12} & \sigma_2^2 \end{pmatrix}$$

The model's likelihood can be shown to be :

$$L \ = \ \prod_1^T \ \varphi \ (Y - a'_1 \ X_1, \sigma_1) \left(1 - \phi \left(\frac{Y - a'_2 \ X_2 \ - \dfrac{\sigma_{12}}{\sigma_1^2} \ (Y - a'_1 \ X_1)}{\sigma_1^2 \ - \dfrac{\sigma_{12}^2}{\sigma_2^2}} \right) \right)$$

$$+ \quad \varphi \ (Y - a'_2 \ X_2, \sigma_2) \left(1 - \phi \left(\frac{Y - a'_1 \ X_1 \ - \dfrac{\sigma_{12}}{\sigma_2^2} \ (Y - a'_2 \ X_2)}{\sigma_2^2 \ - \dfrac{\sigma_{12}^2}{\sigma_1^2}} \right) \right)$$

where :

> $\varphi(X, \sigma)$ = density of the normal distribution with zero mean and standard deviation x.
>
> Φ = cumulative function of the reduced normal zero-mean distribution.
>
> T = number of observations.

We can also calculate E [Min $(a'_1 x_1 + \varepsilon_1, a'_2 x_2 + \varepsilon_2)$]. This mathematical expectation will serve to determine the standard statistics (R^2, DW, standard deviation) of the estimates that will be evaluated here on the basis of the difference Y - E (Min $(a'_1 x_1 + \varepsilon_1, a'_2 x_2 + \varepsilon_2)$) using conventional formulae.

Naturally, in this study, these statistics are purely notional and not truly significant. Using the calculation principle given for (18), we get :

$$
\begin{aligned}
E\,[\,\text{Min}\,(a'_1 X_1 + \varepsilon_1, a'_2 X_2 + \varepsilon_2)\,] \;=\; & a'_1 X_1 \;\; \phi \left(\frac{a'_2 X_2 - a'_1 X_1}{\Sigma} \right) \\
+ \; a'_2 X_2 \;\; \phi \;\; & \left(\frac{a'_1 X_1 - a'_2 X_2}{\Sigma} \right) - \Sigma \;\; \phi_0 \left(\frac{a'_1 X_1 - a'_2 X_2}{\Sigma} \right)
\end{aligned}
$$

$$
\Sigma^2 \;=\; \sigma_1^2 + \sigma_2^2 - 2\sigma_{12}
$$

Φ_o = density of the reduced normal zero-mean distribution.

APPENDIX 2

Differentiated expressions of investment demand functions

The log-linear approximations (12) to (15) used in the econometric estimates rest on the general expression of demand functions in logarithmic differential form. These differentiated expressions apply both to the overall function, when capital is assumed to be totally malleable :

(1) $Q = F(K, L)$

and to the *ex ante* marginal function in the putty-clay hypothesis :

(2) $\Delta Q = F(I, \Delta L)$

For this reason, we shall keep to notation (1), which is easier to handle. Since investment demand is always homogeneous and of degree zero with respect to the price system, we shall take the output price as unit, w being the real wage and c the real cost of capital. σ is the elasticity of substitution and v the returns to scale of the production function. We initially assume the absence of technical progress.

Since F is homogeneous and of degree v, we have the Euler equation :

(3) $Q = F(K,L) = \dfrac{1}{v} (K F_K' + L F_L')$

which, differentiated, gives :

(4) $dQ = \dfrac{1}{v} (K\, dF_K' + L\, dF_L' + F_K'\, dK + F_L'\, dL) = F_K'\, dK + F_L'\, dL$

Elasticity of substitution is :

$$(5) \quad \sigma = - \left(\frac{dK}{K} - \frac{dL}{L} \right) : \left(\frac{dF_K'}{F_K'} - \frac{dF_L'}{F_L'} \right)$$

and the marginal rate of substitution :

$$(6) \quad \left(\frac{dK}{dL} \right)_{Q=ct} = - \frac{F_L'}{F_K'}$$

The last three equations will serve to establish a general formulation of the different demands for capital or investment.

1. Effective demand

Effective demand is the demand for capital that minimizes the production cost for a given level of output Q and of relative capital-labor cost (c/w). Let us first consider a shift with unchanged relative cost. From the definition of returns to scale, we get :

$$(7) \quad Q = K^v . F (1, L/K)$$

Since the capital/labor ratio is constant when the relative cost is constant, we can immediately deduce that the elasticity of capital demand with respect to production is equal to $1/v$.

Let us now consider a shift along the isoquant. At the optimum, the marginal rate of substitution is equal to the ratio of relative costs. For the elasticity of substitution and marginal rate, we therefore get :

$$(5) \quad \sigma = - \left(\frac{dK}{K} - \frac{dL}{L} \right) : \frac{d\left(\frac{c}{w}\right)}{\left(\frac{c}{w}\right)}$$

$$(6) \quad -\frac{c}{w} = \frac{dL}{dK}$$

Cancelling out dL between (5) and (6), we obtain the equation for the elasticity of capital with respect to relative cost :

$$(8) \quad \frac{dK}{K} = -\beta\sigma \frac{d\left(\frac{c}{w}\right)}{\left(\frac{c}{w}\right)}$$

$$\text{with} \qquad \beta = \frac{w\,L}{w\,L + c\,K}$$

The general differentiated form of effective demand is therefore :

$$(9) \quad \frac{dK}{K} = \frac{1}{v} \frac{dQ}{Q} - \beta\sigma \frac{d\left(\frac{c}{w}\right)}{\left(\frac{c}{w}\right)}$$

2. Notional demand (v < 1)

The effective-demand equation (9) holds for notional demand too, but production is not exogenous here. It corresponds to the value that maximizes the firm's profit and therefore complies with the marginal conditions :

$$(10) \quad c = F'_K \qquad w = F'_L$$

Taking these marginal conditions into account, the differentiated form of the Euler equation (4) is written :

$$(11) \quad \left(1 - \frac{1}{v}\right) dQ = K\,dc + L\,dw$$

which yields a differentiated expression of the notional supply of goods :

$$(12) \quad \left(1 - \frac{1}{v}\right) dQ = (1 - \beta)\,\frac{dc}{c} + \beta\,\frac{dw}{w}$$

$$\text{with} \qquad \beta = \frac{w\,L}{w\,L + c\,K}$$

Substituting this expression for dQ/Q in (9), we obtain notional demand for capital :

$$(13) \quad \frac{dK}{K} = -\left(\beta\sigma + \frac{1 - \beta}{1 - v}\right) \frac{dc}{c} - \beta\left(\frac{1}{1 - v} - \sigma\right) \frac{dw}{w}$$

It will be noted that notional demand is an always decreasing function of the capital cost and a generally decreasing function of the labor cost, as $\beta\sigma$ is usually smaller than $1 - \beta$.

3. Investment demand with labor constraint

The marginal condition is written :

$$(14) \quad F'_K = c$$

Substituting this condition into the Euler equations (3) and (4) and in the equation defining elasticity of substitution (5), we obtain :

$$(3\ b) \quad Q = \frac{1}{v} (K c + L F_L^{'})$$

$$(4\ b) \quad \left(1 - \frac{1}{v} \right) (c\ dK + F_L^{'}\ dL) = K\ dc + L\ dF_L^{'}$$

$$(5\ b) \quad \frac{dK}{K} = \frac{dL}{L} + \sigma\ \frac{dF_L^{'}}{F_L^{'}} - \sigma\ \frac{dc}{c}$$

Let η be the ratio of capital cost to production :

$$(15) \quad \eta = \frac{K c}{Q}$$

(3b) allows us to calculate the ratio :

$$(16) \quad \frac{L F_L^{'}}{Q} = v - \eta$$

Dividing (4b) by Q, member by member, and taking (16) into account, we get :

$$(17) \quad \left(1 - \frac{1}{v} \right) \left[\eta\ \frac{dK}{K} + (v - \eta)\ \frac{dL}{L} \right] = \left[\eta\ \frac{dc}{c} + (v - \eta)\ \frac{dF_L^{'}}{F_L^{'}} \right]$$

We now need only cancel out dF'_L/F'_L between (5b) and (17) to obtain the demand for capital in differentiated form :

$$(18) \quad \frac{dK}{K} = \frac{v}{\left(1 - \dfrac{1}{v}\right)\eta - \dfrac{v - \eta}{\sigma}} \frac{dc}{c} + \left[\frac{1 - \dfrac{v}{\eta}}{1 - \dfrac{v}{\eta\left(1 + \sigma - \dfrac{\sigma}{v}\right)}}\right] \frac{dL}{L}$$

When returns to scale are unitary ($v = 1$), this equation is greatly simplified :

$$(19) \quad \frac{dK}{K} = - \frac{\sigma}{1 - \eta} \frac{dc}{c} + \frac{dL}{L}$$

APPENDIX 3

For information, the estimate of the model $I = Min (I_{EFF}, I_{PRO})$ is given below :

$$\text{(13 c)} \quad \text{Log}(I_{EFF}) = a_o + a_1 T + \sum_i a_2^i \text{Log}(\Delta Q)_{-i} + \sum_j a_3^j \text{Log}\left(\frac{w}{c}\right)_{-j} + \varepsilon_E$$

$$\text{(23 c)} \quad \text{Log}(I_{PRO}) = b_o + b_1 T + \sum_i b_2^i \text{Log}\left(\frac{\Pi}{p^I}\right) + \varepsilon_P$$

I = investment
ΔQ = gross change in output
w = wage cost
c = user cost of capital
Π = profit
p_I = investment price
T = time

The estimate yields :
(Standard deviation in brackets)

a_0 = 3.97 (0.95)	a_1 = 0.0013 (0.0025)	Σa_2^i = 1.27 (0.09)	Σa_3^j = 0.23 (0.14)
b_0 = 9.08 (0.20)	b_1 = 0.0028 (0.0003)	Σb_2^i = 0.38 (0.06)	σ_2 = 0.0133 (0.0030)
R^2 = 0.986	DW= 1.05	SEE = 1.55 %	σ_1 = 0.0176 (0.0038)

The regime probabilities are given in Table 5.

TABLE 5.   **Effective demand and profit**

	Effective demand	Profit
1968	100	0
1969	100	0
1970	100	0
1971	100	0
1972	96	4
1973	32	68
1974	16	74
1975	93	7
1976	53	47
1977	57	43
1978	16	84
1979	0	100
1980	5	95
1981	18	82

CHAPTER 9
Production capacity, factor demands and demand uncertainty*
by
Patrick Artus

Introduction

Malinvaud [1983] has shown that by taking into account the uncertainty of demand for firms' output, one can construct an investment model in which installed capacity depends on profitability and the capital coefficient depends on the factors' relative cost. Many authors have already studied firm-behavior models with demand uncertainty. Nickell [1977], for example, looks at the investment behavior of a firm that knows demand will change, but at an undetermined date. Pindyck [1982] introduces a demand function dependent on prices and a stochastic process. The following chapter takes up Malinvaud's model in the standard intertemporal context of putty-clay production functions. The resulting model of factor-choices by firms differs from those generally obtained (see INSEE [1981] and Chapter 8 above), as expected demands are no longer just an exogenous constraint but are represented by a probability distribution. In the long run, the production capacity of firms is not necessarily equal to demand, as in the conventional models, but depends on the assumed characteristics of demand distribution. After defining the model, we determine the optimality conditions, the stationary and steady-state-growth solutions, and the general solution for factor demand and installed capacity. This will enable us to proceed to the estimation phase, for which we specify the marginal production function and the demand probability distribution.

* Originally published as "Capacite de production, demande de facteurs et incertitude sur la demande," Annales de l'INSEE 53:3-29, 1984.

1. The model and the optimality conditions

In each period (written t_0) firms determine an optimal path over $[\,t_0\,,\,\infty\,]$ by taking as given their situation in t_0 (capacity, etc.) and setting expectations for the producer price, wage per capita, and capital-goods price for all future periods. The model could easily be generalized in the event of less frequent path revision (in t_0 , $t_0 + k$, $t_0 + 2\,k$ and so on).

Firms maximize the mathematical expectation of the discounted sum of dividends (from which we have eliminated debt incurred at the rate of interest r); observed and expected prices and wages are assumed to be exogenous:

$$\text{Max } E \sum_{t=t_0}^{\infty} \frac{1}{(1+r)^t} \left[p_t\,Y_t - w_t\,N_t - p_t^{\text{I}}\,I_t \right]$$

where:
Y_t = production;
N_t = employment (number of workers);
I_t = investment;
p_t = expected producer price for period $\underline{t}$;
w_t = expected wage cost per capita;
$p_t{}^{\text{I}}$ = expected capital-goods price.

The technology is putty-clay. Total employment corresponding to full capacity utilization changes according to:

$$N_t^* = N_{t-1}^*\,(1 - \delta) + L_t^*$$

where L_t^* is the employment allocated to the new equipment vintage, assuming full capacity utilization.

Capacity follows:

$$\bar{Y}_t = \bar{Y}_{t-1}\,(1 - \delta) + \bar{Q}_t$$

where $\bar{Q}_t$ is the period's contribution to production capacity, with the marginal production function :

$$\bar{Q}_t = f(L_t^*, I_t)$$

The employment allocated to existing vintages, N_t , adjusts to the capacity utilization rate:

$$N_t = N_{t-1}^* \frac{Y_t}{\bar{Y}_{t-1}}$$

(during the period t, the capacity is $\bar{Y}_t$ and full-utilization employment is N^*_{t-1}).

In the short term, production does indeed take place with constant coefficients:

$$\left(\frac{N_t}{Y_t} = \frac{N_{t-1}^*}{\bar{Y}_{t-1}}\right)$$

Capital vintages are therefore differentiated at the input stage (the technology measured by $I_t / \bar{Q}_t$ and $L_t / \bar{Q}_t$ is calculated for each vintage at the time of purchase). Subsequently, the vintages are "merged" in an undifferentiated aggregate, which depreciates at the common rate δ and in which the utilization rate is identical for all vintages. We therefore take only partial advantage of the putty-clay hypothesis, owing to this extreme but customary simplification, intended to make the problem manageable. As a result, we do not introduce the notion that scrapping and utilization depend on the performance specific to each level of equipment, the least profitable being scrapped earlier and being the first to go when demand falls.

Expected demand D_t is random and characterized for each period by an expected cumulative function P_t :

$$(P_t (u) = \text{Prob} (D_t \leq u))$$

Ex post, actual production is:

$$Y_t = \text{Min} (\bar{Y}_{t-1}, D_t)$$

If demand exceeds capacity, production is limited to that capacity.

The firms' program is therefore written:

$$
\left\{
\begin{array}{l}
\text{Max E } \displaystyle\sum_{t=t_0}^{\infty} \frac{1}{(1+r)^t} \left[p_t\, Y_t - w_t\, N_{t-1}^* \frac{Y_t}{\tilde{Y}_{t-1}} - p_t^{\mathrm{I}} I_t \right] \\[1.2em]
N_t^* = N_{t-1}^* (1-\delta) + L_t^* \qquad \text{(multiplier : } \dfrac{\lambda_t}{(1+r)^t} \quad) \\[1.2em]
\tilde{Y}_t = \tilde{Y}_{t-1}(1-\delta) + f(L_t^*, I_t) \qquad \text{(multiplier : } \dfrac{\mu_t}{(1+r)^t} \quad)
\end{array}
\right.
$$

The endogenous variables are $\quad N_t,\ \tilde{Y}_t,\ I_t,\ L_t^*;\ N_{t_0-1}^* \qquad$ and $\quad \tilde{Y}_{t_0-1}$ are known.

$$
\text{E}\left[p_t Y_t - w_t \frac{N_{t-1}^*}{\tilde{Y}_{t-1}} Y_t - p_t^{\mathrm{I}} I_t \right]
$$

equals:

$$
\left[p_t - w_t \frac{N_{t-1}^*}{\tilde{Y}_{t-1}} \right] \left[(1 - P_t(\tilde{Y}_{t-1}))\, \tilde{Y}_{t-1} + \int_{-\infty}^{\tilde{Y}_{t-1}} u\, dP_t(u) \right] - p_t^{\mathrm{I}} I_t
$$

since $\text{E}(Y_t)$ breaks down into two terms:

$$
(1 - P_t(\tilde{Y}_{t-1}))\, \tilde{Y}_{t-1}
$$

when demand exceeds capacity;

$$
\int_{-\infty}^{\tilde{Y}_{t-1}} u\, dP_t(u)
$$

when capacity exceeds demand.

The Lagrangian is written:

$$
\mathcal{L} = \sum_{t=t_0}^{\infty} \frac{1}{(1+r)^t} \left[\left(p_t - w_t \frac{N_{t-1}^*}{\tilde{Y}_{t-1}} \right) \left((1 - P_t(\tilde{Y}_{t-1}))\, \tilde{Y}_{t-1} + \int_{-\infty}^{\tilde{Y}_{t-1}} u\, dP_t(u) \right) - p_t^{\mathrm{I}} I_t \right]
$$

$$
- \frac{\lambda_t}{(1+r)^t} (N_t^* - N_{t-1}^*(1-\delta) - L_t^*) - \frac{\mu_t}{(1+r)^t} (\tilde{Y}_t - \tilde{Y}_{t-1}(1-\delta) - f(L_t^*, I_t))
$$

Deriving $\mathcal{L}$ with respect to the $\quad N_t^*, \bar{Y}_t, I_t, L_t^* \quad$ values, we obtain the necessary optimality conditions:

(1) $\quad (N_t^*) \;:\; -w_{t+1}\left((1 - P_{t+1}(\bar{Y}_t) + \frac{1}{\bar{Y}_t}\int_{-\infty}^{\bar{Y}_t} u\, dP_{t+1}(u)\right)$

$$-\lambda_t(1+r) + \lambda_{t+1}(1-\delta) = 0$$

(2) $\quad (\bar{Y}_t) \;:\; w_{t+1}\frac{N_t^*}{\bar{Y}_t^2}\left((1 - P_{t+1}(\bar{Y}_t))\,\bar{Y}_t + \int_{-\infty}^{\bar{Y}_t} u\, dP_{t+1}(u)\right)$

$$+ \left(p_{t+1} - w_{t+1}\frac{N_t^*}{\bar{Y}_t}\right)(1 - P_{t+1}(\bar{Y}_t))$$

$$-\mu_t(1+r) + \mu_{t+1}(1-\delta) = 0$$

(3) $\quad (I_t) \;:\; -p_t^I + \mu_t f_L'(L_t^*, I_t) = 0$

(4) $\quad (L_t^*) \;:\; \lambda_t + \mu_t f_L'(L_t^*, I_t) = 0$

(for $t = t_0, \ldots, \infty$)

(3) yields:

$$\mu_t = \frac{p_t^I}{f_I'(L_t^*, I_t)}$$

(4) yields:

$$\lambda_t = \frac{-p_t^I f_L'(L_t^*, I_t)}{f_I'(L_t^*, I_t)}$$

which, substituted into (1), gives:

(5) $\quad -w_{t+1}\,T_{t+1}(\bar{Y}_t) + \frac{(1+r)\,p_t^I f_L'(L_t^*, I_t)}{f_I'(L_t^*, It)} - \frac{(1-\delta)\,p_{t+1}^I f_L'(L_{t+1}^*, I_{t+1})}{f_I'(L_{t+1}^*, I_{t+1})}$

where:

$$T_{t+1}(\bar{Y}_t) = 1 - P_{t+1}(\bar{Y}) + \frac{1}{\bar{Y}_t}\int_{-\infty}^{\bar{Y}_t} u\, dP_{t+1}(u)$$

is the mathematical expectation of the capacity utilization rate; and, substituted into (2), gives:

(6)
$$w_{t+1} \frac{N_t^*}{\bar{Y}_t} T_{t+1}(\bar{Y}_t) + \left(p_{t+1} - w_{t+1} \frac{N_t^*}{\bar{Y}_t}\right)(1 - P_{t+1}(\bar{Y}_t))$$

$$-\frac{(1+r)\,p_t^I}{f_I'(L_t^*, I_t)} + \frac{p_{t+1}^I(1-\delta)}{f_I'(L_{t+1}^*, I_{t+1})} = 0$$

The $N_t^*, \bar{Y}_t, I_t, L_t^*$ values solve (5), (6) and:

(7)
$$N_t^* = N_{t-1}^*(1-\delta) + L_t^*$$

(8)
$$\bar{Y}_t = \bar{Y}_{t-1}(1-\delta) + f(L_t^*, I_t) \qquad (t = t_0, \ldots, +\infty)$$

$N_{t_0-1}^*$ and $\bar{Y}_{t_0-1}$ being known.

(5) relates the marginal labor productivity / marginal capital productivity ratio to the relative cost of factors corrected for the capacity utilization rate.

(6) expresses the notion that the additional profit to be expected in t + 1 from an increase in investment in t:

$$\left[\frac{f_I'}{1+r}\left(w\frac{N}{\bar{Y}}T(\bar{Y}) + \left(p - w\frac{N^*}{\bar{Y}}\right)(1 - P(\bar{Y}))\right)\right]$$

is equal to the cost of that investment, taking into account the resale value in t+1 corrected for the variation in the marginal productivity of capital between the two periods:

$$\left[p_t^I - \frac{1-\delta}{1+r}p_{t+1}^I \frac{f_I'(t)}{f_I'(t+1)}\right]$$

To determine if these necessary optimality conditions are also sufficient, we examine the Hessian of *L* (given in Appendix 1). The Hessian is semi-defined negative with respect to the control variables if the production function fulfills the standard conditions:

$$(f''_{I2} < 0, \; f''_{L2} < 0, \; f''_{I2}f''_{L2} - (f''_{LI})^2 > 0),$$

which will be the case for the production functions used in our estimate. The equations (1), (2), (3) and (4) would therefore effectively seem to be necessary and sufficient optimality conditions. However, in the case of continuous-time maximization problems, it is correct that the concavity with respect to the control variables implies that (1)-(4) are sufficient conditions. In a discrete-time problem, one would have to verify case by case the optimality of the solution found. We have done that here only for stationary paths using complex calculations omitted for lack of space.

2. Stationary solution and steady-state growth

The study of the stationary solution allows us to spell out the significance of equations (5) and (6), and can also serve as a reference point for the subsequent linearization of the system (5)-(8). In a second step, we shall examine steady-state growth paths.

In stationary long-term equilibrium, (5), (6), (7) and (8) are written:

(5')
$$w T (\bar{Y}) = p^I \frac{f'_L}{f'_I} (r + \delta) \quad \text{soit} : \frac{f'_L}{f'_I} = \frac{w T (\bar{Y})}{p^I (r + \delta)}$$

(6')
$$w \frac{N^*}{\bar{Y}} T (\bar{Y}) + \left(p - w \frac{N^*}{\bar{Y}} \right) (1 - P (\bar{Y})) = \frac{p^I (r + \delta)}{f'_I (L^*, I)}$$

$$= p (1 - P (\bar{Y})) + \frac{w N^*}{\bar{Y}} \frac{1}{\bar{Y}} \int_0^{\bar{Y}} u \, dP (u)$$

(7')
$$\delta N^* = L^*$$

(8')
$$\delta \bar{Y} = f (L^*, I) = f (\delta N^*, I)$$

Equation (5') means that the marginal-productivities ratio is equal to the relative cost of factors corrected for the mathematical expectation of the capacity utilization rate $T(\overline{Y})$. Equation (6') means that the cost of one additional unit of capital ($p^I (r + \delta)$) is equal to the sum of two terms: the first is the value of the additional products sold ($p\, f'_I$) multiplied by the probability of excess demand ($1 - P(\overline{Y})$); the second is the reduction in the wage cost, for a given optimal employment N^*, due to rising capacity. If the capacity is too large, $P(\overline{Y}) = \text{Prob } (D > \overline{Y})$ tends toward unity, and additional profit (($p - wN/Y$) ($1 - P(\overline{Y})$)) tends to disappear. In this case, the cost of the investment exceeds the profit it generates, and we have an overcapacity cost. If the capacity is too small, $P(\overline{Y})$ is low and investment, if larger, could yield higher profits: we then have an undercapacity cost. The purpose of optimization is precisely to eliminate these two costs. The second term is derived from the hypothesis that firms adjust employment to match the capacity utilization rate ($N = N^* \, Y / \overline{Y}$). With this formulation, if capacity expands, but not demand, firms are not obliged to employ more labor. The reader will find in Appendix 2 the equivalent conditions if firms were required to maintain employment at full capacity N^*. (6') corresponds to system (10) in Malinvaud [1983].

Taking the stationary system (5'), (6'), (7') and (8'), and replacing L^* and Y by their values in (7') and (8'), we get:

$$(9) \qquad \frac{f'_L}{f'_I} = \frac{wT\left(\frac{1}{\delta} f(L^*, I)\right)}{p^I (r + \delta)}$$

$$(10) \qquad \frac{w L^* T\left(\frac{1}{\delta} f\right)}{f(L^*, I)} + \left(p - w\frac{L^*}{f}\right)\left(1 - P\left(\frac{1}{\delta} f\right)\right) = \frac{p^I (r + \delta)}{f'_I (L^*, I)}$$

Replacing $w\, T\, /(p^I (r + \delta))$ in (10) by its value in (9), we get:

$$(11) \qquad \frac{L^* f'_L}{f} + \frac{f'_I}{p^I (r + \delta)}\left(p - w\frac{L^*}{f}\right)\left(1 - P\left(\frac{1}{\delta} f\right)\right) = 1$$

(9) and (11) can be used later to calculate long-term L^* and I.

The analytical study of the system (9), (11) yields no unambiguous sign for the derivatives of L^* and I with respect to w, p^I and p. The response of the endogenous variables' long-term values to the exogenous variables' values will be studied numerically after the model estimate.

We shall now assume that from the period t_0 considered onward, the volume values $(\bar{Y}, I)$ grow at the rate g; that the demand probability distribution is distorted over time in such a manner that $T(Y)$ and $P(Y)$ remain constant over time; that the real wage (w/p) increases at the same rate as labor productivity $(\overset{*}{N}/\bar{Y}$ or $\overset{*}{N}/I)$; that prices (p^I, p) grow at the rate ρ; that f combines L^*, I and any technical-progress trends so as to grow at the rate g (here we shall be able to write $f = f(L_t^*, I_t, t)$. Substituting these steady-state-growth conditions into (5), (6), (7) and (8) gives us:

$$(12) \qquad w_{t_0} T_{t_0} (\bar{Y}_{t_0-1}) = \frac{p_{t_0}^I f_L' (L_{t_0}^*, I_{t_0}, t_0)}{f_I' (L_{t_0}^*, I_{t_0}, t_0)} \left(\frac{1+r}{(1+\rho)(1+\gamma)} - (1-\delta) \right)$$

$$(13) \qquad w_{t_0} \frac{N_{t_0-1}^*}{\bar{Y}_{t_0-1}} T_{t_0} (\bar{Y}_{t_0-1}) + \left(p_{t_0} - w_{t_0} \frac{N_{t_0-1}^*}{\bar{Y}_{t_0-1}} \right) (1 - P_{t_0}(\bar{Y}_{t_0-1}))$$

$$= \frac{p_{t_0}^I}{f_I' (L_{t_0}^*, I_{t_0}, t_0)} \left(\frac{1+r}{1+\rho} - 1 - \delta \right)$$

$$(14) \qquad N_{t_0-1}^* \left(\frac{1+g}{1+\gamma} - (1-\delta) \right) = L_{t_0}^*$$

$$(15) \qquad \bar{Y}_{t_0-1} (\delta+g) = f(L_{t_0}^*, I_{t_0})$$

where $\bar{Y}_{t_0-1}, N_{t_0-1}^*, L_{t_0}^*, I_{t_0}$ represent the starting points of the constant-rate paths for the endogenous variables, $w_{t_0}, p_{t_0}^I, p_{t_0}$ those for the exogenous variables.

Substituting (14) and (15) into (12) and (13), we find:

$$(16) \qquad wT \left(\frac{f}{\delta+g} \right) = p^I \frac{f_L'}{f_I'} \left(\frac{1+r}{(1+\rho)(1+\gamma)} - (1-\delta) \right)$$

$$(17) \qquad \frac{L^* f_L'}{f} \frac{\left(\frac{1+r}{(1+\rho)(1+\gamma)} - (1-\delta) \right) (\delta+g)}{\left(\frac{1+r}{1+\rho} - (1-\delta) \right) \left(\frac{1+g}{1+\gamma} - (1-\delta) \right)} + \frac{f_I'}{p^I \left(\frac{1+r}{1+\rho} - (1+\delta) \right)}$$

$$\left(p - \frac{wL^*}{f} \frac{\delta+g}{\frac{1+g}{1+\gamma} - (1-\delta)} \right) \left(1 - P \left(\frac{f}{\delta+g} \right) \right) = 1$$

which are the equivalents of (9) and (11) for calculating L* and I in the case of steady-state growth.

3. SPECIFICATION FOR THE ECONOMETRIC ESTIMATION

3.1. Linearization

In order to obtain a specification that can be estimated econometrically, it is useful to linearize the system (5)-(6)-(7)-(8) around a reference path starting in $t = t_0$, for example the stationary path defined by ((9)-(11)-(7')-(8') or the steady-state-growth path calculated with (16)-(17)-(14)-(15). Let $\widehat{N}_t, \widehat{Y}_t, \widehat{I}_t, \widehat{L}_t$ be the values of N^*, $\widehat{Y}$, I, L* on this reference path. In the case of a stationary reference path, we can start directly from the system (5)-(6)-(7)-(8). In the case of a steady-state-growth reference, it is useful to change the variables by dividing each by its trend: this will enable us to obtain a fixed-coefficient differential-equation system. The linearization of (5)-(6)-(7)-(8) gives the following result, after calculation and resolution:

$$
(18) \qquad
\begin{pmatrix}
N_t^* - \widehat{N} \\
\widehat{Y}_t - \widehat{Y} \\
L_{t+1} - \widehat{L} \\
I_{t+1} - \widehat{I}
\end{pmatrix}
= A
\begin{pmatrix}
N_{t-1}^* - \widehat{N} \\
\widehat{Y}_{t-1} - \widehat{Y} \\
L_t - \widehat{L} \\
I_t - \widehat{I}
\end{pmatrix}
\; ; \; t = t_0, \; \ldots \infty
$$

where the matrix A (given in Appendix 3) is composed of elements all calculated at the point $(\widehat{N}, \widehat{Y}, \widehat{L}, \widehat{I})$ and for the assumed values of the exogenous variables (for the stationary path: constant values equal to those in t_0; for the steady-state-growth path: values obtained after the variable change described above). The matrix A is given in Appendix 3 for the stationary reference, which, as we shall see, yields better results. In the other case, the notation is similar but made cumbersome by the presence of terms incorporating $(1+\rho)$, $(1+g)$ and $(1+\rho)(1+\gamma)$.

To estimate the model, we will require eigen values and vectors for A. After handling, we obtain the following form of the characteristic equation for the stationary reference:

$$
\begin{vmatrix}
1-\delta-\lambda & 0 & 1 & 0 \\[2ex]
0 & 1-\delta-\lambda & 0 & \dfrac{f_{\text{I}}'\,\lambda}{1-\delta} \\[2ex]
(1-\delta)\,\varepsilon_2 & \varepsilon_1 & -\lambda+\dfrac{1+r}{1-\delta}+\varepsilon_2 & 0 \\[2ex]
0 & \varepsilon_3 & \left(\dfrac{f_{\text{L}}'}{f_{\text{I}}'}+\dfrac{1}{V}\right)\left(\lambda-\dfrac{1+r}{1-\delta}\right) & -\lambda+\dfrac{1+r}{1-\delta}+\varepsilon_3\dfrac{f_{\text{I}}'}{1-\delta}
\end{vmatrix} = 0
$$

where λ denotes the eigen values and:

$$
\varepsilon_1 = \frac{1}{\Delta}\,\frac{\widehat{w}\,\text{T}'\,(\widehat{\text{Y}})\,f_{\text{I}}'^{\,2}}{\widehat{p\text{I}}\,(f_{\text{LI}}''f_{\text{L}}'-f_{\text{L}^2}''f_{\text{I}}')} - \frac{\text{V}}{\Delta}\frac{f_{\text{I}}'}{f_{\text{I}^2}''}\frac{1}{\widehat{p\text{I}}}\left(2w\,\frac{\widehat{\text{N}}}{\widehat{\text{Y}_3}}\int_{-\infty}^{\widehat{\text{Y}}} u\,d\text{P}\,(u) + \left(\widehat{p}-\widehat{w}\,\frac{\widehat{\text{N}}}{\widehat{\text{Y}}}\right)\text{P}'\,(\widehat{\text{Y}})\right)
$$

$$
\varepsilon_2 = \frac{\text{V}}{\Delta}\frac{f_{\text{I}}'^{\,2}}{f_{\text{I}^2}''}\frac{1}{\widehat{p\text{I}}}\frac{\widehat{w}}{\widehat{\text{Y}^2}}\int_{-\infty}^{\widehat{\text{Y}}} u\,d\text{P}\,(u)
$$

$$
\varepsilon_3 = -\frac{1}{\text{V}}\frac{\widehat{w}\,\text{T}'\,(\widehat{\text{Y}})\,f_{\text{I}}'^{\,2}}{\widehat{p\text{I}}\,(f_{\text{LI}}''f_{\text{L}}'-f_{\text{L}^2}''f_{\text{I}}')}
$$

$$
\text{V} = \frac{f_{\text{I}^2}''f_{\text{L}}'-f_{\text{LI}}''f_{\text{I}}'}{f_{\text{L}}''^2 f_{\text{I}}'-f_{\text{LI}}''f_{\text{L}}'} > 0; \quad \Delta = 1+\frac{f_{\text{LI}}''}{f_{\text{I}^2}''}\text{V} > 0
$$

By calculating the successive derivatives of the characteristic polynomial, one can show that there are always two and only two real roots lying between -1 and +1 (and therefore stable), one of these lying between 0 and 1 - δ, the other between 1 - δ and 1. The other two roots are either conjugate complex or real, and their modulus is always greater than 1. This gives us two transversality conditions (zero value of the integration constants linked to the two divergent eigen values), which, when combined with the initial conditions $\bar{Y}_{t_0-1}$, $N^*_{t_0-1}$ allow a single calculation of the two other integration constants and of $L^*_{t_0}$ and I_{t_0}. As a result, the uniqueness of the optimal path is ensured.

3.2. Estimate specifications

We have taken as a marginal production function a Cobb-Douglas function:

$$(19) \qquad \bar{Q}_t = Q_0 \, I_t^a \, L_t^{*b} \, (1+\gamma)^{bt} \, (1+g)^{(1-a-b)t} \, ; \, a+b < 1$$

that allows steady-state growth at the rate g with a technical progress embodied in labor at the rate γ. When the reference solution is stationary, the $(1+g)$ and $(1+\gamma)$ terms must disappear. For this purpose, we alter the variable concerning w and L in a manner that maintains the wage cost wL and eliminates real-wage and productivity gains (w_t is divided by $(1+\gamma)^t$ and L_t multiplied by $(1+\gamma)^t$). We also assume $g = 0$ starting at t_0 on the reference path. For the demand probability distribution in t we have chosen a normal distribution with (m_t, σ_t) moments. The mean m_t is determined by :

$$(20) \qquad m_t = \left[\frac{1}{N} \sum_{i=1}^{N} D_{t_0-i}(1+\bar{g})^i\right] \cdot m \cdot (1+g)^{t-t_0}$$

from the observed demand values for the pre-t_0 periods corrected for the mean growth rate of demand over the N periods preceding t_0 (g), multiplied by a coefficient to be estimated m and by the expected growth rate on the reference path (in a static reference, $g = 0$ but $\bar{g}$, which is observed and not expected, subsists). The parameter to be calculated (m) is therefore the estimated ratio between the mean of the expected distribution of demand used by firms and the empirical trend-corrected mean of past demand. σ_t is the empirical standard deviation (with respect to m_t) on the N pre-t_0 observations of demand D, multiplied by a coefficient to be estimated s (similar to m in significance) and by the expected growth rate on the reference path.

$$(21) \qquad \sigma_t = \left[\frac{1}{N} \sum_{i=1}^{N} (D_{t_0-i}(1+\bar{g})^i - m_{t_0})^2\right]^{1/2} \cdot s \, (1+g)^{t-t_0}$$

σ_t effectively measures the size of the demand's deviations from its trend. If Φ stands for the cumulative function of the normal distribution and φ for normal distribution, we have:

(22)
$$P_t(\bar{Y}) = \Phi\left(\frac{\bar{Y}-m_t}{\sigma_t}\right)$$

and:

(23)
$$T_t(\bar{Y}) = 1 - \Phi\left(\frac{\bar{Y}-m_t}{\sigma_t}\right)(1-(m_t/\bar{Y})) - (\sigma_t/\bar{Y})\,\varphi\left(\frac{\bar{Y}-m_t}{\sigma_t}\right)$$

When $\bar{Y}$ grows at the rate g, $\dfrac{\bar{Y}-m_t}{\sigma_t}, \dfrac{m_t}{\bar{Y}}, \dfrac{\sigma_t}{\bar{Y}}$ are indeed constant, as are

$P_t(\bar{Y})$ and $T_t(\bar{Y})$. This is a prerequisite for steady-state growth.

4. ESTIMATION

4.1. Principle

The estimation is based on the equations resulting from the integration of (18). To obtain these, we calculate A's eigen values and vectors. As we have seen earlier, there are always two eigen values with a modulus greater than 1. The transversality conditions, which enable the system to converge toward the long-term solution, oblige us to assign the value 0 to the integration constant of these two eigen values. The two initial conditions are thus:

(24)
$$\begin{cases} b_{11}(N^*_{t_0-1}-\hat{N}) + b_{12}(\bar{Y}^*_{t_0-1}-\hat{Y}) + b_{13}(L_{t_0}-\hat{L}) + b_{14}(I_{t_0}-\hat{I}) = 0 \\ b_{21}(N^*_{t_0-1}-\hat{N}) + b_{22}(\bar{Y}_{t_0-1}-\hat{Y}) + b_{23}(L_{t_0}-\hat{L}) + b_{24}(I_{t_0}-\hat{I}) = 0 \end{cases}$$

where b_{ij} is the jth coordinate of the eigen vector linked to the eigen value number i in the base $(N^*_t-\hat{N}, \bar{Y}_t-\hat{Y}, L_{t+1}-\hat{L}, I_{t+1}-\hat{I})$. Here, we have assigned the numbers 1 and 2 to the two eigen values whose modulus is greater than 1.

Using (24), we can calculate $L_{t_0}-\hat{L}$ and $I_{t_0}-\hat{I}$, which are not known, since only $N^*_{t_0-1}$ and $\bar{Y}_{t_0-1}$ are givens for firms at the time the optimal path is calculated. It is therefore entirely necessary to have only two eigen values with a modulus smaller than 1 in order to define a single optimal path based on $N^*_{t_0-1}$ and $\bar{Y}_{t_0-1}$ and the stability condition. We can then calculate the integration constants (c_3 and c_4) linked to the stable eigen values (nos. 3 and 4) by :

$$(25) \begin{cases} b_{31} (N^*_{t_0-1} - \widehat{N}) + b_{32} (\bar{Y}_{t_0-1} - \widehat{Y}) + b_{33} (L_{t_0} - \widehat{L}) + b_{34} (I_{t_0} - \widehat{I}) = c^\varepsilon \\ b_{41} (N^*_{t_0-1} - \widehat{N}) + b_{42} (\bar{Y}_{t_0} - \widehat{Y}) + b_{43} (L_{t_0} - \widehat{L}) + b_{44} (I_{t_0} - \widehat{I}) = c^\flat \end{cases}$$

where $L_{t_0} - \widehat{L}$ and $I_{t_0} - \widehat{I}$ are identified with the aid of (24).

The solution system for (18) is thus:

$$(26) \qquad B \begin{pmatrix} N^*_t - \widehat{N} \\ \bar{Y}_t - \widehat{Y} \\ L_{t+1} - \widehat{L} \\ I_{t+1} - \widehat{I} \end{pmatrix} = \begin{pmatrix} 0 \\ 0 \\ c_3 \, \lambda_3^{t'} \\ c_4 \, \lambda_4^{t'} \end{pmatrix} \quad \text{where } t' = t - t_0 + 1$$

B is the matrix of the b_{ij} values, c_3 and c_4 are calculated using (25), and λ_3 and λ_4 are the stable eigen values.

As the firm follows the optimal path calculated in t_0 , between t_0 and t_0+1, the estimate is made using the equations (26) at the point $t = t_0$. In fact the estimate uses the two equations for $N^*_{t_0}$ and $\bar{Y}_{t_0}$ derived from (26) by eliminating $L_{t_0+1} - \widehat{L}$ and $I_{t_0+1} - \widehat{I}$, since L_{t_0+1} and I_{t_0+1} are not observed, the firm having calculated a new optimal path in t_0+1 . The estimate is obtained by maximizing the likelihood of the two equations so obtained for N* and $\bar{Y}$, to which one simply adds the Gaussian, zero-mean random variables ε_N and ε_γ , whose standard deviations are σ_N and σ_γ. We have therefore refrained from introducing the random terms into the model's structural form. This constitutes a considerable simplification without which, in particular, the random terms found for the estimated form would be correlated, as the correlation coefficient depends on the model's total parameters and variables. The likelihood maximization is performed by means of an iterative change in the parameters. The estimated parameters are:

Q_0, a, b, γ : coefficients of the marginal production function (19);

m, s : multiplicative coefficients of the expected-demand distribution's mean and its standard deviation ((20) and (21)) ;

σ_N and σ_γ : standard deviations of the random terms ε_N and ε_γ of the equations for N* and Y.

For each parameter value and each period, the estimation program calculates:

- the stationary or steady-state-growth reference path by numerical resolution of the system (9)-(11)-(7)-(8') or (16)-(17)-(14)-(15), which requires the use of (20)-(21)-(22)-(23). In the second case, the program effects changes in the variables by taking for γ the parameter's present value, and for g and ρ the average growth rates observed for output and prices during the previous two years (this two-year period was obtained by using an iterative procedure);

- the matrix A, with its eigen values and vectors ;

- the integration constants c_3 and c_4 , separating stable eigen values from divergent eigen values ;

- the coefficients of the N* and $\overline{Y}$ equations derived from (26) and the likelihood value finally obtained.

In these two final equations, $N_t^* - \widehat{N}$ and $\overline{Y}_t - \widehat{Y}$ are a function of $\lambda_3 c_3$ and $\lambda_4 c_4$ (since we are considering the period after the starting point of the optimal path, hence t' = 1), and consequently of $N^*_{t-1} - \widehat{N}$ and $\overline{Y}_{t-1} - \widehat{Y}$ with coefficients derived from the eigen value and vector calculation. We also prepared a less constrained estimate for:

(27)
$$\begin{cases} N_t^* - \widehat{N} = n_0\,(N_{t-1}^* - \widehat{N}) + n_1\,(\overline{Y}_{t-1} - \widehat{Y}) + \varepsilon_N \\[2mm] \overline{Y}_t - \widehat{Y} = y_0\,(N_{t-1}^* - \widehat{N}) + y_1\,(\overline{Y}_{t-1} - \widehat{Y}) + \varepsilon_Y \end{cases}$$

where n_0 , n_1 , y_0 , y_1 , are freely estimated. The model parameters (Q_0 , a, b, γ , m, s) are used only to calculate $\widehat{Y}$ and $\overline{N}$ and not, as in the general case, to calculate the coefficients of the two equations.

4.2.   Results

The optimal-employment equations for full-capacity utilization (N*) and for capacity $\overline{Y}$ were estimated for France on quarterly data covering the period 1965.I to 1981.IV. We used the following series:

- $\overline{Y}$ was calculated as the sum of the potential value added in manufacturing (manufacturing value added divided by the capacity utilization rate extracted from the business surveys) and potential non-manufacturing value added (simple smoothing of non-manufacturing value added) (in millions of 1970 FFr) ;

- N* was calculated using the hypothesis developed here: $N* = N \overline{Y} / D$ where N is total business-sector employment, $\overline{Y}$ the potential output calculated above, D total value added;

- r is the private-sector bond interest rate;

- p is the value-added deflator (1970 = 1);

- w is the wage cost per capita (including net wages and social security contributions); w and N have been rebased to make w = 1 in 1970 (as with p) and convert N into millions of 1970 FFr ;

- p^I is the business-sector investment price corrected for the impact of tax incentives for investment;

- d is the capital depreciation rate.

4.2.a. Intermediate results

It is interesting to examine the matrix A and its eigen values. At the optimum for the complete model, using a stationary reference, the matrix's mean value, calculated at the 68 points of the sample for each of its coefficients, is:

$$
\underset{(N,\ Y,\ L,\ T)}{\tilde{A}} \ = \ \begin{pmatrix} 0.989 & 0 & 1 & 0 \\ 0 & 0.989 & 1.243 & 0.050 \\ -0.001 & 0.003 & 1.031 & 0.0001 \\ -0.022 & 0.049 & 0.039 & 1.031 \end{pmatrix}
$$

Again at the optimum, we found that at all points of the sample A had four real eigen values, of which two were smaller than 1 and two greater than 1. This result tallies with the analytical calculation performed earlier. Table 1 below gives the eigen values' mean and extreme values for the 68 periods.

TABLE 1

	Mean	Lowest value	Highest value
Eigen value no 1....................	1.085	1.072	1.240
Eigen value no 2....................	1.040	1.028	1.059
Eigen value no 3....................	0.989	0.988	0.991
Eigen value no 4....................	0.922	0.840	0.953

We see that eigen values 1 and 4 undergo fairly wide swings over time. Eigen value 3 is always very slightly greater than $1 - \delta$: it therefore represents a dynamic that is convergent, albeit very slowly (mean adjustment lag: 12-20 years). The convergence is more rapid with eigen value 4 (from 5 quarters to 5 years). The inspection of the eigen values for each period shows a faster convergence in the final years (1978-1981) than in the first years (1965-1970).

4.2.b. Structural equation results

The estimates were carried out with the stationary reference path and the steady-state-growth path. We shall only report here the results obtained with the stationary path, as they were consistently of much higher quality than those reached by linearizing around the steady-state-growth path. This result may come as a surprise, considering the non-stationary character of the observed paths. The superiority of the stationary reference to the steady-state reference is doubtless due to the high variability of the steady-state-growth series, in which the denominators include very volatile terms such as $r-\rho+\delta$

(r: interest rate; ρ : inflation rate) ; by contrast, in the stationary case, the terms in the example chosen, $r+\delta$, become stabler. This superiority therefore has a numerical and a non-numerical origin. It should nevertheless be recalled that, on the stationary path, w, L and N underwent a change of variable for the purpose of eliminating technical progress $(1+\gamma)^t$. We shall begin by examining the estimate of (27), where the coefficients of $N^*_{t-1} - \hat{N}$ and $\overline{Y}_{t-1}-\hat{Y}$ have been left free (Table 2, column 1).

The production function displays slightly diminishing returns to scale (a+b = 0.946) and fairly strong technical progress (3.6% a year). Expected demand has a distribution whose mean is equal to 0.998 times — in other words, is practically identical to — the trend-corrected observed mean of past demand. By contrast, the standard deviation of demand apparently used by firms is distinctly larger (by 40%) than the empirical standard deviation. This suggests that firms fear that demand swings will be sharper than those they have recently observed. Equation accuracy is fairly high; the equation for optimal full-capacity employment seems to be more accurate than the equation for production capacity. The s coefficient differs significantly from 0, implying a rejection of the usual no-uncertainty model (where m = 1, s = 0).

We can now examine the complete model (derived from (26)), in which the coefficients of $N_{t-1} - \hat{N}$ and $Y_{t-1} - \hat{Y}$ follow from A's eigen values and vectors obtained for each period. The coefficients of the marginal production function are very close to those obtained by estimating (27). The expected-demand distribution mean is 2.1% lower than the mean recorded on recent (and trend-corrected, see (20)) observations. As in the results reported in the preceding paragraph, the standard deviation of expected demand exceeds the observed standard deviation (by 26%). We can calculate the mean coefficients of $N^*_{t-1} - \hat{N}$ and $\overline{Y}_{t-1} - \hat{Y}$ in the $N^*_t - \hat{N}$ and $\overline{Y}_t - \hat{Y}$ equations and compare them to those yielded by the estimate of (27). We find considerable differences: in particular, y_1 is on average distinctly smaller than 1 here (0.928 versus 1.165 earlier). The free estimate of the cross-adjustment pattern does not, therefore, seem very robust, and the adjustment coefficients obtained are very different from those yielded by the theoretical model.

TABLE 2

(Values in parentheses under coefficients are their *t* statistics)	Estimate of (27) (free coefficients)	Estimate of (26) (complete model)
Production function		
Q_0	0.992 (0.6)	1.022 (0.8)
a	0.404 (3.4)	0.385 (3.2)
b	0.542 (144)	0.560 (12.0)
γ	0.0089 (26.8)	0.0086 (23.8)
Demand distribution		
m	0.998 (98.4)	0.979 (32.4)
s	1.40 (6.7)	1.26 (5.1)
Standard deviations of the equations		
σ_n	803 (7.2)	731 (6.1)
(σ_n *as % of* N^*)	*0.90*	*0.82*
σ_y	2 412 (8.0)	2 854 (6.1)
(σ_y *as % of* $\bar{Y}$)	*1.22*	*1.44*
DW of the equations		
Equation for $N^* - \hat{N}$	0.67	0.78
Equation for $\bar{Y} - \hat{Y}$	1.51	1.56
Coefficients of (27)		Mean coefficients
n_0	0.855 (17.8)	0.988
n_1	0.100 (5.0)	0.027
γ_0	- 0.283 (1.9)	- 0.029
γ_1	1.165 (18.8)	0.928

We can calculate the stationary series consistent with the estimated coefficients (optimum $\hat{N}$ and $\hat{Y}$) and compare them with the observed series (see Graphs 1 and 2, which plot $\hat{N}$, N*, $\overline{Y}$ and $\hat{Y}$). Observed capacity is lower than long-term capacity (toward which it converges) from 1971 to 1973, and always exceeds it thereafter. Optimal employment at full capacity is lower than optimal long-term employment from 1965 to 1973 and consistently higher thereafter. The gap between observed and long-term series is particularly wide in 1974-1975, 1976-1977 and 1980, and narrower in 1975-1979-1981. This would imply that since the first oil crisis, firms have been choosing optimal change paths on which employment and production capacity move down to long-term levels lower than those inherited from the past. From one period to the next, however, the paths are revised upward owing to changes in expected demand and in prices and costs. But, for given values of prices and expected-demand characteristics in each period, firms would appear to regard their production capacity as excessive. If we look at the replies to the production-capacity question in the business surveys, we find the same break at the time of the first oil crisis. Before 1974, a majority of manufacturers considered their production capacity inadequate: the subtraction of "inadequate" from "more than adequate" replies yields a percentage varying between -6% and -20%. From 1975 on, manufacturers consistently regard their production capacity as excessive: the subtraction results range from +10% in early 1980 to +40% in early 1981. The cross-over between observed and long-term series recorded here in 1973 therefore seems plausible.

In order to verify this observation, we have regressed the net balance of opinion on production capacity (OPI) on the differential $\overline{Y}_t{}^* - \hat{Y}$ between existing capacity and long-term capacity (OPI is positive when a majority of manufacturers regards existing production capacity as excessive). We get:

$$OPI = \underset{(4,9)}{- 10,36} + \sum_{j=0}^{3} \alpha_j\,(\overline{Y}_t - \hat{Y})_{-j}$$

$$R^2 = 0,783$$

$$\sum_{j=0}^{3} \alpha_j = \underset{(12,0)}{0,00084}$$

$$DW = 1,65$$

which confirms the close link between the opinion on capacity and the $\overline{Y}_t - \overline{Y}$ differential obtained in the estimates reported here.

GRAPH 1 : **Production capacity**

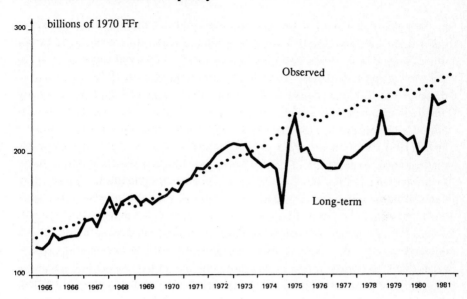

GRAPH 2 : **Optimal employment at full capacity**

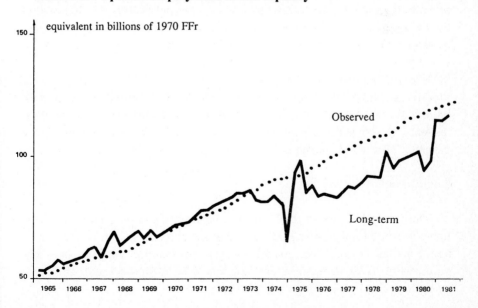

4.2.c. *Effects of exogenous variables on long-term values*

We also calculated — on the stationary path — the long-term effect on investment, optimal employment and production capacity of changes in the model's exogenous variables: production price p, wage cost w, investment price p^I, expected demand mean m_t, (that is, in fact, the sum total of past demands D_{to-i}), the standard deviation of expected demand σ_t , and the discount rate r (Table 3). The effects were calculated for the start of each period (for the average of the years 1965-1969), for the end of the period (1978-1981) and on an average basis (1965-1981). A 1% increase in the mathematical expectation of demand increases long-term production capacity by an average of only 0.5%. By contrast, in a model that did not incorporate demand uncertainty, the long-term rise in capacity would have been identical to that of demand. It should be noted that this is a partial model, as it analyzes only domestic output. If capacity expands in the long run by only 50% of the demand average, this means either that demand is rationed or that imports are substituted for domestic output. Naturally, the model tells us nothing about the rationing scheme at work here. Furthermore, the average figure of 50% fluctuates considerably. For example, it exceeds 80% in the more recent period. All exogenous-variable changes that help improve profitability (higher production prices, lower wage costs, lower discount rates) entail a long-term rise in production capacity. We also observe the customary effects of capital-labor substitution. The increase in demand uncertainty, represented by a rise in expected-demand variance, causes capacity — and consequently investment and employment — to contract.

The pure substitution effects, stemming from the Cobb-Douglas marginal production function, are very close to those adopted for standard specifications. All the other effects (profitability, uncertainty, incomplete response to expected-demand rises) are new and can be attributed to the inclusion of demand uncertainty.

Conclusion

This study has shown that demand uncertainty can be integrated in the standard firm production-function model of the putty-clay type. As a result — unlike in the conventional model — firms' production capacity does not necessarily match demand in the long run. The effects of profitability —

summed up by Malinvaud in Tobin's q — and of relative production-factor costs appear simultaneously. Of course, one could make this model more realistic by endogenizing prices or inventories (as in Maccini [1981]), or by a fuller treatment of taxation.

TABLE 3 : **Effects (in %)**

Of a 1% Rise in	At the start of the period on			At the end of the period on			Mean effects on		
	Investment	Employment	Production capacity	Investment	Employment	Production capacity	Investment	Employment	Production capacity
Production price	+ 0.27	+ 0.68	+ 0.48	+ 0.67	+ 1.01	+ 0.81	+ 0.32	+ 0.75	+ 0.53
Wage cost	+ 0.56	- 0.69	- 0.14	+ 0.14	- 1.06	- 0.51	+ 0.48	- 0.78	- 0.23
Investment price	- 0.87	- 0.03	- 0.37	- 0.95	- 0.11	- 0.44	- 0.90	- 0.07	- 0.40
Expected-demand	+ 0.74	+ 0.99	+ 0.58	+ 0.92	+ 0.85	+ 0.83	+ 0.63	+ 0.46	+ 0.51
Expected-demand standard deviation	- 0.15	- 0.01	- 0.07	- 0.17	- 0.11	- 0.13	- 0.26	- 0.03	- 0.12
1 point discount rate	- 7.41	- 0.66	- 3.41	- 5.29	- 1.00	- 2.70	- 7.01	- 0.88	- 3.37

APPENDIX 1
Hessian of the problem

$$\mathcal{H} = \begin{pmatrix}
\mu_t f''_{L^2}(L_t^*, I_t) & \mu_t f''_{LI}(L_t^*, I_t) & 0 & 0 \\[1em]
\mu_t f''_{LI}(L_t^*, I_t) & \mu_t f''_{I^2}(L_t^*, I_t) & 0 & 0 \\[1em]
0 & 0 & \dfrac{-2 w_{t+1}}{(1+r)^{t+1}} \dfrac{N_t^*}{\bar{Y}_t^3} \displaystyle\int_{-\infty}^{\bar{Y}_t} u\, dP_{t+1}(u) - \dfrac{1}{(1+r)^{t+1}}\left(p_{t+1} - w_{t+1}\dfrac{N_t^*}{\bar{Y}_t}\right) P'_{t+1}(\bar{Y}_t) & \dfrac{1}{(1+r)^{t+1}} \dfrac{w_{t+1}}{\bar{Y}_t^2} \displaystyle\int_{-\infty}^{\bar{Y}_t} u\, dP_{t+1}(u) \\[2em]
0 & 0 & \dfrac{1}{(1+r)^{t+1}} \dfrac{w_{t+1}}{\bar{Y}_t^2} \displaystyle\int_{-\infty}^{\bar{Y}_t} u\, dP_{t+1}(u) & 0
\end{pmatrix}$$

$$(P' > 0).$$

APPENDIX 2
Optimality conditions when firms must preserve employment N*
(perfect rigidity of employment)

(5″)
$$w_{t+1} = \frac{p_t^I (1+r) f_L' (L_t^*, I_t)}{f_I' (L_t^*, I_t)} - \frac{p_{t+1}^I (1-\delta) f_L' (L_{t+1}^*, I_{t+1})}{f_I' (L_{t+1}^*, I_{t+1})}$$

(6″)
$$p_{t+1} (1 - P_{t+1} (\bar{Y}_t)) = \frac{(1+r) p_t^I}{f_I' (L_t^*, I_t)} - \frac{(1-\delta) p_{t+1}^I}{f_I' (L_{t+1}^*, I_{t+1})}$$

or, in the long term:

(5‴)
$$\frac{f_L'}{f_I'} = \frac{w}{p(r+\delta)}$$

(6‴)
$$p(1 - P(\bar{Y})) = \frac{p(r+\delta)}{f_I'}$$

APPENDIX 3
Matrix A (equation (18))

$$A_{N_t^*,\,N_{t-1}^*} = 1-\delta \qquad\qquad A_{\overline{Y}_t,\,N_{t-1}^*} = 0$$

$$A_{N_t^*,\,\overline{Y}_{t-1}} = 0 \qquad\qquad A_{\overline{Y}_t,\,\overline{Y}_{t-1}} = 1-\delta$$

$$A_{N_t^*,\,L_t} = 1 \qquad\qquad A_{\overline{Y}_t,\,L_t} = f_L'$$

$$A_{N_t^*,\,I_t} = 0 \qquad\qquad A_{\overline{Y}_t,\,I_t} = f_I'$$

$$A_{L_{t+1},\,N_{t-1}^*} = \frac{V}{\Delta}\frac{f_I'^2}{f_{I^2}''}\frac{1}{\widehat{p^I}}\frac{\widehat{w}}{\widehat{Y}^2}\int_{-\infty}^{\widehat{Y}} u\,dP(u) < 0 \quad\Bigg|\quad \text{où } V = \frac{f_{I^2}''f_L' - f_{LI}''f_I'}{f_{L^2}''f_I' - f_{LI}''f_L'} > 0$$

$$\Delta = 1 + \frac{f_{LI}''}{f_{I^2}''}V > 0$$

$$A_{L_{t+1},\,\overline{Y}_{t-1}} = \frac{1}{\Delta}\frac{\widehat{w}\,T'(\widehat{Y})f_I'^2}{\widehat{p^I}\,(f_{LI}''f_L' - f_{L^2}''f_I')}$$

$$- \frac{V}{\Delta}\frac{f_I'}{f_{I^2}''}\frac{1}{\widehat{p^I}}\left(2\widehat{w}\frac{\widehat{N}}{\widehat{Y}^3}\int_{-\infty}^{\widehat{Y}} u\,dP(u) + \left(\widehat{p} - \widehat{w}\frac{\widehat{N}}{\widehat{Y}}\right)P'(\widehat{Y})\right)$$

$$A_{L_{t+1},\,L_t} = \frac{V}{\Delta}\frac{f_I'^2}{f_{I^2}''}\frac{1}{\widehat{p^I}(1-\delta)}\frac{\widehat{w}}{\widehat{Y}^2}\int_{-\infty}^{\widehat{Y}} u\,dP(u) + \frac{1}{\Delta}\frac{\widehat{w}\,T'(\widehat{Y})f_I'^2 f_L'}{(1-\delta)\,\widehat{p^I}\,(f_{LI}''f_L' - f_{L^2}''f_I')}$$

$$- \frac{V}{\Delta}\frac{f_I'^2 f_L'}{f_{I^2}''}\frac{1}{\widehat{p^I}(1-\delta)}\left(2\widehat{w}\frac{\widehat{N}}{\widehat{Y}^3}\int_{-\infty}^{\widehat{Y}} u\,dP(u) + \left(\widehat{p} - \widehat{w}\frac{\widehat{N}}{\widehat{Y}}\right)P'(\widehat{Y})\right) + \frac{1+r}{1+\delta}$$

$$A_{L_{t+1},\,I_t} = \frac{1}{\Delta}\frac{\widehat{w}\,T'(\widehat{Y})\,(f_I')^3}{(1-\delta)\,\widehat{p^I}\,(f_{LI}''f_L' - f_{L^2}''f_I')}$$

$$- \frac{V}{\Delta}\frac{(f_I')^3}{f_{I^2}''}\frac{1}{\widehat{p^I}(1-\delta)}\left(2\widehat{w}\frac{\widehat{N}}{\widehat{Y}^3}\int_{-\infty}^{\widehat{Y}} u\,dP(u) + \left(\widehat{p} - \widehat{w}\frac{\widehat{N}}{\widehat{Y}}\right)P'(\widehat{Y})\right)$$

$$A_{I_{t+1}, N^*_{t-1}} = \frac{1}{\Delta} \frac{f_I'^2}{f_{I}''^2} \frac{1}{\widehat{p^I}} \frac{\widehat{w}}{\widehat{Y}^2} \int_{-\infty}^{\widehat{Y}} u \, dP(u) < 0$$

$$A_{I_{t+1}, \bar{Y}_{t-1}} = \frac{1}{\Delta} \frac{\widehat{w} \, T'(\widehat{Y}) f_I'^2}{\widehat{p^I} \, (f_{LI}'' f_L' - f_{L}''^2 f_I')} \cdot \frac{f_{LI}''}{f_{I}''^2} - \frac{f_I'^2}{f_{I}''^2} \frac{1}{\widehat{p_I}} \frac{1}{\Delta} \left(2 \, \widehat{w} \, \frac{\widehat{N}}{\widehat{Y}^3} \int_{-\infty}^{\widehat{Y}} u \, dP(u)\right.$$

$$\left. + \left(\widehat{p} - \widehat{w} \frac{\widehat{N}}{\widehat{Y}}\right) P'(\widehat{Y})\right)$$

$$A_{I_{t+1}, L_t} = \frac{1}{\Delta} \frac{f_I'^2}{f_{I}''^2} \frac{1}{\widehat{p_I}(1-\delta)} \frac{\widehat{w}}{\widehat{Y}^2} \int_{-\infty}^{\widehat{Y}} u \, dP(u) - \frac{1}{\Delta} \frac{\widehat{w} \, T'(\widehat{Y}) f_I'^2 f_L' f_{LI}''}{(1-\delta) \, \widehat{p^I} \, (f_{LI}'' f_L' - f_{L}''^2 f_I') f_{I}''^2}$$

$$- \frac{f_I'^2 f_L'}{f_{I}''^2} \frac{1}{\widehat{p_I}(1-\delta)} \cdot \frac{1}{\Delta} \left(2 \, \widehat{w} \, \frac{\widehat{N}}{\widehat{Y}^3} \int_{-\infty}^{\widehat{Y}} u \, dP(u) + \left(\widehat{p} - \widehat{w} \frac{\widehat{N}}{\widehat{Y}}\right) P'(\widehat{Y})\right)$$

$$A_{I_{t+1}, I_t} = -\frac{1}{\Delta} \frac{\widehat{w} \, T'(\widehat{Y}) \, (f_I')^3 f_{LI}''}{(1-\delta) \widehat{p^I} \, (f_{LI}'' f_L' - f_{L}''^2 f_I') f_{I}''^2} - \frac{(f_I')^3}{f_{I}''^2} \frac{1}{\widehat{p^I}(1-\delta)} \frac{1}{\Delta}$$

$$\cdot \left(2 \, \widehat{w} \, \frac{\widehat{N}}{\widehat{Y}^3} \int_{-\infty}^{\widehat{Y}} u \, dP(u) + \left(\widehat{p} - \widehat{w} \frac{\widehat{N}}{\widehat{Y}}\right) P'(\widehat{Y})\right) + \frac{1+r}{1-\delta}$$

EPILOGUE

Econometric models in France:
recent developments

The preceding chapters have shown that in the early 1980s there was a certain consensus in France as to the most suitable model for investment. The best econometric model seemed to be the flexible accelerator, with a relative-factor-cost effect and a high elasticity of substitution (close to unity) if a putty-clay technology was adopted. Profits could be introduced as a supplementary factor playing an additive role (by modifying only the pace of implementation of the required investment). The attempts to re-estimate the basic model after 1985 have yielded disappointing results thet challenge the model's stability.

1. INSTABILITY OF THE TRADITIONAL MODEL

A re-estimation of the basic model for the 1970-1986 period produced the following findings (Artus and Sicsic [1988]):

- the relative capital-labor cost loses all significant impact; sometimes its influence actually runs counter to the conventional substitution effect;
- the accelerator-effect coefficient is greatly diminished, with the elasticity of capital relative to output falling well below unity; moreover, the estimated value of this coefficient seems to be driven even higher by the simultaneity of output and investment (Bennett [1988]).

These results are easy to understand if we compare the observed investment rate with the one that would result from the simplest flexible accelerator model, particularly assuming a constant marginal capital coefficient (1.8) and a constant replacement rate. With the standard adjustment lags (embodied in the long-term growth rate), the continuous slowdown in growth ought to have induced a sharp fall in the investment rate. But Table 1 shows that, at the end of the period, the observed rate remained more than three points higher than the calculated rate. This indicates either a strong increase in the marginal capital coefficient of accelerating obsolescence (and consequently a rising replacement rate).

TABLE 1: **Comparison of the observed investment rate derived from the accelerator principle (with constant capital coefficient and replacement rate)**

			Averages per period	
	70-73	74-78	79-83	84-87
Investment rate (%)				
— observed	16.1	14.6	13.5	12.5
— calculated	16.1	12.5	10.4	8.8
Growth rate (%)				
— observed	5.4	2.6	1.7	1.8
— long term	5.5	3.6	2.4	1.5

Notes :
• The investment rate is the ratio of firms' investment to GDP
• $Tc = 6.5 + 1.8\ q^*$ with $q^* = 0.12\ q + 0.25\ q_{-1} + 0.2\ q_{-2} + 0.17\ q_{-3} + 0.12\ q_{-4} + 0.08\ q_{-5} + 0.06\ q_{-6}$

Also, the relative capital-labor cost, which had risen sharply from 1970 to 1975 (in particular because the high rate of inflation kept real interest rates low), shrank from 1976 to 1978 and then remained stable. These changes, therefore, cannot explain the excess of investment relative to the growth rate in the 1980s.

Many attempts — some successful, others not — have been made to alter the basic model and give it a fresh relevance. We shall discuss the most interesting of these attempts below.

1.1. A few popular clichés refuted by economic analysis

It has become commonplace in France to explain the recent pattern of investment by the following notions:

- firms have accelerated their scrapping rate to modernize their capital;
- the repeated rises in energy prices in 1973 and 1979 have led to a substitution of capital for energy, thereby braking capital productivity;

- the very attractive level of financial — asset yields has diverted firms from investing in productive assets (it will be noted that this argument contradicts the one needed to explain the high relative level of investment);

- disinflation has increased the firms' real debt burden and slowed investment (this too is a counter-argument);

- firms remain over-indebted — despite the improvement in gross operating surpluses, whose full effects have not yet been felt at the balance-sheet level — and as a result their investment opportunities are limited.

However, neither the introduction of a higher capital scrapping rate after the second oil crisis, nor the inclusion of the relative energy price, nor the substitution of periodical bond yield (that is, including capital gains and losses) for yield to maturity in the user cost of capital, nor the inclusion of balance-sheet ratios have yielded significant results (Artus and Sicsic [1988]; Malecot and Hamon [1986]).

It would seem that:

- the capital replacement rate has remained stable;
- capital and energy are complementary, not substitutable;
- French firms have not effected trade-offs between tangible and financial assets the growth of financial investments is simply due to the increase in corporate resources generated by wage restrictions;
- in recent years, debt has not impeded investment.

Economists are still debating whether disinflation has adversely affected investment by eliminating the inflation-induced cut in the real corporate debt burden. While this notion is refuted by econometric investigations on time series, it has received some support from findings on panel data (Legendre and Morin [1987]).

1.2. Three promising approaches: capital inertia, structural effects and taxation

The disappearance of capital-labor substitution effects in the econometric estimates is explained by the divergent curves for the relative capital-labor cost and the mean productivities of capital and labor. The relative capital-labor cost fell at an annual rate of 6.8% from 1960 to 1974. Between 1974 and 1985, the rate of decrease was only 1.6%. With a Cobb-Douglas function and a wage share of value added of $\beta = 0.6$, this five-point break in the curve should have lowered labor-productivity growth by three points and capital-productivity growth by two points a year. In fact, however, the French data indicate a simultaneous slowdown in labor-productivity growth (– 2.4% a year) and an accelerating fall of mean capital productivity (– 1.3%). This apparent slowdown is due to lags in adjusting to slower growth (in particular as regards capital). But these lags, which are taken into account in econometric models, are inadequate to reconcile the cost and long-term productivity curves. However, if the model allows both for inter-industry factor mobility and for adjustment lags (Henry, Leroux and Muet [1988]), the cost curve once again becomes qualitatively consistent with long-term factor productivities, as shown by the following breakdown:

	average labor productivity	average capital productivity
observed break (average annual rate)	-2.4%	– 1.3%
impact:		
- adjustment lags............	– 0.1%	– 1.1%
- inter-industry mobility....	– 0.6%	– 1.2%
- capital obsolescence.......	– 0.3%	0
long-term break.........................	-1.4 %	+ 1.0%

This parallel plotting of changes in relative costs and mean productivities is relevant in the putty-putty hypothesis of complete substitution. But it can give a misleading picture of real substitution effects when these result solely from the capital-replacement process (putty-clay model). Because of the slowness of the substitution process, the rise in marginal capital productivity after 1974 in response to the cost curve is not reflected in mean productivity until 1981. When we take into account the changes in inter-industry capital mobility since 1974, we once again find a positive elasticity of substitution of 0.1 in the putty-putty hypothesis, 0.2-0.3 in the putty-clay hypothesis.

A more detailed assessment of the impact of tax incentives (Muet and Avouyi-Dovi [1987a]: see Appendix below) modifies the findings of earlier studies, which did not distinguish between the specific effect of tax incentives and that of other capital-cost components. The estimates that make such a distinction (Muet and Avouyi-Dovi [1987b]; Artus and Sicsic [1988]) show that while the elasticity of investment with respect to other components is very weak, or even non-existent, its elasticity with respect to tax incentives is close to 1.5. In other words, a 1-franc incentive leads to 1.5 francs of additional investment, even taking into account a possible future adjustment.Taxation thus seems to be the only important component of relative cost. The explanation may be that the gain from a tax incentive linked to a capital-goods purchase is immediately and distinctly perceived, whereas the changes in other cost components must be projected over a long period, corresponding to the equipment's lifetime. These expectations, however, can differ considerably from the observed variations. For example, changes in the depreciation systems — which require the firm to discount future costs and benefits — prove less efficient than direct deductions as regards impact on capital cost.

Despite some promising approaches, the difficulties encountered in properly reproducing the investment curve with the aid of the conventional model have led econometricians to explore two directions that reconcile the effects of profitability and demand. The first, the estimation of disequilibrium models, is a direct extension of the model reported in Chapter 8. The estimates have generally concerned a two-regime model: flexible accelerator and profit/interest rate (Artus and Sicsic [1988]; Muet and Avouyi-Dovi [1987b]). Other studies have argued that greater allowance should be made for demand constraint so as to avoid the bias toward an acceptance of the Keynesian regime resulting from an approximation of demand by output

(Poret [1986]; Lambert [1987]). The second line of research is a more direct inclusion of profitability, either through "Tobin's q"-type models or through the introduction of demand uncertainty as in Chapter 9.

2 - MODELS BASED ON PROFITABILITY

2.1. Tobin's q

The rise in stock-market prices during recent years has prompted econometricians to re-test models based on Tobin's q, the ratio of firms' market value to their capital's replacement value. Higher share prices mean a lower user cost of capital, since the firm's long-standing shareholders can sell new shares at a high price without affecting dividends paid. This should result in additional investment. By regressing the accumulation rate on Tobin's q, Chan Lee and Torres [1987] have indeed found a significant effect: they calculate that a 10% rise in share prices entails 2.5% extra investment. However, Artus [1988] questions the robustness of their findings. He shows that if we add to the Tobin's q variable the standard determinants of the basic model (such as the economic growth rate and the profit rate) the weight of Tobin's q becomes extremely small or even non-existent. Furthermore, the post-1984 "stock-market bubble" has not generated any visible extra investment. Artus concludes that simple current profits — and not their questionably efficient translation into share prices — seem to be the significant variable.

Sneesens and Maillard [1988] specify the Tobin's q model by spelling out this variable. They take a context of disequilibrium where the labor supply, demand, and each firm's supply of goods are subjected to random variation. In the short run, the production technique is rigid and the price is determined prior to the observation of random factors in order to maximize profits in a monopoly-competition environment. The production technique is chosen with a view to maximizing long-term profit. Entry is free, and profits cancel out in the long run. Investment is proportional to the profits that appear in each period (if profits are positive, productive capacity rises until profits disappear). The authors show that in this case investment depends on gross operating profits, the capacity utilization rate and relative factor costs. They therefore reconstruct the standard determinants of investment within the logic of a Tobin's q model. But, in the model form obtained by the authors, the relative factor cost exerts a significant effect, unlike in the standard model.

2.2. Uncertainty on future demand

We saw in Chapter 9 that the model based on the incorporation of uncertainty on future demand, and in which installed capacity depends on profitability, seemed fairly applicable to the French case. More recent econometric studies substantiate this impression. Artus and Sicsic [1988] have completed the model by adding the bankruptcy risk. If demand proves very low, not only is capacity under-utilized as in the standard model, but firms can go bankrupt. Their shareholders then lose their equity while creditors collect the firms' residual value and bear a bankruptcy cost. The bankruptcy probability is chosen endogenously and depends on interest rates and bankruptcy cost. The results are promising and greatly enhance our understanding of investment changes especially in the 1970s.

Lambert and Mulkay [1987] try to combine the investment-disequilibrium and the demand-uncertainty approaches. The traditional disequilibrium approaches to investment (Chapter 8 above; Mulkay [1983]; Gerard and Vandenberghe [1984]; Dormont [1986] on panel data) treat aggregate investment as the minimum or the weighted average of the investments corresponding to each regime. This implies the scarcely credible assumption that firms naively extrapolate the operating regime of the economy that they observe in the short run. For example, a firm suffering from classical unemployment would assume it will never encounter a demand constraint.

Lambert and Mulkay introduce uncertainty on future demand in the disequilibrium model. This means that the firm cannot know precisely how much capacity it will need in the future, and must use profitability as a yardstick for determining the optimal probability that demand will match available capacity. The expected capacity utilization rate thus becomes one of the model's key variables. The authors identify it *ex post* with the aggregate utilization rate resulting from a disequilibrium model of French manufacturing. In fact, this identification raises certain problems of consistency. The estimate shows that profitability plays an important part in the 1980s, whereas its effect on investment in the 1970s is negligible.

On the whole, we can see that recent econometric research on investment in France has brought both disappointments and satisfactions. The conventional model cannot be salvaged except at the price of often debatable complications such as very long lags and a highly specific role for taxation.

However revamped, the model apparently requires a very sharp curtailment of capital-labor substitution opportunities. The work performed on more sophisticated alternatives such as the demand-uncertainty and disequilibrium models demonstrates the potential of these approaches.

APPENDIX
The user-cost-of-capital series

To define the user cost of capital, we return to the determination of investment presented in Chapter 8. The investment function is putty-clay, with :

I_v: volume of equipment acquired and installed at date v;
q_v: equipment purchase price;
$w^*(t,v)$ expected wage rate for period t, including social-security contributions;
$N(t,v)$ labor required, at date t, to operate equipment I_v;
r expected long-term interest rate;
$Q(t, v)$ at date t;
$p^*(t, v)$ production price for period t expected at date t.

The choice of production techniques is represented by a production function with substitutable factors (*ex-ante* production function) that possesses the conventional properties of differentiability and concavity:

$$Q_v = f(I_v , N_v)$$

Once the equipment is installed, the production techniques have fixed coefficients. The equipment depreciates at a constant rate δ (wear and tear). The equipment-related labor and output at date t are therefore:

$$N(t,v) = N_v \, e^{-\delta(t-v)}$$

$$Q(t,v) = Q_v \, e^{-\delta(t-v)}$$

where Q_v and N_v stand for the initial labor and output linked to equipment I_v. Independent of wear and tear, the equipment is scrapped after T_E years, once the productivity of its required labor falls below the real wage. This is due to the technical progress embodied in new equipment and to the increase in the real wage.

The tax depreciation is approximated by an exponential distribution with parameter α. Let T_f be the tax lifetime of the equipment. The distribution density is :

$$g(t) = \frac{\alpha e^{-\alpha t}}{1 - e^{-\alpha T_f}}$$

The discount rate adopted is the bond yield (r) net of tax. Taking into account the average rate of corporate tax β, the discount rate becomes $(1 - \beta) r$ for the firm.

The profit net of tax yielded by the equipment I_v and discounted over its economic lifetime is therefore :

$$P = (1-\beta) \left(\int_{v}^{v+T_E} p^*(t,v)\, Q(t,v)\, e^{-(1-\beta)r(t-v)} dt - \int_{v}^{v+T_E} w^*(t,v)\, N(t,v)\, e^{-(1-\beta)r(t-v)} dt \right)$$

discounted value added   discounted wage cost

$$- (1 - k_1 - \beta k_2) q_v I_v + \frac{(1 - k_1)\,\beta\alpha}{1 - e^{-\alpha T_f}} \int_{v}^{v+T_f} I_v q_v\, e^{-(\alpha + (1-\beta)r)(t-v)}\, dt$$

Investment net of tax deductions   discounted value of
                                                         tax depreciation

where k_1 and k_2 stand for the rates of tax deduction :

- k_1 is tax-deductible and reduces the depreciation base ;
- k_2 reduces the financial-year profit without altering the depreciation base.

A few additional hypotheses are needed to simplify the model's resolution. In particular, we assume that firms expect a constant rate of growth for prices and wages :

$$w^* (t,v) = w_v\, e^{w(t-v)}$$
$$p^* (t,v) = p_v\, e^{p(t-v)}$$

Firms determine the volume of their investment I_v by maximizing their discounted profit net of tax (P).

Using the change of variable :

$$c = q_v\, \frac{1}{1-\beta}\left(1-k_1-k_2\,\beta+\left(\frac{(1-k_1)\alpha\beta}{1-e^{-\alpha T_f}}\right)\left(\frac{1-e^{-(\alpha+(1-\beta)r)T_f}}{\alpha+(1-\beta)r}\right)\right)\left(\frac{\delta-\dot{w}+(1-\beta)r}{1-e^{-(\delta-\dot{w}+(1-\beta)r)T_E}}\right)$$

$$p' = p_v\left(\frac{1-e^{-(\delta-\dot{p}+(1-\beta)r)T_E}}{\delta-\dot{p}+(1-\beta)r}\right)\left(\frac{\delta-\dot{w}+(1-\beta)r}{1-e^{-(\delta-\dot{w}+(1-\beta)r)T_E}}\right)$$

$$w = w_v$$
$$N = N_v$$
$$Q = Q_v$$
$$I = I_v$$

The program is simply equivalent to the static maximization :

$$\text{Max P} \quad\Leftrightarrow\quad \text{Max } (p'Q - w\,N - c\,I)$$

$$Q \le f(\,I\,,\,N)$$
$$Q \le \bar{Q}$$
$$N \le \bar{N}$$
$$I \le \bar{I}$$

If we confine ourselves to the determination of investment, four main regimes are possible (see chapter 8):

a) Notional demand $N < \bar{N}, Q < \bar{Q}$

$$f_I' = \frac{c}{p} \, , \, f_N' = \frac{w}{p} \, , \, Q = f(I,N)$$

b) Effective demand (given demand) $N < \bar{N}, Q = \bar{Q}$

$$\frac{f_I'}{f_N'} = \frac{c}{w} \qquad \bar{Q} = f(I,N)$$

c) Labor-market demand $N = \bar{N}, Q < \bar{Q}$

$$f_I' = \frac{c}{p} \qquad f(I,\bar{N}) = Q$$

d) Financial constraint $(I = \bar{I})$

The real user cost of capital is an implicit price that can always be broken down into three elements :

- the relative price of equipment ;
- the tax index (F) ;
- a discount index (AC).

In the absence of demand constraints and financial constraints (a and c), the marginal productivity of the investment is equal to the real cost of capital (c/p). In this expression, the relative price is the ratio of the capital-goods to the output price and the discount index incorporates the rate of increase of the production price :

$$AC' = \frac{\delta - \dot{p} + (1 - \beta)r}{1 - e^{-(\delta - \dot{p} + (1 - \beta)r)T_E}}$$

If demand is constrained, the marginal rate of substitution is equal to the relative capital-labor cost (c/w). The relative price is the ratio of the investment price to the wage rate (q/w), and the discount index incorporates the rate of wage increase (w).

$$AC = \frac{\delta - \dot{w} + (1 - \beta)r}{1 - e^{-(\delta - \dot{w} + (1-\beta)r)T_E}}$$

By contrast, the tax index is invariable in every case :

$$F = \frac{1}{1-\beta} \left[1 - k_1 - k_2\beta + \left(\frac{(1-k_1)\alpha\beta}{1-e^{-\alpha T_f}} \right) \left(\frac{1 - e^{-(\alpha + (1-\beta)r)T_f}}{\alpha + (1-\beta)r} \right) \right]$$

The values of the coefficients k_1, k_2 and α are listed in Table 2.

The series for the user cost of capital and its breakdown into three components :

$$c = q \quad AC \quad F$$

are given in Table 3.

Also listed in Table 3 are the value of the tax index at a constant interest rate (FISC) and the effect of interest-rate changes on the discounted value of tax depreciations (AMORT)

$$F = FISC \quad AMORT$$

The FISC variable, which exclusively charts the effects of tax policy, is used to measure the specific effect of tax incentives.

	k_1 %	k_2 %	α
60.0	0	0	0.10
to			
66.1	0		
66.2	1.5		
66.3	3.0		
66.4	3.0		
67.1	0		
to			
68.2	0		
68.3	0.6		
68.4	2.5		
to			
69.3	2.5		
69.4	0		
to			
74.2			0.10
74.3			0.0124
to			
75.1	0		0.0124
75.2	2.6		0.10
75.3	7.7		
75.4	10.0		
76.1	0		
to			
76.4			0.10
77.1			0.17
77.2			0.17
77.3			0.10
to			
79.2		0	
79.3		1.6	
79.4		1.6	
80.1		1.2	
80.2		1.2	
80.3		1.2	
80.4		3.8	
to			
81.4		3.8	
82.1		4.8	
to			
82.4		4.8	0.10
83.1		0	0.20
to			
84.4	0	0	0.20

Source : Muet and Avouyi-Dovi [1987a] pages 158-159

	User cost of capital	Price of equipment	Discount index	Tax index	Tax index Effects of tax policy	Tax index Effects of interest-rate changes
	c	q	A C	F	FISC	AMORT
601	.7554	1.002	.7696	.9786	1.000	.9786
602	.8067	1.039	.7936	.9774	1.000	.9774
603	.8483	1.062	.8195	.9739	1.000	.9739
604	.8245	1.073	.7886	.9736	1.000	.9736
611	.8642	1.083	.8175	.9753	1.000	.9753
612	.8698	1.103	.8095	.9738	1.000	.9738
613	.8794	1.117	.8075	.9745	1.000	.9745
614	.8904	1.121	.8145	.9749	1.000	.9749
621	.8995	1.109	.8325	.9740	1.000	.9740
622	.8955	1.094	.8394	.9747	1.000	.9747
623	.8423	1.072	.8075	.9723	1.000	.9722
624	.8716	1.068	.8394	.9719	1.000	.9719
631	.8819	1.069	.8494	.9708	1.000	.9708
632	.8939	1.059	.8693	.9704	1.000	.9704
633	.9088	1.054	.8883	.9703	1.000	.9703
634	.8941	1.044	.8803	.9719	1.000	.9719
641	.8965	1.048	.8793	.9726	1.000	.9726
642	.9125	1.065	.8803	.9728	1.000	.9728
643	.9425	1.085	.8933	.9719	1.000	.9719
644	.9727	1.109	.9022	.9717	1.000	.9717
651	.9872	1.127	.8953	.9783	1.000	.9783
652	1.009	1.138	.9022	.9825	1.000	.9825
653	1.012	1.141	.9042	.9805	1.000	.9805
654	1.019	1.149	.9042	.9815	1.000	.9815
661	1.030	1.163	.9012	.9826	1.000	.9826
662	1.043	1.181	.9102	.9700	.9850	.9848
663	1.055	1.203	.9172	.9565	.9700	.9861
664	1.080	1.219	.9252	.9574	.9700	.9870
671	1.133	1.225	.9391	.9854	1.000	.9854
672	1.134	1.223	.9411	.9853	1.000	.9853
673	1.131	1.219	.9431	.9837	1.000	.9837
674	1.104	1.218	.9202	.9845	1.000	.9845
681	1.066	1.213	.8923	.9852	1.000	.9852
682	1.081	1.215	.9022	.9861	1.000	.9861
683	1.064	1.192	.9122	.9786	.9940	.9845
684	.9899	1.134	.9072	.9617	.9750	.9863
691	.9322	1.085	.8883	.9668	.9750	.9916
692	.9077	1.031	.9082	.9689	.9750	.9938
693	.9057	1.005	.9272	.9715	.9750	.9964
694	.9592	1.006	.9561	.9972	1.000	.9972
701	.9685	1.005	.9611	1.001	1.000	1.001
702	1.000	1.000	1.000	1.000	1.000	1.000
703	.9966	.9935	1.005	.9972	1.000	.9972
704	1.006	.9853	1.018	1.002	1.000	1.002
711	.9871	.9680	1.021	.9978	1.000	.9978
712	.9761	.9529	1.025	.9984	1.000	.9984
713	.9674	.9395	1.031	.9978	1.000	.9978
714	.9646	.9261	1.043	.9978	1.000	.9978
721	.9695	.9218	1.055	.9961	1.000	.9961
722	.9905	.9372	1.066	.9907	1.000	.9907
723	1.006	.9469	1.073	.9899	1.000	.9899
724	1.012	.9522	1.071	.9925	1.000	.9925

	User cost of capital	Price of equipment	Discount index	Tax index	Tax index Effects of tax policy	Effects of interest-rate changes
	c	q	A C	F	FISC	AMORT
731	1.020	.9446	1.084	.9962	1.000	.9962
732	1.024	.9277	1.104	.9994	1.000	.9994
733	1.024	.9058	1.124	1.005	1.000	1.005
734	1.025	.8756	1.161	1.008	1.000	1.008
741	1.069	.8563	1.224	1.020	1.000	1.020
742	1.067	.8087	1.286	1.025	1.000	1.025
743	1.053	.7531	1.336	1.045	1.013	1.032
744	1.026	.7039	1.394	1.045	1.013	1.031
751	.9854	.6614	1.431	1.040	1.013	1.026
752	.9095	.6293	1.452	.9949	.9740	1.021
753	.8579	.6099	1.495	.9405	.9230	1.019
754	.8338	.6059	1.498	.9183	.9000	1.020
761	.9281	.6034	1.509	1.019	1.000	1.019
762	.9987	.6185	1.583	1.019	1.000	1.019
763	1.066	.6358	1.641	1.021	1.000	1.021
764	1.134	.6499	1.701	1.025	1.000	1.025
771	1.155	.6648	1.717	1.011	.9896	1.021
772	1.206	.6829	1.728	1.021	.9930	1.029
773	1.268	.7040	1.752	1.028	1.000	1.027
774	1.340	.7237	1.798	1.029	1.000	1.029
781	1.388	.7433	1.806	1.034	1.000	1.034
782	1.441	.7617	1.842	1.027	1.000	1.027
783	1.484	.7710	1.886	1.020	1.000	1.020
784	1.506	.7730	1.917	1.016	1.000	1.016
791	1.534	.7742	1.957	1.012	1.000	1.012
792	1.571	.7718	2.002	1.016	1.000	1.016
793	1.585	.7701	2.021	1.018	.9884	1.029
794	1.627	.7687	2.068	1.023	.9884	1.035
801	1.715	.7638	2.153	1.042	.9913	1.051
802	1.702	.7439	2.195	1.042	.9913	1.051
803	1.705	.7296	2.245	1.040	.9913	1.049
804	1.685	.7191	2.279	1.028	.9725	1.057
811	1.737	.7100	2.367	1.033	.9725	1.062
812	1.837	.7127	2.453	1.050	.9725	1.080
813	1.866	.7137	2.474	1.056	.9725	1.086
814	1.899	.7069	2.549	1.054	.9725	1.084
821	1.948	.6996	2.668	1.043	.9652	1.080
822	1.942	.6912	2.699	1.040	.9652	1.078
823	1.941	.6834	2.738	1.037	.9652	1.074
824	1.996	.7003	2.757	1.033	.9652	1.070
831	2.120	.7291	2.795	1.040	.9854	1.055
832	2.262	.7534	2.892	1.038	.9854	1.053
833	2.360	.7806	2.920	1.035	.9854	1.050
834	2.421	.7976	2.931	1.035	.9854	1.051
841	2.497	.8086	2.988	1.033	.9854	1.048
842	2.568	.8377	2.968	1.032	.9854	1.048
843	2.774	.8745	3.079	1.029	.9854	1.045
844	2.883	.9103	3.100	1.021	.9854	1.036
851	3.020	.9501	3.118	1.019	.9854	1.034
852	3.154	.9848	3.150	1.016	.9854	1.031
853	3.224	1.016	3.120	1.016	.9854	1.031
854	3.328	1.057	3.106	1.012	.9854	1.027

CONCLUSION

As the final chapters have shown, the estimation of models with rationing makes it possible today to combine several approaches for explaining investment that were merely juxtaposed in earlier analyses. This constitutes an advance in business-cycle analysis. Similarly, the integration of future-demand uncertainty reintroduces in a consistent manner the influence of profitability on investment. However, many research paths must still be explored before we can obtain models that are both more general and closer to firms' actual decision-making process.

The first requirement is to relate investment to the entire complex of the firm's decision-making areas: these include not only employment and the other production factors whose interdependence we have analyzed here, but also finance, pricing, wages and inventory management.

Secondly, one can seek to improve the accuracy of the analysis of how demand and relative-price expectations are formed. However sophisticated the specification of expectations may be in the present volume, these are always of the regressive type, based on past observation. The treatment of direct data on long-term expectations remains the stumbling-block of investment econometrics. Business surveys provide valuable data on agents' short-term expectations, but tell us nothing about the long run. As for security prices, they reflect long-term expectations more closely, but are poor indicators of the marginal profitability of capital. This is shown by the empirical difficulties encountered in applying the approach introduced by Tobin.

The third problem concerns disequilibrium dynamics. One must take into account but only perceived disequilibriums, but also those expected in the future. This requires introducing capital accumulation in a complete dynamic disequilibrium model that incorporates the intertemporal dimension.

The final problem remains the analysis of what Feldstein calls "the other half of investment": scrapping. The capital-vintage models that inform most of the empirical studies presented in this volume allow a theoretical treatment of a crucial aspect of capital accumulation: obsolescence. Now the exponential-scrapping assumption implicit in most investment models bypasses this issue entirely. Of course, we could improve the analysis by endogenizing firms' scrapping behavior. However, because of the lack of direct information on scrapping, the estimation of a large number of parameters using the investment series alone would become very precarious.

Admittedly, one can always complicate a model to improve the theoretical description of the phenomenon studied. In applied econometrics, the limit is seldom on the theoretical side. To ensure the effective advancement of knowledge, the main priority is to accumulate more observations. Without the patient work of the statistician, theory soon becomes an empty shell.

References

Abel, A.B. [1980], "Empirical investment equations: an integrative framework," *Carnegie-Rochester Conference Series on Public Policy* 12, North-Holland, Amsterdam.

Abel, A.B, and Blanchard, O.-J. [1983], "An intertemporal model of saving and investment," *Econometrica* 51, May.

Alcantara, G. d' [1979], "Specification, estimation and simulation of a putty-clay production model," Bureau du Plan, Brussels.

Allen, R. [1938], *"Mathematical Analysis for Economists,"* Macmillan, London.

Ando, A. K., Modigliani, F., Rasche, R. and Turnovsky, S.J. [1974], "On the role of expectations of price and technological change in an investment function," *International Economic Review* 15 (2): 384-414.

Appelbaum, E. [1979], "On choice of functional forms," *International Economic Review* 20: 449-457, June.

Artus, P. [1984a], "Capacité de production, demande de facteurs et incertitude sur la demande," *Annales de l'INSEE* 53: 3-29 and Chapter 9 of this volume.

Artus, P. [1984b], "Comment fonctionne le marché du crédit: diverses analyses dans un cadre de déséquilibre," *Revue Economique* 4, July.

Artus, P. [1988], "Une note sur la validité du modèle de q de Tobin pour le France," *Cahiers Economiques et Monétaires* 29: pp 33-48, Banque de France.

Artus, P. and Bismut, C. [1980], "Substitution et coûts des facteurs: un lien existe-t-il ?," *Economie et Statistique* 127.

Artus, P., Laroque, G. and Michel, G. [1984], "Estimation of a quarterly macroeconomic model with quantity rationing," *Econometrica* 52 (6): 1387-1414.

Artus, P. and Migus, B. [1986], "Dynamique de l'investissement et de l'emploi avec coûts d'ajustement sur le capital et le travail," *Annales d'Economie et de Statistique* 2: 75-101 and Chapter 6 of this volume.

Artus, P. and Muet, P.-A. [1980a], "Une étude de l'influence de la demande, des coûts de facteurs et des contraintes financières sur l'investissement," mimeographed paper 8015, CEPREMAP, Paris.

Artus, P. and Muet, P.-A. [1980b], "Un retour sur la comparaison des hypothèses 'putty-putty' et 'putty-clay' dans l'estimation des demandes effectives d'investissement," *Annales de l'INSEE* 38-39: 193-205 and Chapter 3 of this volume.

Artus, P. and Muet, P.-A.[1981], "Fiscal policy and private investment in France in the 1970's: an econometric study," CNRS-ISPE-NBER Conference on the Taxation of Capital, paper 8117, CEPREMAP, Paris, June.

Artus, P. and Muet, P.-A. [1982], "Politique conjoncturelle et investissement dans les années 70," *Observations et Diagnostics Economiques* 1: 61-90, June and Chapter 4 of this volume.

Artus, P. and Muet, P.-A. [1983], "Investissement, contraintes de débouchés, d'emploi, contraintes financières: estimation d'un modèle à plusieurs régimes," OFCE, *Document de travail no. 83-03* (see below, Artus and Muet [1984a]).

Artus, P. and Muet P.-A. [1984a], "Investment, output and labor constraints, and financial constraints: the estimation of a model with several regimes," *Recherches Economiques de Louvain* 50 (1-2): 33-52 (this translation of Artus and Muet [1983] is reproduced, in a slightly revised and expanded form, as Chapter 8 of this volume).

Artus, P. and Muet P.-A. [1984b], "Un panorama des développements récents de l'économétrie de l'investissement," *Revue Economique* 35 (5): 791-821 and (with revisions) Chapter 1 of this volume.

Artus, P. and Muet P.-A. [1986], *"Investissement et emploi,"* Economica, Paris (original edition of this volume)..

Artus, P., Muet, P.-A., Palinkas, P. and Pauly P. [1981], "Economic policy and private investment since the oil crisis: a comparative study of France and Germany," *European Economic Review* 16: 7-51, April.

Artus, P. and Peyroux, C. [1981], "Fonction de production avec facteur énergie : estimation pour les grands pays de l'OCDE," *Annales de l'INSEE* 44 : 3-39 and Chapter 7 of this volume.

Artus, P. and Sicsic P. [1988], "Modèles économétriques traditionels et nouveaux de l'investissement en France: peut-on comprendre les évolutions des années quatre-vingt ?," *Essai en l'honneur d'E. Malinvaud,* Economica, Paris.

Artus, P. and Sterdyniak, H. [1980], "Comportement des entreprises et modèles macroéconomiques," *Annales de l'INSEE* 40.

Artus, P., Sterdyniak, H. and Villa, P. [1980], "Investissement, emploi et fiscalité," *Economie et Statistique* 127.

Autume, A. d' and Michel, P. [1984], "Evaluation du capital en présence de contraintes anticipées sur les achats de biens d'équipement," *Annales de l'INSEE* 54: 101-114.

Avouyi-Dovi, S. and Sterdyniak, H. [1986], "Une série de coût d'usage du capital," *Observations et Diagnostics Economiques* 15, April.

Bennett, A. [1988], "The accelerator model of investment: an appraisal on French data," *Revue Economique* (forthcoming).

Bernard, A. [1977], "Le coût d'usage du capital productif: une ou plusieurs mesures ?," *Annales de l'INSEE* 28: 3 - 38, Oct.-Dec.

Berndt, E. [1980], "Energy price increase and the productivity slowdown in United States manufacturing," in Federal Reserve Bank of Boston, *The Decline in Productivity Growth,* Conference series, no.22.

Berndt, E. and Christensen, L. [1973a], "The internal structure of functional relationships: separability, substitution and aggregation," *Review of Economic Studies* 40 (3): 403-410.

Berndt, E. and Christensen, L. [1973b], "The translog function and the substitution of equipment structures and labor in US manufacturing," *Journal of Econometrics* 1: 81-113.

Berndt, E., Darrough, M. and Diewert, W. [1977], "Flexible functional forms and expenditure distributions: an application to Canadian consumer demand functions," *International Economic Review* 18: 651-675, Oct.

Berndt, E. and Wood, D. [1975], "Technology, prices and derived demand of energy," *Review of Economic Studies* 52 (3): 259-268.

Berndt, E. and Wood, D. [1978], "Engineering and economics approaches to industrial energy conservation and capital formation: a reconciliation," in International Energy Agency, OECD, *Workshops on Energy Supply and Demand*, pp. 278-314.

Bischoff, C.W. [1969], "Hypothesis testing and the demand for capital goods," *Review of Economics and Statistics,* 51 (3).

Bischoff, C.W. [1971], "The effects of alternative lag distributions," in Fromm, G., ed.,*Tax Incentives and Capital Spending*, pp. 61-130, Brookings Institution, North-Holland, Amsterdam.

Bitros, G.C. [1976], "A model and some evidence on the interrelatedness of decisions underlying the demand for capital services," *European Economic Review* 7.

Blanchard, O.-J. and Sachs, J. [1982], "Anticipations, recessions and policy: an inter-temporal disequilibrium model," *Annales de l'INSEE* 47-48: 117-144.

Bosshardt, M.-O. and Mairesse, J. [1980], "Le comportement de déclassement des entreprises: quelques estimations," *Annales de l'INSEE* 38-39, April-Sept.

Bournay, J. and Laroque, G.[1979], "Les comptes trimestriels 1949-1959," *Collections de l'INSEE,* C series no. 70, March.

Brechling, F. [1975], "*Investment and Employment Decisions*," The University Press, Manchester.

Brefort, D. [1973], "Le comportement d'investissement des entreprises: analyse économétrique," doctoral dissertation, Université de Paris-Dauphine.

Brefort, D. [1974], "Le comportement d'investissement des entreprises: quelques nouveaux résultats," *Revue Economique* 25 (3), May.

Britto, R. [1970], "Durability and obsolescence in putty-clay models," *International Economic Review*, Oct.

Bruno, M. [1978], "An analysis of stagflation in the industrial countries: some preliminary results," Falk Institute Discussion Paper, no. 788, July.

Bruno, M. and Sachs, J. [1979a], "Macroeconomic adjustment with import price shocks: real and monetary aspects," NBER Working paper no. 340, April.

Bruno, M. and Sachs, J. [1979b], "Supply versus demand approaches to the problem of stagflation," NBER Working paper no. 382, Aug.

Bucher, A. and Sterdyniak, H. [1983], "Un investissement relativement soutenu," *Observations et Diagnostics Economiques* 5, Oct.

Chan-Lee, J. and Torres, R. [1987], "q de Tobin et taux d'accumulation en France," *Annales d'Economie et de Statistique,* 5: 37-48.

Christensen, L. and Jorgenson, R. [1970], "The measurement of US real capital input 1929-67," *Review of Income and Wealth* 15 (4): 293-320.

Christensen, L., Jorgenson, D. and Lau, L. [1973], "Transcendental logarithmic production function," *Review of Economic Studies* 55 (1): 28-45.

Coen, R.M. [1969], "Tax policy and investment behavior: a comment," *American Economic Review* 59, June.

Coen, R.M. [1971], "The effect of cash-flow on the speed of adjustment," in Fromm, G., ed., *Tax Incentives and Capital Spending*, Brookings Institution, North-Holland, Amsterdam.

Coen, R.M. and Hickman, B.G. [1970], "Constrained joint estimation of factor demand and production functions," *Review of Economics and Statistics* 52 (3).

Courbis, R. [1968], "Le comportement d'autofinancement des entreprises," *Economie Appliquée* 21 (3-4).

Courbis, R. [1973], "Le comportement d'autofinancement des entreprises et le modèle FIFI," *Annales de l'INSEE* 12-13.

Coutière, A. and Nizet [1981], "Les aides fiscales à l'investissement mises en œuvre en France," CNRS-ISPE-NBER, Conference on the Taxation of Capital, June, Paris.

Desplats-Redier, D. [1971], "Les investissements industriels et le principe d'accélération," *Collection de l'INSEE,* E 7.

Diewert, W.E. [1971], "An application of the Shephard Duality Theorem: a generalized Leontief production function," *Journal of Political Economy* 79 (3): 481-507.

Diewert, W.E. [1973], "Separability and a generalization of the Cobb-Douglas cost, production and indirect utility functions," Technical report 86, Institute for Mathematical Studies in the Social Sciences, Stanford University, California.

Diewert, W.E. [1974], "Application of duality theory," in Intrigilator, M.D. and Kendrick, D.A., eds., *Frontiers of Quantitative Economics* 2, 106-171, North-Holland, Amsterdam.

Dormont, B. [1983], "Substitution et coûts des facteurs: une approche en termes de modèles à erreur sur les variables," *Annales de l'INSEE* 50.

Dormont, B. [1986], "Emploi et contrainte de débouchés: Estimation d'un modèle de demande de travail à deux régimes sur données microéconomiques," Paper delivered at 3èmes Jounées de Microéconomie Appliquée, Nantes, 29-30 March.

Duharcourt, P. [1970], "*La fonction d'investissement,*" Sirey, Paris.

Echard, J.-F. and Hénin, P.-Y. [1970], "Une étude économétrique de la décision d'investir et des structures financières dans l'entreprise," *Economie et Sociétés*, Cahiers de l'ISEA, July-Aug.

Eisner, R. [1967], "A permanent income theory for investment: some empirical explorations," *American Economic Review* 57 (3).

Eisner, R. [1978a], "Factors in business investment," NBER, General Series, 102, Ballinger, Cambridge, USA.

Eisner, R. [1978b], "Cross section and time series estimates of investment functions," *Annales de l'INSEE,* 30-31.

Eisner, R., and Nadiri, M.I. [1968], "Investment behaviour and neoclassical theory," *Review of Economics and Statistics 50 (3).*

Eisner, R. and Nadiri, M.I. [1970], "Neoclassical theory of investment behaviour: a comment," *Review of Economics and Statistics* 52(2), May.

Eisner, R. and Stroz, R.H. [1963], "Determinants of business investment," in Commission on Money and Credit, *Impacts of Monetary Policy*, Prentice Hall, pp.59-337.

Faini, R. and Schiantarelli, F. [1984], "A unified framework for firm's decisions theoretical analysis and empirical application to Italy 1970-1980," *Recherches Economiques de Louvain* 50, 1-2.

Fair, R.C., and Jaffee, D.M. [1972], "Methods of estimation for markets in disequilibrium," *Econometrica* 40.

Feldstein, M.S. and Fleming, J.S. [1971], "Tax policy, corporate savings and investment behaviour in Britain," *Review of Economic Studies* 38.

Feldstein, M. and Foot, D. [1971], "The other half of gross investment: replacement and modernization expenditures," *Review of Economics and Statistics* 1.

Feldstein, M. and Rothschild, M. [1974], "Towards an economic theory of replacement investment," *Econometrica,* May.

Findlay, R. and Rodriguez, C. [1977], "Intermediate imports and macroeconomic policy under flexible exchange rates," *Canadian Journal of Economics*, May.

Fouquet, D., Charpin, J.-M., Guillaume, H., Muet, P.-A. and Vallet, D. [1978], « DMS modèle dynamique multi-sectoriel," *Collections de l'INSEE*, C series, no. 64-65.

Furstenberg, G. Von [1977], "Corporate investment: does market valuation matter in the aggregate ?," Brookings Papers on Economic Activity 1.

Fuss, M. and Mac Fadden, D. [1979], "*Production Economics: A Dual Approach to Theory and Application*," North-Holland, Amsterdam.

Gardner, R. and Sheldon, R. [1975], "Financial conditions and the time path of equipment expenditures," *Review of Economics and Statistics,* May.

Gerard, M. and Vanden Berghe, C. [1984], "Econometric Analysis of sectoral investment in Belgium (1956-82)," *Recherches Economiques de Louvain* 50 1-2.

Ginsburgh, V., Tishler, A. and Zang, I. [1980], "Alternative estimation methods for two-regime models," *European Economic Review* 13.

Girod, J. [1976], "*La demande d'énergie: modélisation, méthodes et techniques*," CNRS, Paris.

Gould, J.P. [1968], "Adjustment costs in the theory of investment of the firm *Review of Economic Studies* (35) 1.

Gould, J.P. [1969], "The use of endogenous variables in dynamic models of investment," *Quarterly Journal of Economics*.

Gould, J.P and Waud, R.N.[1973], "The neoclassical model of investment behaviour: another view," *International Economic Review* 14 (1).

Gouriéroux, C. [1981], "Modèles à variables dépendantes limitées," mimeographed, ENSAE, Paris, Nov.

Griffin, J. and Gregory, P. [1976], "An intercountry translog model of energy substitution responses," *American Economic Review*, Dec, 845-857.

Griliches, Z. [1967], "Distributed lags: a survey," *Econometrica* 35 (1).

Grossman, H. [1972], "A choice theoretic model of an income investment accelerator," *American Economic Review*, Sept.

Gubian, A., Guillaumat-Tailliet, F. and Le Cacheux, J. [1986], "Fiscalité des entreprises et décision d'investissement," *Observations et Diagnostics Economiques, 16*, July.

Guillaume, H. and Muet, P.-A. [1979], "Simulations et multiplicateurs dynamiques du modèle DMS," *Revue Economique*, March.

Hall, R.E. and Jorgenson, D.W. [1967], "Tax policy and investment behavior," *American Economic Review* 57(3).

Hall, R.E. and Jorgenson, D.W. [1969], "Tax policy and investment behavior," *American Economic Review* 59.

Hanoch, G. [1975a], "CRESH production function," *Econometrica* 39: 695-712.

Hanoch, G. [1975b], "Production and demand models with direct or indirect implicit additivity," *Econometrica* 43: 395-420.

Hardy, G.H., Littlewood, J.E. and Polya, G. [1959], "*Inequalities*," Cambridge University Press, Cambridge, UK.

Hayashi, F. [1982], "Tobin's marginal q and average q: a neo-classical interpretation," *Econometrica* 50: 213-224, Jan.

Helliwell, J. [1976], "Aggregate investment equations: a survey of issues," in Helliwell, ed., *Aggregate Investment*, Penguin Modern Economics Readings.

Helliwell, J. and Glorieux, G. [1970], "Forward-looking investment behaviour," *Review of Economic Studies* 37 (4): 499-516.

Helliwell, J. and Mc Rae, R. [1980], "*Output, Potential Output and Factor Demands in an Aggregate Open Economy Model with Energy and Capital Bundled Together*," mimeographed University of British Columbia, Oct.

Henry, J., Leroux, V. and Muet P.-A. [1988], "Coût relatif capital-travail et substitution: Existe-t-il encore un lien ?," *Observations et Diagnostics Economiques*, July, pp. 163-182.

Hicks, J.R. [1946], "*Value and Capital*," Clarendon Press, Oxford.

Hogan, W. [1980], "Dimensions of energy demand," in Landsberg, H., ed., *Selected Studies on Energy*, Ballinger, Cambridge, USA.

Hotelling, H. [1932], "Edgeworth's taxation paradox and the nature of demand and supply functions," *Journal of Political Economy* 40: 577-616.

Houthakker, H.S. [1955], "The Pareto distribution and the Cobb-Douglas production function in activity analysis," *Review of Economic Studies* 23.

Hudson, E.A. and D.W. Jorgenson, "U.S. Energy Policy and Economic Growth, 1975-2000," *Bell Journal of Economics*, 5 (Autumn, 1974), 461-541.

INSEE [1981], "*METRIC, une modélisation de l'économie française*," INSEE, Paris.

Johansen, L. [1972], "Production Functions," North-Holland, Amsterdam.

Jorgenson, D.W. [1963], "Capital theory and investment behaviour," *American Economic Review* 53.

Jorgenson, D.W. [1966], "Rational distributed lag functions," *Econometrica* 32 (1).

Jorgenson, D.W. and Stephenson, J.A. [1969], "Issues in the development of the neo-classical theory of investment behaviour," *Review of Economics and Statistics* 51 (3).

Kalecki, M. [1937], "The principle of increasing risk," *Economica* 4 (16): 440-447.

King, M. [1972], "Taxation and investment incentives in a vintage investment model," *Journal of Public Economics* 1: 121-147.

Klein, L.R. [1974], "Issues in econometric studies of investment behaviour," *Journal of Economic Literature.*

Krainer, R. [1966], "Interest rates, investment decisions and external financing », *Oxford Economic Papers.*

Kuh, E. [1963], "*Capital Stock Growth: A Microeconometric Approach,*" North-Holland, Amsterdam.

Laffont, J.J. and Garcia, R. [1977], "Disequilibrium econometrics for business loans," *Econometrica*, July.

Laffont, J.-J. and Monfort, A. [1976], "Econométrie des modèles d'équilibre avec rationnement," *Annales de l'INSEE* 53: 31-60.

Lambert, J.-P. [1987a], "*Disequilibrium macroeconomic models: Theory and estimation of rationing models using business survey data*", Cambridge University Press, Cambridge.

Lambert, J.-P. [1987b], "Conflicting Specifications for Investment Functions in Rationing Models: A Reconciliation", *Recherches Economiques de Louvain*, 53 (2): 135-146.

Lambert, J.-P. and Mulkay, B. [1987], "Investissement et profitabilité dans un modèle complet de déséquilibre," Working paper, CORE, November.

Lau, L. [1974], "Comments on application of duality theory," in Intriligator, M.D. and Kendrick, D.A., eds., *Frontiers of Quantitative Economics* 2: 176-199, North-Holland, Amsterdam.

Legendre, F. and Morin, P. [1988], "L'investissement dans un contexte de faible croissance et de taux d'intérêt élevés," *Recherches Economiques de Louvain*. (forthcoming).

Le Marois, M. [1979], "Une étude économétrique trimestrielle sur l'investissement des entreprises," *Annales de l'INSEE* 35: 135-151, July.

Loranger, J.G. [1976], "Problems of identification and estimation of the demand for capital," *Review of Economics and Statistics* 63 (2), May.

Lucas, R.E. [1967], "Optimal investment policy and the flexible accelerator," *International Economic Review* 8.

Maccini, L.S. [1981], "On the theory of the firm underlying empirical models of aggregate price behavior," *International Economic Review*, Oct, 609-623.

Mac Fadden, D. [1964], "Estimation techniques for the elasticity of substitution and other production parameters," Meeting of the Econometric Society, mimeographed.

Magnus, J. [1979], "Substitution between energy and non-energy inputs in the Netherlands 1950-1976," *International Economic Review* 20: 465-483, June.

Mairesse, J. [1972], "Evaluation du capital fixe productif," *Collections de l'INSEE,* C series, no. 18-19.

Malgrange, P. and Villa, P.[1984], "Comportement d'investissement avec coûts d'ajustement et contraintes quantitatives," *Annales de l'INSEE* 53: 31-60.

Malecot, J.-F. and Hamon, J. [1986], "Contraintes financières et demande d'investissement des entreprises," *Revue Economique*, Sept. pp. 149-174.

Malinvaud, E. [1971], "Peut-on mesurer le coût d'usage du capital productif ?," *Economie et Statistique* 22: 5-20, April.

Malinvaud, E. [1978], "Nouveaux développements de la théorie macro économique du chômage," *Revue Economique,* Jan.

Malinvaud, E.[1980], *"Profitability and Unemployment,"* Cambridge University Press, Cambridge, UK.

Malinvaud, E. [1981], *"Théorie Macroéconomique,"* vol.1, Dunod, Paris.

Malinvaud, E. [1982], *"Théorie Macroéconomique,"* vol. 2, Dunod, Paris.

Malinvaud, E. [1983], "Profitability and investment facing uncertain demand », ENSAE and INSEE Unité de Recherche, Working paper 8303.

Malkiel, B.G., Furstenberg, G. von and Watson, H.S. [1979], "Expectations, Tobin's q and industry investment," *Journal of Finance* 34 (2): 549-564.

Melitz, J. [1976], "Un modèle pour la détermination du stock de monnaie et son application à la France," *Annales de l'INSEE* 24.

Ménil, G.de and Porcher, R. [1977], "Les anticipations d'inflation à long terme », in ' METRIC ', *Annales de l'INSEE* 26-27: 261-273.

Ménil, G.de and Yohn, F. [1977], "La formation de capital fixe par les entreprises," *Annales de l'INSEE* 26-27: 115-161.

Muet, P.-A. [1978a], "Croissance, profits et investissement: une étude économétrique," doctoral dissertation, Université de Paris I, mimeographed, INSEE - CEPREMAP.

Muet, P.-A. [1978b], "Les modèles à retards échelonnés: fondements théoriques, spécifications et méthodes d'estimation," mimeographed paper no.7901, CEPREMAP, Paris, Nov.

Muet, P.-A. [1979a], "Les modèles néo-classiques et l'impact du taux d'intérêt sur l'investissement," *Revue Economique*, March.

Muet, P.-A. [1979b], "Les modèles à retards échelonnés: fondements théoriques, spécifications et méthodes d'estimation," *Cahier du Groupe de Mathématiques Economiques,* 2, Universités de Paris I, Paris VI, Sept.

Muet, P.-A. [1979c], "Modèles économétriques de l'investissement: une étude comparative sur données annuelles," *Annales de l'INSEE* 35: 85-133 and Chapter 2 of this volume.

Muet, P.-A. and Zagamé, P. [1976], "Fonction d'investissement et retards échelonnés," *Annales de l'INSEE*, 21, 85-133.

Muet, P.-A., Villa, P. and Boutillier, M. [1980], "Modélisation et estimation simultanée des demandes d'investissement et d'emploi," mimeographed paper no. 8001, CEPREMAP, Paris.

Muet, P.-A. and Zagamé, P. [1980], "L'effet du taux d'intérêt sur l'investissement: un essai d'analyse par les modèles de contraintes," *Economie et Sociétés*, MO2.

Muet, P.-A. and Avouyi-Dovi, S. [1987a], "L'effet des incitations fiscales sur l'investissement," *Observations et Diagnostics Economiques*, Jan. pp 149-174.

Muet, P.-A. and Avouyi-Dovi, S. [1987b], "L'investissement productif dans les années 1980: Diagnostic et perspectives,"ˌRevue d'Economie Industrielle, no. 40-41, 2nd and 3rd quarter.

Mukerji, G. [1963], "A generalised SMAC function with constant ratio of elasticities of substitution," *Review of Economic Studies* 30 (3): 233-236.

Mulkay, B. [1983], "Fonctions d'investissement néo-classiques dans un modèle microéconomique avec rationnement," *Recherches Economiques de Louvain*, 49(3): 247-276.

Nadiri, M.I. and Rosen, S. [1969], "Interrelated factor demand functions," *American Economic Review* 59 (4).

Nadiri, M.I. and Rosen, S. [1974], "A disequilibrium model of demand for factors of production," *American Economic Review*, Papers and Proceedings, 64 (2).

Nickell, S. [1977], "Uncertainty and lags in the investment decisions of firms," *Review of Economic Studies*: 44 (137): 249-263.

Nickell, S.J. [1978], *"The investment decisions of firms,"*Cambridge University Press, Cambridge, U.K.

Nishimizu, M., Quandt, R. and Rosen, H. [1982], "The demand and supply for investment goods: does the market clear ?," *Journal of Macroeconomics 4 (1)*, Winter.

Nordhaus, W. [1980], "Oil and economic performance in industrial countries," Brookings Papers on Economic Activity, no.2.

Obstfeld, M. [1980], "Intermediate imports, the terms of trade and the dynamics of the exchange rate and current account," *Journal of International Economics* 10.

Oudiz, G. [1978], "Investment behavior of French industrial firms: a study on longitudinal data," *Annales de l'INSEE* 30-31.

Perloff, J. and Wachter, M., [1979], "A production function — non-accelerating inflation approach to potential output," *Journal of Monetary Economics, Supplement*, pp.113-133.

Pindyck, R. [1979], "Interfuel substitution and the industrial demand for energy : an international comparison," *Review of Economic Studies,* 61 (2): 169-179.

Pindyck, R. [1982], "Adjustment costs, uncertainty and the behavior of the firm », *American Economic Review*, June pp.415-427.

Pouchain, M. [1980], "Estimation de demandes de facteurs en termes d'ajustements croisés," *Annales de l'INSEE* 38-39.

Quandt, R.E. [1982], "Econometric disequilibrium models," *Econometric Review* 1.

Rothschild, M. and Stiglitz, J. [1971], "Increasing risk II. Its economic consequence," *Journal of Economic Theory* 3: 66-84.

Roy, R. [1942], *"De l'utilité: contribution à la théorie des choix,"* Hermann, Paris.

Russel, R. [1975], "Functional separability and partial elasticities of substitution," *Review of Economic Studies*, Jan. pp.79-86.

Samuelson, P.A. [1947], *"Foundations of Economic Analysis,"* Harvard University Press, Cambridge, USA.

Sarantis, N. [1979], "Relative prices, investment incentives, cash-flow and vintage investment functions," *European Economic Review* 12 (3), July.

Sato, K. [1967], "A two-level constant elasticity of substitution production function," *Review of Economic Studies* 34: 201-218, April.

Sato, K. [1975], *"Production Functions and Aggregation,"* North-Holland / American Elsevier, Amsterdam.

Schiantarelli, F. [1983], "Investment models and expectations: some estimates for the Italian industrial sector," *International Economic Review* 24 (2).

Schramm, R. [1972], "Neoclassical investment models and French private manufacturing investment," *American Economic Review* 62, Sept.

Shephard, R.W.[1953], *"Cost and Production Functions,"* Princeton University Press, Princeton.

Shephard, R.W. [1970], *"Theory of Cost and Production Functions,"* Princeton University Press, Princeton.

Sneessens, H. [1985] "A macroeconomic rationing model of the Belgian economy," Working Paper no. 8540, London School of Economics.

Sneessens, H. and Maillard, B. [1988], "Investment, sales constraints and profitability in France 1957-1985," Working paper no. 8803, Université Catholique de Louvain.

Stegman, T. [1982], "The estimation of an accelerator-type investment function with a profitability constraint, by the technique of switching regressions," *Australian Economic Papers* 39, Dec.

Sterdyniak, H. and Villa, P. [1977], "Du côté de l'offre de monnaie," *Annales de l'INSEE* 25.

Thollon-Pommerol, V. and Malinvaud, E. [1971], "L'effet d'accélération dans les investissements industriels français," *Annales de l'INSEE* 7.

Tobin, J. [1969], "A general equilibrium approach to monetary theory," *Journal of Money, Credit and Banking.*

Uzawa, H.[1962], "Production functions with constant elasticities of substitution," *Review of Economic Studies* 29: 291-299, Oct.

Uzawa, H. [1964], "Duality principles in the theory of cost and production," *International Economic Review* 5: 216-220.

Uzawa, H. [1969], "Time preference and the Penrose effect in a two-class model of economic growth," *Journal of Political Economy* 77, July.

Vilares, M.J. [1986], "Un modèle macroéconomique pour l'étude des changements structurels: théorie et application à l'économie française," Fitoussi, J.-P. and Muet, P.-A., eds., *Macrodynamique et déséquilibres*, Economica, Paris.

Villa, P., Muet, P.-A. and Boutillier, M. [1980], "Une estimation simultanée des demandes d'investissement et de travail," *Annales de l'INSEE* 38-39: 237-258 and Chapter 5 of this volume.

Yoshikawa, H. [1980], "On the q theory of investment," *American Economic Review*.

Zagamé, P. [1977], "L'investissement en déséquilibre," in de Boissieu, C., Parguez, A. and Zagamé, P., *Economie du déséquilibre*, Economica, Paris.

SUBJECT INDEX